It was said of Leptis Magna, "Nature failed to support man. The truth is exactly the opposite. Man failed to support nature."

Sir David Attenborough
from
"The First Eden"

Front Cover picture of Flat Rock Tower by Damian Goodman

Inside Sketch of Shannondale Tower by Tania Gray courtesy Max Gorman

© 2019 by Bob Frakes. All rights reserved.
Words Matter Publishing
P.O. Box 531
Salem, Il 62881
www.wordsmatterpublishing.com

No part of this publication may be reproduced, stored in a retrieval system, or transmitted in any way by any means—electronic, mechanical, photocopy, recording, or otherwise—without the prior permission of the copyright holder, except as provided by USA copyright law.

ISBN 13: 978-1-949809-52-7

Library of Congress Catalog Card Number: 2019954641

Contents

Dedication v

Acknowledgments vi

Forward x

Glossary xii

The Lessons of Leptis 1

Missouri a Century Ago 3

The Time Had Come 7

Involvement & Information 13

Smokey Bear – 101 15

The "pioneering" Pioneer Forest – information supplied by Terry Cunningham 22

Lookouts Not Towers 25

Wooden Towers 31

Jim Ruble and Vulcan Tower 39

Kelleter Tower and Ed Christopher 49

Chris Polka – The Google Map Project 55

Panther Hill Tales with Charley Santhuff 58

Jim Parker Interview 62

Lawrence Buchheit At Perry Tower 67

Glenn Skinner – Knob Lick Fire Warden 70

Jerry Presley 74

Kerwin Hafner 77

Ron "Woody" Woodland 79

Steel Towers	83
Contribution to Book on Lookout Towers by Jim Sorenson	104
Bucksnort by Shari Wolford	110
Everett Chaney and Tram Tower	112
Our U.S.F.S. Life by Shari Wolford	115
My Best Friend and a Life Close to High Tower by Shari Wolford	120
Shannondale Tales Information from Max & Trudy Gorman	123
Interview with Marvin and Pat Brawley – 3/6/2019 by Teena Ligman	133
Geodetic Markers	135
What's In a Name?	137
A Good Mystery Scrapbook	140
George Graham	151
Earl (Minnie) Lutes	153
"Dozers"	158
On The Move	162
Drone Shots	169
Hello Down There/Hello Up There	173
Managing Fire Tower Sites on Federal land: The Mark Twain National Forest by James Halpern	175
Travelogue	182
Gone, But Not (here) Forgotten	233
Ellsinore Forest Lookout Tower with Barbara Kingen Alcorn	237
The Evolution of the Fire Tower in the Missouri Ozarks A Look at Then and Now by Steve Orchard	239
Picture Credits	242
Bibliography/References Cited	244
Index	246
Epilogue	254
The Author	255

Dedication

I would like to dedicate this book to my many friends in Forestry and Conservation. I have not asked for, even once, help that they were not ready to find an answer. Missouri is so much better off for their efforts. Give them a pat on the back and get out and enjoy the outdoors of one of the greatest conservation success stories in the nation. I would also like to dedicate the book to the people of Missouri, who on several occasions have voted to make Missouri the Conservation success story it is.

Lest we forget!

Acknowledgments

Although I have spent some time in the libraries and courthouses, it dawned on me early on that "getting the memories down" of those who worked and lived at the lookouts would be of value. It was obvious some of the stories were being lost and needed to be preserved. It was also obvious that my interest in the lookouts crossed paths with those who had experienced the "special time and place" and we often seemed to hit it off. Following are some I need to recognize.

My wife Brenda-as we headed up another lookout road she often remarked, "You need to get a Jeep!" She has been a good partner. Her aptitude test in Junior College showed, "Forest Ranger."

Jim Lyon-Jim started firefighting with the Conservation Commission in 1963, fought fires in California for a couple of seasons, and eventually spent 14 seasons running fire lookouts with his wife Flo in five different western states, ending in 2016. He did some of the early work to index what lookouts had existed in Missouri.

Chris Polka-Chris is a tech guy in St. Louis and the creator of a Google Map Project, (http://tinyurl.com/mofiretowers). Chris has visited all the standing towers in Missouri. I have emailed many a tower question and received many a tower answer. It was his map that allowed me to make some real progress on my lookout visits and research. I am proud to contribute to it now and then.

Ron Kemnow-Ron has studied the lookouts for years and is the author of (RonKemnow.Weebly.com). It is one of the largest collections of tower information out there. Ron has always been ready to help me with my lookout questions.

A special thanks to **those I interviewed – Max Gorman, Jim Parker and Lawrence Buchheit.**

Also, **those who contributed** all or parts of interviews and/or submitted topics – **Terry Cunningham, Jim Ruble, Frances (Christopher) Long, Eddie Long, Chris Polka, Jack Skinner, Kerwin Hafner, Jim Sorenson, Bill and Shari Wolford, Ruth Graham, The Lutes Brothers, Teena Ligman, Steve Orchard, Kathleen Boulay-Eaton, Laura Kampschroeder, Janet Shannon, Barbara Alcorn, Charley Santhuff and James Halpern.**

The Missouri Department of Conservation and Mark Twain Forest - A big thanks to the present and past Conservation **workers who have helped me** with all my questions. These are some I have used, no particular order-

Acknowledgments

Doug Gall, David Lane, James Murrell & Ron Woodland who passed recently – Thanks for all your help!

Max Gorman	Jim Parker
Terry Cunningham	Steve Orchard
Jim Sorenson	Francis Main
Mike Hoffman	John Tuttle
Mac Roberts	James Halpern
Ben Webster	Charles Tatum
Justine Gartner	Lindell Tucker
Tom Draper	Howard Brawley
Bob Cunningham	Travis Mills
Kevin Cox	William Konen
Leon Peterson	Mark Davis
Wes Swee	Elsie & Curt Patterson
Rob Miley	Richard Stirts
Jim Voyles	Keith Smith
John Strange	Jason Stotler
John Timmermann	Joyce Barrett
Greg Painter	Curt Patterson
Cody Norris	William Whitacre
Becky Ewing	Elizabeth Barrera
Teena Ligman	Jeremiah Privett
Mike Fiaoni	Jennifer Behnken
Rocky Hayes	Tom Draper
Lisa Allen	Holly Dentner
Paul Johnson	Mark Johanson
Mike Mitchell	Bill Altman
Gary Gognat	Gayle Todd
Stan Lovan	Shane Rice
Mark Pelton	Lawrence Buchheit
Terry Thompson	Dwaine Hillhouse
Steven Laval	Cindy Ganer
Ross Glenn	Shane Botard
Aaron Holsapple	Skyler Bockman
Cindy Garner	David Hurlbut
Gene Brunk	Ed Ponder

The people of Missouri we have crossed paths with and received lots of help.

Bill & Shari Wolford	Marguerite Barkley
Jim Ruble	Jack Skinner
Gregg Mendenhall	Lutes Brothers
Gerald Angel	Verlin & Faye Beasley
Tom Aley	Delane Dunn

Phil Turner	Helen Lamb
Owen Brown	Richard Brown
Zachery Gillihan	Viola Crites & the Quilters
Michael Pomeroy	James Schearrer
Larry Newton	Francis (Christopher) Long
Eddie Long	Connie Holland
Carole Goggin	Steve Zulpo
Bruce Baron	Dewayne Botkin
Ken Beck	Zach Smith
Sharon Macormic	Raymond McGarrity
Trish Erzfeld	Damian Goodman
Terry Primas	Roger Dillon
Sharon Vaughn	Kimberly Combs
Jimmy Sexton	Brandi Conrad
Sarah Dye	Tom Botkin
Jerry Clements	Darrell Smith
Minuard Abney	Larry Davis
Kathleen Boulay-Eaton	Laura Kampschroeder
Barbara Alcorn	

The "**coffee club**" at J. Finley Auto Sales & Convenience Store

"The Old Foresters"

My wife and I were fortunate on the 6th of June, 2017 to be invited to attend a gathering of retired forestry workers representing 300 years of experience. As a tower documenter, I was able to ask questions and establish contacts.
Front Row - George Graham, Ed Keyser, Max Gorman, Joe Garvey, and Jerry Presley.
In the Back - Larry Lackamp, Bill Klatt, Charlie Santhuff, Duane Parker, and Randy Herberg.

"Old Foresters" in 2018 – Mr. & Mrs. Charley Santhuff, Mr. & Mrs. Joe Garvey, Mr. & Mrs. Ed Keyser, Kerwin Hafner, Larry Lackamp, Mr. & Mrs. Randy Herberg, Clell Solomon, Mr. & Mrs. Pat Hutchison, Mr. & Mrs. Max Gorman, Shelby Jones, Russell Schmidt, Mr. & Mrs. Bill Klatt and Mr. & Mrs. George Graham.

Thanks to **those I may have missed**!

I could not include all who deserve to be. I hope by job & geography, I have a good sample.

Forward

My Mother, Marge (Kinnison) Frakes, was raised near Rings Creek south of Patterson, Missouri. She was one of eight children of Roy and Ella Kinnison. I spent many a summer at the family farm with my many aunts, uncles and cousins.

Sam A. Baker Park was near and we often made outings to enjoy Missouri and the park. Mudlick Mountain (once called Tip Top) was tipped on its top by Mudlick Lookout, which still stands today. Mudlick is an 85-foot or so steel tower of the MC-39 design (more on that later).

On one of these side trips, I took my first tentative steps into the world of the lookouts. This was more than 50 years ago and I recall that I didn't make it to the top. I did, however, "clear the trees and feel the breeze." I made a mental note at the time that this was fun, and I have noted over the years, by the way, that some people enjoy heights and some don't! I might mention that Mudlick at the time, like many towers, had a picnic table and a sign-in book that contained hundreds of signatures from around the world. It was a different world then. I have been told stories that the school buses used to stop now and then to let the kids climb at some towers.

It would be several years before I would get another tower opportunity. In the early 1970s, I was asked by my friend, Tom Dare, to take part in a father/son canoe trip that was being sponsored by the West Salem Methodist Church. There was a son who wanted to go, but his father did not feel up to the trip. I had, by the way, never canoed. We would float the Current River for two days. Day one would be Baptist Camp to Akers and day two, Akers to Round Spring. It would be a real eye-opener, and I would return to enjoy the Current and Jack's Fork many times. I also would revisit for other reasons.

As we rounded a curve toward the end of the second day, I glanced up to catch a lookout high on a cliff above the river. It was the Shannondale Lookout. I recalled the view from Mudlick and figured this would be a fantastic view! I was also taken by the contrast. At Mudlick I had felt I was "above the forest." Looking up at the tower, you hardly noticed.

The first chance I had on a subsequent trip, I made my way up to the tower and climbed up to scope out the view. I had been right, it was a stunning sight. I took a picture, and I am sure you agree. Unfortunately, the tower is not often open for climbing nowadays. I would always make Shannondale a part of my trip itinerary. On a side note, I compared notes with one of my lookout friends, Max Gorman (retired MDC), and learned that he and his wife Trudy worked and lived at the tower at this very time. In fact, she worked at Carr's Canoe which I rented from many times.

My lookout hobby really kicked into a higher gear after this climb. However, it was to remain sporadic and at times lightly organized. My first attempt to make progress came in the form of old road maps. For many years Missouri road maps contained symbols noting "Forest Lookout Towers" which often served as roadside parks. On my trips here and there in the state, I would use the maps to plan strategy. However, road maps had limitations. You can see the Montauk Tower from halfway to Licking, but you can also park a hundred yards to the west and not see it. Some lookouts I found, some I didn't.

Forward

My searching got a boost 20 years ago when I married. My wife Brenda, the Forest Ranger aptitude tester from high school, enjoyed the lookout search and the back roads of Missouri. She had a real knack for location and finding footings and geodetic markers. We started making some real progress.

It was also about this time I did a word search and came across an index that had been done by Conservationist Jim Lyon. Jim had, by name, county, range, township and section, MDC or USFS, size, and up or down, made a listing of the lookouts he could document. It is an amazing document that I refer to often and others, like me, have noted it as a real boost to their tower searches.

At almost the same time, I crossed paths with Emery Styron of the River Hills Traveler Magazine. He did a short piece on the travels of my wife and me. He also, in what was to be an eventful idea, suggested that I should include contact information. I would, by the way, later write lookout articles for that same magazine.

In short order, I was contacted by Chris Polka, a tech guy working in St. Louis. Chris enjoyed hiking in Missouri and had added the lookouts to his hobby list. As I shared information, it became clear that I would learn much more tower info from him than the other way around. In fact, he had already visited all of the standing towers in the state. He also had entered his information and pictures onto a Google Map Project—(http://tinyurl.com/mofiretowers). We could now organize our outings more effectively, and the pictures that he linked to the site were a real incentive. As I removed many of the "standing tower" pins from my map, I would investigate historic sites, sites planned but never built, lookouts, not towers, and lookout mysteries. Chris would show me "monkey see, monkey do" how to enter the information on the map layers. Some of the steps I had to "tattoo on my forehead" but I would eventually get the hang of it.

I also contacted Ron Kemnow. Ron runs an impressive site, (RonKemnow.weebly.com) where he is documenting lookout sites around the world. I offered, and he accepted, my pictures and information on lookouts in Missouri, Illinois, and Indiana. Ron proved to be a real lookout veteran who was always willing to help me with a question.

I would also begin writing articles on the lookouts in the Reynolds County, Wayne County, Eminence, Van Buren, and Summersville papers. It was obvious there was lots of tower interest out there. I also became a volunteer staff writer for the River Hills Traveler, the magazine that had given my lookout search such a boost.

And as I crossed paths with people from all over Missouri, as noted in the acknowledgments, at times, I would reach out to them, while other times they would contact me. There existed and still does a real interest in this chapter of Missouri history. On more than one occasion, I was urged to gather my papers and stories into a book. I put it off as I worked on my various lookout projects, but as I pushed 70, I realized maybe I needed to get some ideas down before they were forgotten, just as my search had started for much the same reason. I have included two chapters that attempt to "set the table" instead of just dropping in the middle of the lookout story. Chapter One looks at the conservation story as it existed a hundred years ago and Chapter Two discusses the reaction that came to be in the M.D.C., the U.S.F.S., and most importantly the people of Missouri. This is not a detailed examination of either topic. I would urge readers to get a hold of the book, "Missouri Department of Conservation—The First 50 Years." It is a fascinating look at that subject.

So, I hope you enjoy the fruits of the travels that my wife and I have made. I will attempt to tell the back story of the towers, some information about them, and offer some of the personal stories and insight they have evoked.

As I always include—Bob Frakes/frakes2@mvn.net

Glossary

Aermotor – A Chicago, Illinois and Broken Arrow, Oklahoma steel tower manufacturer. Originally involved in the making of windmills, this company found itself well-prepared to shift to tower production when the need arose. Aermotor was the most common maker of Missouri towers, which are often found with an identity tag on the tower legs. It made a variety of tower designs.

A-Frame – A triangle-shaped device used to gain leverage and stability to bring objects to an upright position.

Back-firing – Using fire lines or features to set a counter-fire to put out the problem fire. Location and construction were essential to success. (See Below)

Glossary

Back-pack pump – The five gallons of water was carried by the firefighter who pumped the double hull pump by hand and used the spray or stream nozzle to fight grass fires, addressing hot spots and holding back fires.

Blowers – Offset wheeled models were used because they could go over logs and be lifted over fences. Back-pack models could also be used to create a line or on direct suppression by back blowing. (See Below)

Broom Rake – A special rake used to move leaves and other material to create a fire break. It could also be used to beat out a small fire or to create a backfire. It was a hand tool that was small and springy. The one lick method was used, and the tines were used to do help do the work. (See Below)

Cantilever Sign - Original design involved peeled White Oak and were made right on the district. Tyloses in the wood provide a natural preservative and make the White Oak a very useful tree. (See Below)

Glossary

Carnage – A steel tower manufacturer.

Creosote – Dark brown oil distilled from coal tar and used as a wood preservative. Health concerns related to contact with creosote have made its use today limited or even prohibited. When applied correctly to prepared wood, it greatly increased wood's resistance to the weather.

Cruising Timber – The process of walking the forest to determine by quantity and quality what was there.

Deadening Timber – This refers to girdling or using herbicides to kill selected trees to be dealt with later. The use of herbicides would be phased out over safety concerns.

Dispatch Map – A large map that allowed information called or sent by radio from a lookout to be plotted to determine a fire's location and to dispatch fire crews. (See Below)

Drift Pin (Spud Bar) – This was simply called a punch by many. When during construction the holes would not align, a drift pin would be used to line them up to then be clamped, the pin removed, and bolts attached.

Fire Factors - Fuel type, humidity, season, time of day, wind, and topography.

Footings (Piers) – I was schooled by my friend in construction, Jim Carkin, to use the correct term "pier." However, the term "footing" is so widely used; I still use it to avoid confusion. These anchors varied by tower size and provided a firm foundation. (See Below)

Galvanized Steel – This is steel that has been hot dipped in zinc. This is an effective tool for reducing rust and corrosion. Under favorable conditions, this can extend the life of a structure well over a century. However, this same zinc makes welding very dangerous owing to the zinc fumes.

Gin Pole – A gin pole is a supported pole which uses a pulley or block and tackle on its upper end to lift loads. When used in tower construction, the gin pole can be detached, raised, and re-attached to the just completed segment in order to lift the next. This process of jumping is repeated until the topmost portion is completed. A tag rope may be used to pull the lifted segment away from the tower while a piece is lifted. Gin poles can also be used with pulley and block and tackle arrangements to move items laterally.

Increment Borer – Device that takes a "core" from a tree to allow the counting of rings and estimation of age. (See Below)

International Derrick and Equipment – IDM is another popular tower maker in Missouri. Many IDM towers were assembled oil derrick frames with cabs on top. They also made, under license, models similar to Aermotor designs.

Lookout – As in "looking out" for a fire or smoke. However, it can get much more complicated from there. There seems to be a tendency to add "tower" to the term lookout, and there are many more lookouts than towers. At times, you will even see "tower" attached to tree lookouts or single pole lookouts. Compounding the confusion is that some locations had bare areas, tree and/or single pole, wooden-legged, steel legged, or existing structures such as water towers all used for lookout purposes on the same site at different times with the same name. Further, the term "crow's nest" is used at times to reference a platform in a tree, but at other times used for any lookout platform that is not an enclosed cab. So, even a short steel tower with only a platform and no cab may be said to have a "crow's nest" at its top. Platform and "crow's nest" can mean the same in some usage. So, with multiple uses for "tower" and "crow's nest," we create multiple combinations of descriptors that can lead to uncertainty. The reader must just read carefully and not insert words that are not there.

Osborn Fire Finder – A device used to obtain information in degrees that could be communicated to locate a fire. (See Below)

Panama Pump – A pump that ran off a vehicle that could be very useful depending on terrain.

Fire Parts – head, flanks, and tail

Primary Tower – One of two types of towers. The primary tower was a center of operations year round.

Riser – A flight of steps that goes from platform up to another platform. Different tower designs have varying amounts and lengths of risers.

Secondary Tower – Was called into usage in times of higher fire danger. These towers were often shorter 50 footers.

Swatter – Used to beat out a fire.

TSI – These three letters stand for Timber Stand Improvement. This is the process of determining by soil and location the type and number of trees that would work best in an area.

Types of Fires – Surface, crown, and spot

Visibility Assessment – Visiting a site firsthand to gain information about how useful it might be for a lookout.

Windmill Tower – A 50-foot or so metal tower that was very common in Missouri. Most were Aermotor designs that provided secondary or spot coverage. Basically, it's an Aermotor windmill with the vanes removed and replaced by a platform. A few had small canvas cabs. The platform was reached by rungs or ladders attached to the outside, providing an "interesting" climb.

A tower, truck, broom rake, blower, and backpack – Five instruments of detection and suppression.

The Lessons of Leptis

What is may not be what was. What will be is often to be determined. Let us consider the "Leptis Magna Principle."

Leptis Magna was a Roman province in what is modern-day Libya on the north shore of Africa. It grew to include the surrounding province in its sphere of influence. It was allowed to coin its own currency and enjoyed a prosperous trade. Its advantages included remarkably fertile soil where it was said you could plant one grain of wheat and produce one-hundred fifty. Its wealth was tied to the land. Leptis grew to the point that it was supplying a majority of the grain for the city of Rome. The motivation was to cut more trees and plant more land. Eventually, the harbor silted up and what soil was left blew away. Today it is largely abandoned except for the occasional archeologist.

Although subjected to several setbacks, it is often written that nature failed to support man but the truth is exactly the reverse—man failed to support nature. The people of Leptis raised the same crops decade after decade, broke the land, and today it holds no agricultural value and few people.

One can find other examples of the population affecting their surroundings. Illinois is known as "The Prairie State" although little of the tall grass prairies are left. The Australian state of Tasmania displays the "Tasmanian Tiger," or Thylacine, on its flag and coat of arms. This is the same animal likely today extinct with part of that equation being bounties that were placed on it.

Although meant to address the near extinction of the American bison, the book "The Extinction of the American Bison" written by William Hornaday in 1889, in fact, talked about more than that. The book noted that "The primary cause of the buffalo's extinction was the direct result of civilization with all its elements of destructiveness upon the whole of the country inhabited by that animal." That statement has to do with more than bison, perhaps. In the modern world, conservation depends on our support.

Humans possess the ability to alter the environment, for better or worse.

Missouri a Century Ago

Sometimes lost today is the fact that the Missouri one views today is in many ways much different than a century ago. Few can recall those days and as "seeing is believing" that is in some ways understandable. People tend to view "what is as what has always been." However, let's not go so fast.

I will present some of these differences with an emphasis on the Forestry and Lookouts that were the basis of my hobby and travels. Of course, it is not always easy to separate. If you take soil erosion, for example, there was an obvious connection to the gravel and soil that eroded from poor cover and poor fishing that occurred in streams and rivers that today run clean. Diminished timber also had a marked effect on game.

The combination of massive timber harvest, large numbers of free-roaming livestock and annual burning had a major effect on Ozark soils, streams, and of course, wildlife. Forest wildlife was hunted year-round, and it dwindled as the forests were cut over and competition from livestock reached a peak. By the 1930s only about 2,000 deer were thought to exist in the state and turkeys declined to a few thousand birds in scattered flocks. For all practical purposes, bear, ruffed grouse and passenger pigeons ceased to exist, and most other species were in dire straits (Keefe 1987). Let's turn the clock back a century and take a closer look.

Whether or not Native Americans used yearly burning is a matter of which book you read. There are many works (Steyermark 1959) that contend, contrary to popular belief, that this practice probably was not used. It most likely did not exist as an annual and organized effort. It is cited on occasion, however, as evidence of a certain "natural" past to the practice. Regardless, the small number of Native Americans involved made the consequences likewise, small.

It is also thought that some settlers brought the practice in for a variety of reasons. Some of these included: suppressing ticks and snakes, destroying crop insects, reducing predators, and in improving range and hunting. None of these worked in fact over a period of time. Fires started by landowners for their parcel often ended up as multi-acre disasters. As the first State Forester George O. White put it, "we can cut and use our forests over and over again so long as their progeny, which is called second growth, is protected from the many fires set by man and the comparatively few set by Jehovah" (Hoffman/ No Date).

Some of the early settlers also practiced the "European" style of agriculture. It had, in effect, not worked that well for the Europeans. Time was when trees grew right down the shores of Italy and Spain, for example. The trapping of beaver was common.

In Spain, the Merino Sheep emerged. Its wool was like no other, and only the Spanish had it. The king taxed each sheep, and each pound of wool and the removal of a single head from the country was punishable by death. Because the sheep needed to move from the lower coastal areas to the hills to graze at different times of the year, laws were passed banning fences and trees were felled wholesale to provide grass to graze on. Eventually, this practice spread up to the highest elevations leaving a Spain today that bears little resemblance to history. Of course, the soil washed away to silt the harbors, the tops of the highlands turned to bare rock, and food production fell. The Merino would eventually be transported to Italy to help turn Southern Italy into the environment we recognize today.

Italy was also symbolic of other problems. There was a time when, just in the area of Venice, large forests grew. These trees were a major source of fuel and lumber. The ships of the day needed oak for ribbing, walnut for rudders, elm for the capstan, beech for oars, and spruce for masts. The Venetian Flagship at the Battle of Lepanto, El Real, contained 39 beech trees, 300 pines, and 300 oak for that one ship alone. It is estimated at that one battle, 250,000 trees were lost. In fact, shipbuilding would shift north leaving southern Italy with few trees and a difficult agriculture (The First Eden, The Mediterranean World and Man - B.B.C. Documentary 1987).

Now, the "free range" style of grazing in Missouri would not have such a dramatic story, but in some ways, it was a similar one. The destruction by grazing or the clearing by fire would leave bare hilltops, broken soil, silted streams, and only scrub foliage left behind.

Paul Kelleter observed, "Destructive logging, woods burning, and overgrazing—working hand in hand, caused such an impoverishment of the productive capacity of the soil as to result in declining communities and low incomes with all of their attendant social and economic problems. Fire alone has caused untold losses by the destruction of trees, habitats for wildlife, forage for livestock, and the leaf litter which has, in turn, resulted in the erosion of the top layer of soil. Even a small fire scar on a tree destroys enough bark to admit diseases into the tree and cause its decay; large ugly scars on trees are the result of frequent burning and usually make the trees valueless for high-grade timber" (Kelleter 1936).

The same need for fuel that had helped level the forests of Europe was at work here in America. It was said the at one time a squirrel could travel from the Atlantic Coast to the Mississippi River and never touch the ground. Those days were over to the east and squirrels were afoot more and more in Missouri as well. At first, trees were cut near the banks of the rivers to fuel the steamships. Soon, forests that had grown right up to the edge of the Mississippi were gone. The soil began to wash, and it fast became the "Muddy Mississippi."

"Free Range" grazing in the Clark National Forest

Interior forests began to be cut. The effects of "clear cutting" could be devastating. Train lines were run to bring the timber out. It was the golden age of the railroad in America with an endless need for ties. The timbering produced "timber towns" that sprang up and prospered, for the moment. Grandin was home to the largest sawmill in the world. Good size communities today were even larger. Some large communities then, no longer exist. They show on an old topography map but not a computer word search. The influx of unbridled timbering quickly shifted the economy and layout of the Ozarks, only to shift it back just as fast as the timber ran out. I recall my search for the Horton Tower. Horton it seems was a timber town at one time, gone today. When a retired U.S.F.S. worker helped me locate the tower site, there is a Horton Cemetery, but no Horton. The conservation of Missouri was under stress, from many angles.

Missouri Rivers also were used to float cut timber out. Timber would be made into "rafts" and floated out to collection points.

United States Senator Everett Dirksen once observed, "Stronger than all the armies on earth is an idea whose time has come." Education, protection, and detection were on the conservation horizon.

The Time Had Come

As the 1920s ended and the 1930s began in Missouri, it had become clear to many the "the time had come" to get an organized conservation effort underway. Decades of abuse and poor practices had left much of the Missouri landscape ravaged. Timber had been "mined" for quick profit, the soil was heavily eroded, rivers and streams were full of silt, and wildlife had all but vanished. Deer and turkey numbers had fallen to a few thousand each and the season on both was canceled for years.

The country was also plummeted into the Great Depression. You had large numbers of young people in cities with nothing to do which contrasted with the rural conservation scene where there was lots to do. From both state and federal angle, conservation in Missouri was about to get organized.

It is difficult to decide if the state or federal effort should be addressed first. In fact, the two would overlap here and there. For example, a National Forest could not be established in the state until the state enacted legislation that would allow such an undertaking. Some of this work would have consequences that linger even today. For example, the original Consent Act set limits on land acquisition in terms of acres per tract and total per county.

Since a certain number was deemed necessary for a working ranger district, it became common to lay out purchases that overlapped several counties (Crowell 1953). This partly explains the at times odd looking layout of what emerged as the Mark Twain, even today.

The state effort would also encompass forestry, fishery, and wildlife. This is the triangle on the Missouri Department of Conservation badge. The federal effort would focus more on the forests.

From a Forest Lookout standpoint, it would mean a tower hobbyist like me would encounter lookouts that were likewise state and federal. I would have to go hunting information in two locations. I have flipped my coin, and the Missouri Department of Conservation will be first on the runway.

STATE OF MISSOURI EFFORTS—Although some departments and agencies existed before the mid-1930s, these tended to be style over substance. From 1925 to 1931 Missouri had a State Forester post in the Board of Agriculture to address wildfires. State Forester Frederick Dunlap resigned in 1931 when the state legislature failed to appropriate funds for forestry.

It was the hunters who first exerted their influence. Healthy forests would be essential to the recovery of fish and wildlife in the state (Hoffman /No Date). In the fall of 1935, a group of sportsmen met in Columbia to ponder the dwindling wildlife resources. This led to the formation of the Conservation Federation of Missouri. A year later, voters would approve the single most important concept in getting conservation efforts off the launch pad. This would be Amendment 4.

Amendment 4 was approved in November of 1936 and went into effect a year later. The vote surprised even its supporters and showed how widespread the belief in an organized conservation effort was. The final tally was 879,213 (71%) yes and 351,962 (29%) no. Many people in the state were ready for some substance.

The Conservation Federation would be heavily involved in the amendments promotion and wording. Amendment 4 would call for an agency, the Conservation Commission, to make rules and regulations over fish, forests, and wildlife. It would also give that agency the authority to set fines and punishment for violations. The Amendment would likewise direct money from licenses and fees that had previously been siphoned off to stay at home. Direction and resources were established. Although some provisions of the Amendment would be challenged, the Missouri Supreme Court would uphold its wording and intent. The wording Conservation Commission/Missouri Department of Conservation would be explained to me as follows by a department expert. Amendment 4 created the Conservation Commission which created the MDC. However, for many years the "Hawthorne" symbol was the logo for the Conservation Commission. In 1970, the MDC "Triangle" logo was adopted, and the Conservation Commission term was replaced with the MDC. The Commission employs the MDC Director and approves all major decisions such as budget and land purchases. The MDC implements the guidance of the Director that is approved by the Commission.

The original "Hawthorne Bloom."

"Wildlife, Fisheries, and Forestry Triangle"

The Missouri Department of Conservation would grow out of these beginnings. To meet the need, situation, and resources, the Department would be organized and reorganized over the years.

The next red-letter date would be in 1976. Finance had been a problem from the start with fees and licenses unable to produce enough revenue for a broad-based effort. Groups like the Conservation Federation and Citizens Committee for Conservation had collected signatures on petitions to put to the votes a one-cent tax on every sixteen ounces of soda they bought. Opposition from the soft drink industry was expected, and the petitions were actually thrown out on a wording technicality.

The various groups then proposed a "Design for Conservation" tax of one-eighth of 1% sales tax devoted to fish, forest, and wildlife conservation. This would provide funds to support a broad-based "Design for Conservation." The measure would pass by some 30,000 votes.

George O. White Nursery near Licking

For a tower hobbyist like myself, this would mean forestry was a part of the equation and early fire detection by lookout a big part of that.

FEDERAL EFFORTS - As I mentioned earlier, the State of Missouri, in the mid-1930s passed several "Consent Acts" allowing the formation of national forests in the state. Each of these Acts was slightly more relaxed in the amount of land that could be purchased. Purchase Units: Clark, Fristoe, Gasconade, and Pond Fork were established and followed by others. What is now known as the Mark Twain National Forest would undergo many changes. In 1933 eight purchase units made up what was called the National Forest in Missouri. Two years later this would be split into the Mark Twain and Clark National Forest. In 1953, the Fristoe and Wappapello would be assigned to the Shawnee National Forest in Illinois with the remaining units in Missouri called the Missouri National Forests. In 1962 the Fristoe and Wappapello would be returned to a Missouri now divided between the Mark Twain and the Clark National Forest. Then, for a brief period, a consolidation period created the National Forests in Missouri before the term Mark Twain National Forest was applied in 1976 to all the holdings. As was and is true on the state level, resources and need would create many divisions and combinations over the years. Ranger Districts and offices would be assigned and reassigned (Malouf 1991).

The national effort was much more a forestry one as contrasted to the state which addressed forestry, fish, and wildlife. Obviously, the various parts can't always be separated. The term "Purchase Unit" meant just that. Vast areas of the state were heavily timbered and the soil eroded. The purchase of these areas provided, many times, the only road to a return to normalcy.

Of course, corresponding to conservation "time had come" was the Great Depression which swept the country at almost the same time. The national government would create any number of "alphabet agencies" to put people to work. Some of these would have a marked conservation design.

Some of these agencies would operate on the fringe of the conservation work. Activities included: roads, telephone lines, buildings, bridges, etc. Of course, the big conservation alphabet agency would be the Civilian Conservation Corps. The C.C.C. was established on March 31, 1933, it remains today in many eyes the most popular and effective program in the New Deal. The first job of the enrollees was to build their housing and camp. Most of a worker's monthly wage was sent home to support those left back in the city.

Life at the camp often led to increased morale and the acquisition of skills. This same training provided a jump start to military service in World War II. Billions of trees would be planted across America. Trails, lodges, roadways, buildings, would be constructed with C.C.C. workers from 28 camps spread across the current Mark Twain Forest. C.C.C. workers would be called upon to fight forest fires, and the technique for that fighting was constantly refined.

For the tower hobbyist like me, the C.C.C. would build 87 towers across what is now the Mark Twain (Price 1940:7). They would also build a tower for the state here and there and experiment with new ideas. The Blooming Rose C.C.C. camp built and experimented with the "single pole" type of lookout. In addition, many of these lookouts were also manned by the "C.C.C. boys."

"Built about twelve miles apart, the towers afford a normal range of vision over the hills of twelve miles. Triangulation between towers will spot the fire within about 400 feet" (Turner 1938). In the following chapters, we will take a look at the variety of "lookouts" that sprung up across Missouri and some of the documentation my wife and I have worked on.

C.C.C. Workers Building a Toolbox

The Tie Capital of the World

Beamer Handle Company

Chess & Waymond Stave Finishing Company - Cuba, Missouri

C.C.C. Workers

Involvement & Information

Both the Forest Service and the Missouri Department of Conservation reached out to involve the public in the conservation effort. One Forest Service program involved the "Ancient and Honorable Order of Squirrel."

Note: On national forest system lands fire towers are not currently open to the public for climbing due to safety concerns

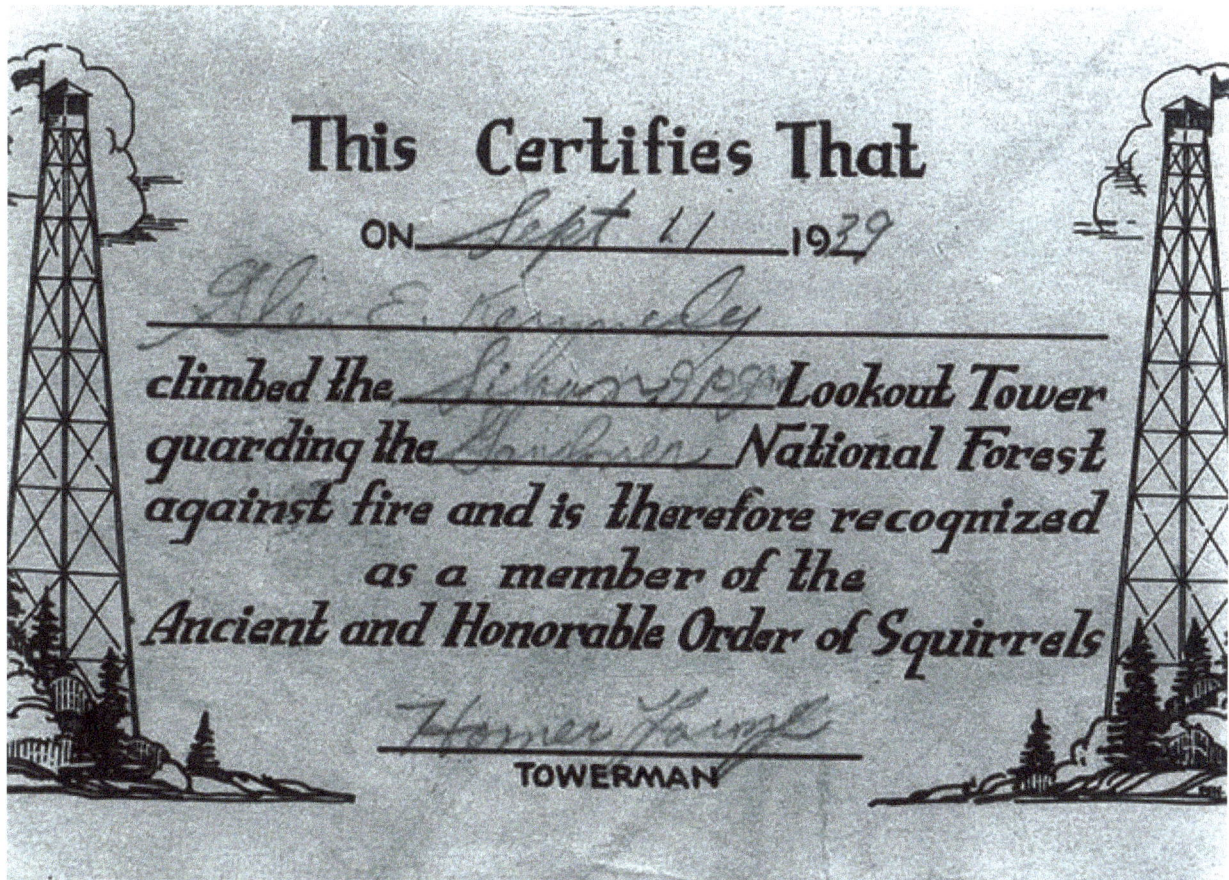

Visitors who climb the Fremont Lookout Tower are being presented with an attractive membership card in the Ancient and Honorable Order of Squirrels, a club initiated for the purpose of reducing the number of man-caused forest fires. There are no formalities to join—you merely climb the 100-foot steel tower "in the interest of fire prevention," and the Forest Service towerman will do the rest. He will demonstrate the method used in detecting and reporting forest fires and furnish each visitor with a membership card giving the name and date on which they climbed the tower.

Membership in the squirrel club is about equally divided between men and women, but the percentage of women who start to climb and reach the top is higher than that of men. Towermen remark that men look down more frequently than women while climbing, which may be one of the reasons why men decide to call it quits at the half-way mark. (Current Local / August 24, 1939)

Smokey Bear – 101

(Note: The name and character of Smokey Bear are the property of the United States, as provided by 16 U.S.C. 580p-1 and 18 U.S.C. 711, and are used with the permission of the Forest Service, U.S. Department of Agriculture.)

I received several requests to not forget "the Bear." Although perhaps not directly connected to the Forest Lookout Towers, I started some research and quickly wanted to add a piece. Jim Sorenson suggested I pick up "Smokey Bear 20252 – a Biography." It was a fun read, and I suggest you get yourself a copy. It is available on Amazon.

One of the more noteworthy efforts in all of Conservation, and even Americana, involved the creation and use of "Smokey Bear." In fact, name a figure: 1) recognized by 90% of the public and, 2) held in universal esteem and, 3) has enjoyed that position since 1944. Introducing - Smokey Bear-

Now, the Smokey Bear concept had a very interesting genesis. Here is Smokey through the years.

1940's – World War II created some simple logic. If we were fighting our enemies, we didn't need to be fighting forest fires. Following the outbreak of the war an enemy submarine surfaced and fired shells near the Los Padres National Forest. This even was parodied in the movie "1941." Then there were the Fu-Go. Incendiary balloons were not a new idea. In fact, both sides used them.

Thousands would be released from Japan using the jet stream to cross the Pacific Ocean in days. A barometric device allowed sand ballast or hydrogen to be released to control altitude. The idea was to ride the winds east and release firebombs on the forests of the northwest United States to create damage and distraction.

The bombs did little damage, although many are surprised to learn a mother and five children died after approaching a downed balloon.

In the early 1940s, a Cooperative Forest Fire Prevention Program had been organized. The Wartime Advertising Council was also charged with helping the cause. The message was simple, prevent fires and help win the war. Americans didn't understand that a million man-hours of labor – enough to build 800 fighter planes – were required each year to fight the nation's fires. Many trucks, bulldozers, tools and other equipment were tied up fighting fires. They could not measure the gallons of fuel needed to power the vehicles, or the cost of that fuel and the labor, food or tools needed to fight fires (Lawter, 1994).

In the mid-1940s, the Walt Disney movie "Bambi" was released. Disney would allow the usage of Bambi but only for a specified time. The effort proved very successful, and soon the Forest Service began the search for a permanent symbol. Symbols such as Little Willie, Ranger Bill, Sapling Sam and Ranger Jim had already been tried. Some felt the squirrel was a natural. The bear emerged as the animal of choice. Artist Albert Staehle was asked to conjure up this first Smokey Bear, and its usage and popularity took off. The Ad Council, the United States Forest Service and the National Association of State Foresters would combine knowledge with delivery to use Smokey Bear in fire prevention.

Several decades later, the problem of trash and an animal response would be considered. It would be decided to not give Smokey new responsibilities, and Woodsy Owl was created. "Give a hoot – don't pollute" and "Lend a hand – care for the land" became the slogans for this effort.

1950's – In the early '50s, a large fire broke out in the Capitan Mountains of New Mexico. A virtual army assaulted the fire and reports came in of a cub wandering near the fire and then high in a burnt tree. The cub was taken to Santa Fe for veterinary care for burns on its paws and hind legs. The original name of "Hotfoot Teddy" would be replaced with Smokey Bear.

This bear would find its way to the National Zoo and become, for the next quarter century, the living symbol of Smokey Bear. A Smokey costume would be stitched together, and over the years that costume codified. Forest Service artist Rudy Wendelin would become famous for his drawing and posters urging people to practice fire safety. Legislation would also be passed to promote the commercial use of the image. Fees and royalties would bring in revenue to help fire prevention. However, Jim Sorenson points out the focus was exposure and the benefit that would bring to the table, not the money brought in.

The 1950s also saw the Junior Forest Ranger Program arrive. Programs and materials were developed to involve young people in the effort. The idea was young people grew up, and if you had a dedicated junior forester, you would eventually have a dedicated adult who could then perpetuate the cause. This "Smokey system" would work for decades as forest fires continue to decrease.

In 1962, "Goldie Bear" was introduced to Smokey with the hopes of perhaps creating a Smokey lineage. Perhaps Smokey's duties were too time consuming, but no young were produced. The possibility existed that the burns from the Capitan fire had left him sterile (Lawter, 1994). A cub from the Lincoln National Forest would be added with the understanding it had been adopted. This became "Little Smokey."

On November 9th, 1976 the original Smokey passed away. His remains were returned to Capitan, New Mexico and he was interred at what is now Smokey Bear Historical Park. Near the interpretive center, you will find this plaque – "This is the resting place of the first living Smokey Bear…the living symbol of wildfire prevention and wildlife conservation." Little Smokey would pass on August 11, 1990.

However, the birth of the concept in 1944 would continue to be celebrated. The 40th, 50th, 60th, and 70th birthdays would see a variety of activities marking the occasion. He moved into new arenas with a website and social media. Smokey Bear Awards are conferred by the United States Forest Service, the National Association of State Foresters and the Ad Council.

Some Smokey Bear Trivia

No "the" is not needed unless you sing. In 1952 Steve Nelson and Jack Rollins had a hit with Eddy Arnold – "Smokey the Bear". They said the "the" was added to help with the song's rhythm. For most other usages, it is just Smokey Bear.

"Only YOU Can Prevent Forest Fires" is in many people's minds synonymous with Smokey. In 2001 however, the slogan was changed to "Only You Can Prevent Wildfires" to cover fires in areas other than forests.

In 1952 the Junior Forest Ranger Program was started. Children were encouraged to write Smokey Bear to talk about fire prevention. In return, they received a Junior Forest Ranger Kit and materials. Soon Smokey was receiving 1,000 letters a day. In response, a Zip Code – 20252 was created to handle the volume.

In addition to fish, Smokey developed a love of peanut butter sandwiches.

The "Smokey Hat" became the inspiration for hats worn by law enforcement and others. He was a trendsetter.

For his 40th birthday, Smokey was honored with his own postage stamp illustrated by Rudy Wendelin. Also, "Smokey Sports" was created, and activities occurred across major league baseball. There was also a "Smokey and the Pros" program.

Though an imposing figure, the living Smokey was not always the playful type. In addition, in 1972, China, in response to President Nixon's openings, had donated Hsing-Hsing and Ling-Ling. Smokey was no longer the only bear on the block and faced stiff competition. There is probably some truth to the idea Smokey got lost in the shuffle a little. His pen, compared to his Chinese stars, was viewed by some as second rate. The fact remains, however, that millions came to see Smokey over the years and many still enjoy the Smokey Bear Historical Park each year.

Firetowers

Smokey demonstrates he can do it all and this bear does not hibernate.

A big "thank you" to Roger Schmidt for sharing his Smokey collection!

The "pioneering" Pioneer Forest – information supplied by Terry Cunningham

Photo Credit – Pioneer Forest

Terry Cunningham sent me the following information on the Brushy Creek Mill that once operated on Brushy Creek. Brushy Creek (this one, Missouri has many a Brushy Creek) flows south and enters the Current River below Round Springs. The mill was run by National Distillers Products who owned the land at the time. It had a Post Office (Brushy, Mo.) and a small mill town and company store. The mill shut down in 1950. The history of the land was: Current River Lumber Company, Pioneer Cooperage, and National Distillers (who called it Seton Porter Forest). In 1954 Leo Drey purchased it and renamed it Pioneer Forest. It has been a true "pioneer" in sustainably managed forestry. Prior to his death, Leo Drey donated it to the LAD Foundation to ensure its protection and management. Pioneer Forest was and is a pioneer in sustainable uneven-aged forest management and at present covers @ 140,000 acres. The mill was visible from Coot Mountain, Shannondale, and Himont Tower.

An airplane view from the north looking south at Brushy Creek

The "pioneering" Pioneer Forest – information supplied by Terry Cunningham

Staves from the stave mill days

Forest Manager Ed Woods pictured with a large White Oak from near Round Springs circa 1950.

Stave bolts being loaded to take to the mill in the early 1950s.

Lookouts Not Towers

Although not as dramatic and noticeable, a number of lookouts that were not wooden or steel towers existed here and there across Missouri. The wood and steel towers left concrete piers or footings behind. Made up of many cubic yards of concrete, seldom were they removed when the tower was and left a "fingerprint" of past existence. The single pole lookouts and crow's nests in the trees are often not listed in documents and not found in the countryside. They were of several types.

Max Gorman recalls an Elliot Lookout near Stegall Mountain. This was in fact just a high bare spot which offered a good view. A worker could be sent to "Elliot" to just observe from their truck during the dry season. There seems to also have been a "portable lookout" that could be moved from place to place but little remembrances remain and no pictures I have found.

What is remembered are places and locations where coverage was needed to see over a ridge or observe an area during the dry season. The "burn index" also factored into this equation. When winds exceeded 20 mph, and humidity was less than 25 percent, these "secondary" lookouts were often called into service. At times these just had to do until a wood or steel tower could be put up.

The simplest of these was just a platform or "crow's nest" in a high tree. Here you see a good example (right) simply listed "in the Winona" area. It could be Low Wassie, Tee, HighwayE/High Knob, or Mud Pond Ridge. Regardless, it gives a good example of the tree lookout experience.

This "lookout" from near Sligo (right) seems to be a private undertaking atop a building that predates any organized state or federal effort.

In fact, the most famous White Oak in Missouri history was a part of the tree lookout brigade. As soon as I began writing lookout articles for the Summersville and Current Wave papers, I received calls that I needed to get a hold of Verlin and Faye Beasley. I called Verlin, and he invited me over for a visit.

His father, Earnest, worked in Conservation, and between the two of them, they were honored many times for their work. These included: two awards from the Texas County Soil and Water Commission, Woodland

Awards in 1981 and 1982, a 25 years silver tree farm certificate for 1977 and 2003, and the Missouri Outstanding Forester for 1983. It was one White Oak that was very interesting.

Verlin began the story at Gist Ranch. The tower there had trouble "seeing over the ridge" that divides South Apple Creek and Big Creek. These "blind spots" were often covered with tree lookouts or single pole lookouts. In 1943 a large White Oak became part of the lookout arsenal. For the next 15 years, the tree would provide coverage. It was often manned by Verlin's Dad Earnest, who worked for the Missouri Conservation Commission.

The Conservation Commission would later erect a famous sign at the site in the memory of Earnest Beasley. This would make that White Oak, since blown down, probably the most famous White Oak in Missouri history. Thanks to Verlin and Faye for the information and the Missouri hospitality.

Pictured at the dedication were: Vergie Langston, Vera Kirkman, Verlin Beasley, Don Beasley, and Roy Beasley.

Another type of coverage lookout was the single pole tower. This involved setting a single pine pole in the ground and putting a platform or even a small cab in the top. Now and then all the limbs would be removed from a tree to form the "pole" in what was a tree lookout variation. When a single pole was used, a close inspection of the picture will often show "guy wires" attached at various points for stability.

The following is from the Rolla Herald. "Plans are now being prepared for erection of a temporary lookout about three miles southeast of Big Piney, on the Piney Ranger District of the Gardner National Forest in Missouri calls for an open "crow's nest" atop a forty-foot pine pole.

The nest will be five feet square with three-foot walls and will not be permanently roofed but will be fitted with an adjustable canvass cover to shelter the lookout man in sudden storms and protect the range finder, maps, radio, or telephone or other equipment at night.

The nest has already been built inside an electrically angle-iron frame fabricated by mechanic Jack Ash at the Blooming Rose C.C.C. camp and will be hoisted to the top of the pole by tackle.

The corner irons project some 6 or 7 feet below the floor of the nest and are bent inward to serve as braces when they are bolted to the floor.

The pole itself will protrude upward through the floor of the nest to a height slightly above the walls and will serve as a support on which to mount the range finder. Cables attached just below the corner braces will guy it four ways, and alternation lag screws on opposite sides of it will serve as a ladder.

Forestry officials state that if this type of temporary lookout proves satisfactory, a large number of other such structures will be erected at strategic points before the beginning of the next fire season." (Rolla Herald 2/4/1937)

It was common for most C.C.C. camps to have some kind of lookout since one of the hats worn by the enrollees was fighting fires. Pole towers were often the first up and at times replaced later by 50 foot or even 100-foot towers. The C.C.C. camps also had water towers, and these served double duty at times providing a lookout use.

Also, existing structures were called into service. The Doniphan water tower was used as a lookout for example.

Here are a few historical pole tower/tree pole examples.

Simpson's Crow's Nest NE of Falcon, Missouri. Note this is a pole/tree hybrid with the "pole" being a tree that has been pruned bare.

Above left is a picture of the Bunker Pole Lookout. It stood south of Bunker. In this case, you notice the lookout had a cab, not common for pole lookouts. A close examination will also show guy wires running up to attach about halfway up and just below the cab. It happened now, and then the high point chosen for a pole lookout would also be used later for a wooden or steel tower.

The second picture is of the Blackjack Pole Lookout that stood NE of Blackjack. Again, if you look close, you can make out the guy wires that ran up from the ground for stability. Evidence of pole towers is almost non-existent, but a cable or small footings for the wires show now and then with close examination.

Above left is a pole lookout that stood near what was later a site for the Vada Tower near Vada.

Above right is Olin Ashleck climbing a pole lookout at C.C.C. Camp # 7731. Again, note the guy wires.

These tree lookouts and pole tower could be found scattered across Missouri at one time. Some, like Mud Pond Ridge, would never evolve into anything else. Others would be replaced by wood towers and those replaced by steel. Some examples:

Asher – a wooden tower and finally a windmill tower

Avon – a pole lookout

Baldridge – a crow's nest to a pole to a windmill

Bee – a pole lookout on Bee Hill

Bell Mountain I – started as a crow's nest

Bell Mountain II – started as a crow's nest

Birch – started as a crow's nest

Centerville – a tree platform

High Knob/E Highway – tree

Hilda – started as a crow's nest

Firetowers

Sullivan Hill – started as a crow's nest

Horn – tree lookout

Lone Pine – started as a tree lookout

Low Wassie – started as a tree lookout

Mud Pond Ridge – tree lookout

Nottinghill – started as a crow's nest

Pike – pole lookout

Rombauer – started as a crow's nest

Simpson – tree with open cab

Tee – tree lookout

Vada – started as a pole lookout

Wooden Towers

Once fire detection and lookouts became a part of the equation to reforest Missouri, tree and pole lookouts sprang up across the state. What also began to appear were wooden towers. The fact that there are @ 60 some steel towers still up by no wooden tells a story of sorts. To assume a uniform pattern of wood to steel however is not true also. During the war years, for example, the shortage of steel turned the tower builders back to wood, at least for the moment. Wood could be stubborn. "The old sentinel didn't fall easily. The fire tower was stronger than Conservation Commission personnel had figured. Supporting braces were sawed away. Bolts were driven out with sledges, power saws partially cut through three of the massive legs. Still, it resisted. The cold Tuesday afternoon dragged on. Time after time, ropes were attached to a small bulldozer and tension applied. Time after time the ropes snapped. Half a dozen times the structure defied the crew, settling back on its concrete base with creaks and groans. Built in 1947, the fire tower near the Reform Community, in southeastern Calloway County, had served its purpose. The 120-foot steel tower south of Gutherie has replaced the 60-foot wooden tower which was rotting and unsafe. The Reform Tower, a familiar landmark in the area, had been scheduled for destruction last Friday. Transportation difficulties gave it four days of grace. It was a cold, damp, and windy day to go. Its time, however, had run out. Nestled in its dark green 20-acre grove of surrounding pine trees, the roar of the dozer and shouts of the crew disturbed the forest stillness as they tried to pull the tower over. The tower stood starkly against the slate-gray sky, a belligerent, frustrating reminder of a time when things were built to last. The dozer won in the end. The leg in the direction of fall was sawed almost completely through almost four feet from the base. A chain was attached to the dozer and tied directly around the base. Revving up the machine, the dozer yanked on this four-foot "plug" at a right angle. Slowly at first, with a loud snapping of timbers and the collapsing of the topmost portion of the structure, the fall began. Then the tilt, inharmonious, chillingly incongruent, with agonizing slowness and finally the crash, cushioned by the pines, comrades for years performing one last favor. Eugene McCormick, Reform, had been the tower man at Reform since its construction and is now assigned to the Gutherie Tower. He was among the workmen at the site" (Jefferson City Post-Tribune, 10/1972).

The sturdiness of the wooden towers owed much to design, the fragility to wood as opposed to galvanized steel. The wooden towers had piers or footings like steel towers. Like steel towers, this meant excavating a large hole to hold many cubic yards of concrete. A difference was that wooden tower had "straps" set in the concrete and not bolts. See the picture on the next page from Proctor Tower.

The wooden leg of the tower would be set between the straps and the leg then bolted to the straps. Much like a steel tower, the footings had to be accurate in spacing and level or problems would compound as the tower went up. Since water and wood don't mix, many of these wood footings had a bevel to them to ensure water ran off.

Getting the wooden leg set between the straps depended on the size of the tower. For small 50 foot or so towers, the tower might be assembled on the ground in a horizontal position. Then using a wench or gin pole, the tower would be set vertical. With a "rocker log" under two of the legs, the tower would pivot vertical, and if all went well, two of the legs would sit down right between two of the straps to be bolted down. See the following U.S.F.S. diagram -

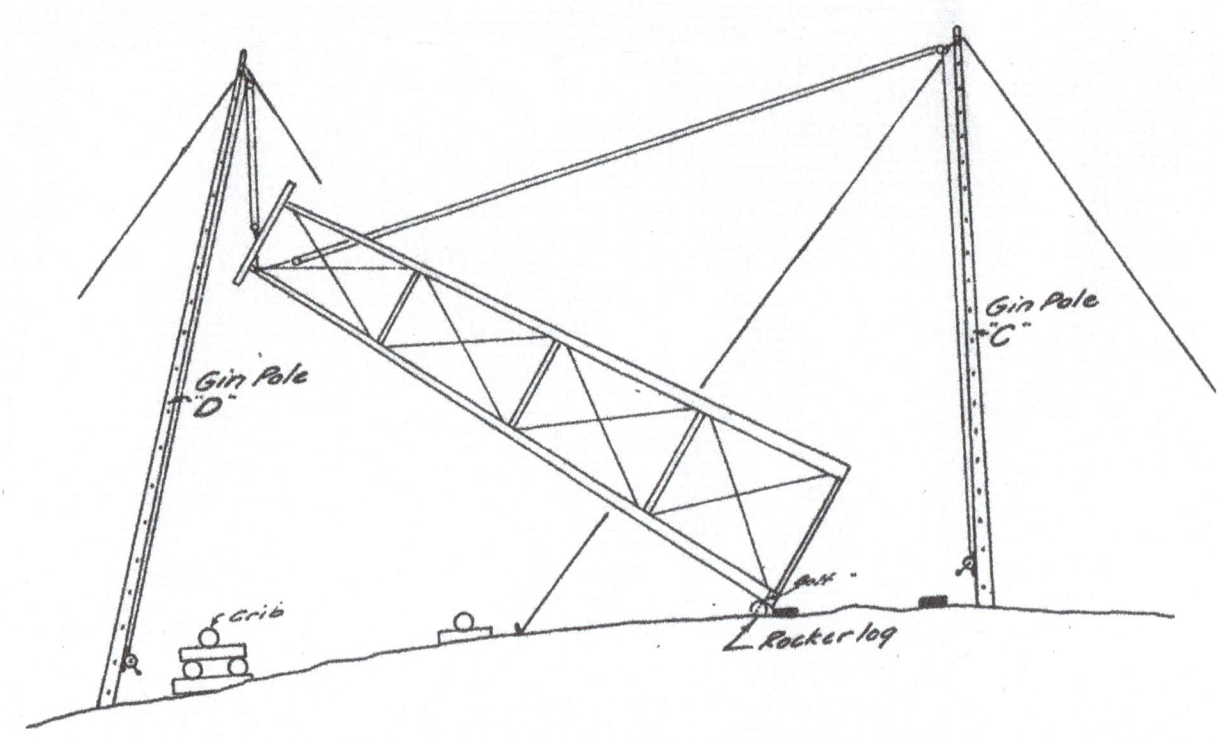

Following this, additional belts and braces would be added. Also, some system for making your way to the top was installed. For these smaller towers, this often meant a ladder that ran up the outside. Commonly, these smaller wooden towers didn't have a cab but only a platform on the top. Some models did have risers and cabs. They usually had no fire finder and were as they were named, only "patrol" towers.

Erecting a larger 100 foot or so wooden tower was a different story. Unlike steel towers where the legs were put up in pieces, the larger wooden towers had four legs set on the footings in a different manner. Of course, the footings for a 100-foot tower were larger than a fifty footer with many more cubic yards of concrete. The same exact spacing and level likewise had to be achieved.

Each leg was in effect a 100 foot or so pine log. To set these vertical, an A-frame was used. In the picture on the following page, you can see an A-frame in the background being used to gain leverage and pull the leg vertical to be bolted to straps already set on each footing. You will notice to gain stability during the erection process, guy wires were attached and remained so after the legs were brought vertical to gain stabilization. In fact, guy wires remained a part of the larger wooden tower design as guy wires would be run away from each leg permanently to gain stability. The tension of these guy wires was set to exact standards.

If you visit a historic wooden tower site, like at Macedonia, you will find smaller footings away from each corner where these guy wires were anchored. If you look close in larger wooden tower pictures, you can make out these cables or sets of cables.

As soon as the four legs were secured, crews would start at the bottom attaching "braces" and "belts" as they worked their way up. You can see all of this in the picture below.

Once the belts and braces were finished, the tower had gained lots of stability. Crews could then go about adding a stairway with risers and platforms. A cab would be constructed on top with radio or telephone for communications. A big focus following the construction of a series of towers would be the running of lines. However, not all towers would have lines in which case the tower worker would simply have to use various portable radios that put the word communication to the test.

Of course, having reported the smoke or fire, the worker then would have to take off to fight the fire. This might have to be done by themselves for a small fire or until others arrived for larger ones.

With wood, of course, the common problem was water or on occasion "dry rot." The answer was creosote. When applied correctly to a well-dried log it could provide good protection against the elements. The pine had a natural center filled with resin which resisted water. Not only would the legs arrive having been creosoted, but the coating would be reapplied by brush periodically. Even the holes for the bolts would be creosoted to resist water. My friend Jim Parker remembers hanging from a "saddle sling" with a can and brush. On one occasion some slack had got bound up where the rope ran through the trap door. When the door was opened the sling dropped several inches. His can and brush dropped to the ground as Jim's blood pressure didn't.

On occasion, looks could be deceiving. Max Gorman told me that on occasion when a wood tower was taken down, people were stunned at how little of the inside of the leg remained. It could make things look good, on the surface. In fact, Jim Parker told me he was always instructed to not creosote the steps. If a step was bad, you needed to see it.

Creosote would later come under scrutiny for health concerns associated with the fumes and with the runoff into the environment. Other preservative methods were tried, but few worked as well as creosote.

I was told by more than one worker who served on even the largest wooden towers, a person today would be amazed just how sturdy and little sway a well-constructed wooden tower actually had.

An iconic and often rendered picture of the Macedonia Tower that stood near the community of Macedonia south of Grandin. Again, note the guy wires visible at a close look.

Wooden Towers

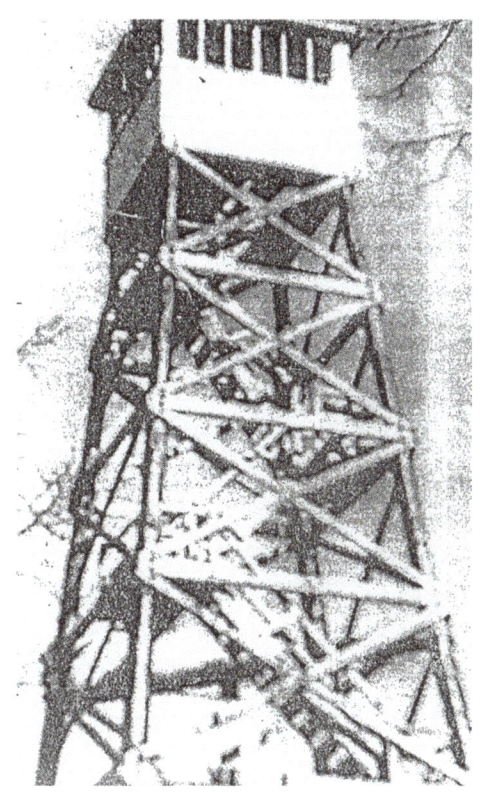 

(Left) This is the original wooden tower at Deer Run, according to Gerald Angel now the Current River Conservation Area. It was later replaced by the current steel tower, reported to be the first steel tower in the state. This tower was the first in the state by some sources (Rose 1990), but the exact nuance of towers at Deer Run remains today a little contradicted. (Right) The original wooden tower at Neosho from a postcard.

The original wooden tower that stood at Mountain View sitting next to the present steel one.

Original wooden tower that stood at Panther Hill north of Ellington

Wooden Lookout that stood atop Stegall Mountain at one time.

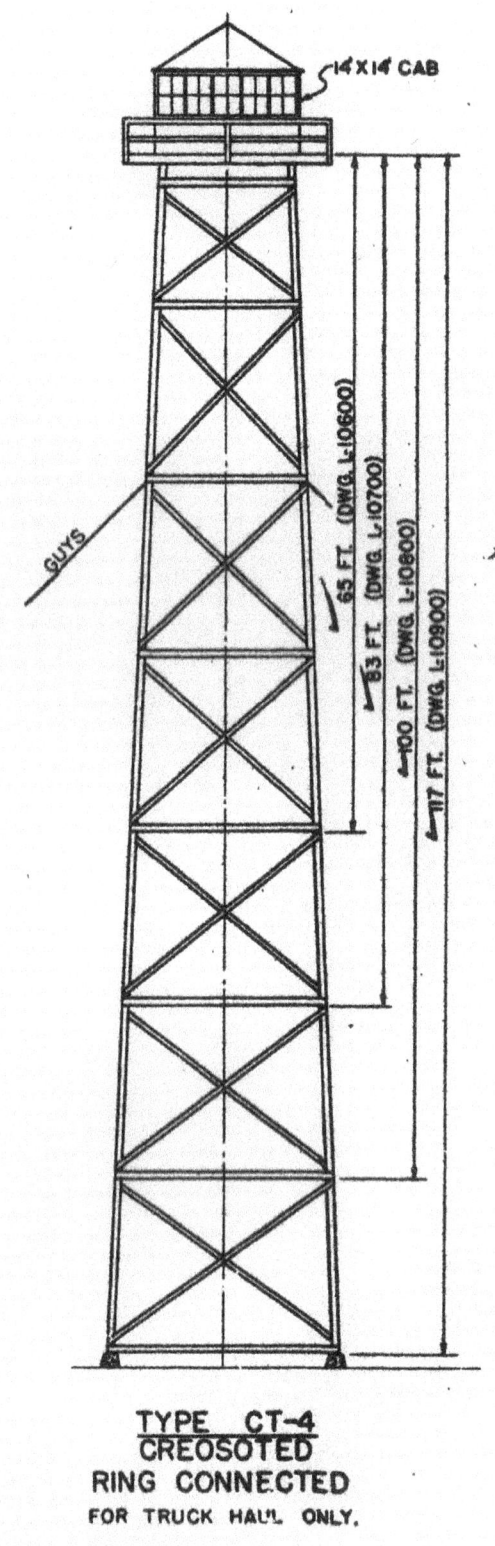

This is a Diagram for a CT-4 wooden U.S.F.S. Tower. The Macedonia Tower seems to be this design, or some variation with the seven segments and guy wire attach points. Note how for a smaller tower, you could just use the top portion or portions.

Here is a picture of the wooden Goodman Tower still up as the steel Goodman is erected. Several sites that would contain steel towers started out as wood. Some of these were: Jenkins, Washburn, Grassy, Hunter, Lone Hill-Meramec, Mountain View, Sunridge, Elkhorn, Powell, Goodman, Joplin, Hercules, Hilltop, Shannondale, Neosho and Greenley.

Jim Ruble recalls Vulcan Tower and his Dad

Avery and Smokey heading up to the first tower at Vulcan

REFLECTIONS OF GROWING UP AT THE MISSOURI CONSERVATION COMMISSION, VULCAN LOOKOUT TOWER, ON MANN MOUNTAIN, VULCAN, IRON COUNTY, MISSOURI.

Written February 2018
By James Adrian (Jim) Ruble

My Dad, James Avery Ruble, was employed by the Missouri Conservation Commission as the Vulcan Towerman on July 1, 1945. I was 10 years old. We lived in Annapolis, Missouri, which was 10 miles from the Tower. There were two routes to the tower. One route was 10 miles of gravel roads by way of Funk Branch, and the other route was 5 miles of blacktop road and 5 miles of gravel road, by way of Vulcan, MO. The tower road was 1 ½ miles long and intersected the Funk Branch Road. In 1945, the tower road was hardly more than a trail. The road was improved about 2 years later.

My Dad (Avery Ruble) was assigned several different vehicles early in his employment. The Conservation Commission was fairly new and had a variety of vehicles. Some that I remember were a 1941 Chevrolet Coupe with the trunk lid removed and a small pickup bed installed, a military weapons carrier, a Dodge Power Wagon, a Willy's pickup (rare), a 1939 Ford pickup, a new 1949 Willys Jeep and a new 1955 Willys Jeep. The fire crew always tried to get as close to the fire as possible, so the vehicles were driven over rough terrain, through the woods, etc. The only accident my Dad (Avery Ruble) had was returning from Piedmont, MO in the 1939 Ford pickup, he hit a patch of "black ice" at Des Arc, MO and hit a guard rail. Piedmont, MO was headquarters for the Sam A. Baker District.

The original Vulcan Tower was a 60 ft. wood tower constructed with 4 wooden telephone-type poles and wood cross members. There was a wood platform landing about 8-10 feet below the bottom of the tower cab. Three steps led to a large trap door in the floor of the cab for access to the cab. You would stand on the steps and push the trap door up to gain access to the cab. You would then close the trap door to make a complete floor in the tower cab.

The tower cab was constructed of wood with a shingle roof. It was approximately 10 X 10 feet square and approximately 8 to 9 feet high. The inside walls were plywood, and the floor was finished oak boards.

There were windows completely around the cab. In the center of the cab, was a wooden stand approximately 2 ft square. The top of the stand was level with the bottom of the windows. Suspended from the ceiling of the cab, over the stand, was a cabinet extending down about 18 inches, leaving a space between the stand and the cabinet. Installed in the cabinet above, was the Communications Radio. Installed on top of the stand was an Osborne Fire Finder (see Fire Finder in later paragraph).

In 1945, the tower was still equipped with a wood ladder made of 2"X4" runners and 1" X 4" rungs, installed straight up the front side of the tower. Later, the ladder was replaced by flights of steps inside the tower frame.

My Dad (Avery Ruble) had a large rope he used to lift equipment to the platform since he could not carry anything up the straight ladder. Since I was 10 years old when I first started climbing the tower, it was a long time before he would let me climb the ladder without tying the rope around me when I climbed the tower.

Radio communication was necessary between the tower, the vehicles and the District Headquarters in Piedmont. The first radio I remember was a box approximately 24" X 18" rectangle and about 6" - 8" deep. One half of the front side hinged open, exposing the switches, antenna connection and the microphone.

The towermen were required to make radio contact with Headquarters every hour during certain times of the year. When my Dad was at home in Annapolis, he would have to drive about 2 miles to the top of Annapolis Hill to make a contact. I first remember using this radio when my Dad had the 1939 Ford pickup. He would take the radio out of the bed box and set it on top of the box. He would then take a piece of strand wire with a weight attached and throw the wire over a limb of a tree for the antenna. He would attach the antenna to a connection on the radio. In order to get the attention of Headquarters, he would "whistle" in the microphone. When contact was made, after each comment, each person would say "over." I think this radio was the only one he had at that time, so he had to pull the radio up the tower with the rope.

The next radios in the tower were two radios from Army tanks. They were installed in the cabinet above the fire finder. The radio in the Jeep looked like a CB radio. A long whip antenna was installed on the back of the Jeep.

In the 1940s, the main purpose of the Forestry Division of the Conservation Commission was the detection and control of wildfires. The area was open range for livestock, so the owners of the land liked to burn off the woods, so a little amount of grass and vegetation would help feed their livestock. A lot of the wildfires were set by landowners, some were caused by control burns, and several were intentionally set. On several occasions, a sack or cloth soaked in flammable liquid would be tied to a horse and fire would be set for miles. They were called string jobs.

The spring fire season, March and April, was the busy time for the towerman. The fall fire season in November was usually not as destructive as the Spring season, but still a very busy time. During fire season, the towerman worked almost 24/7. My Dad had two men who worked almost full time in fire season, Rudy Perry and Vernon Sutton. When a fire was detected, additional firefighters were picked up. Several local men were usually available. Several times, high school students from Annapolis and Des Arc were used. On weekends and after school, I would be on standby. I worked many an hour for 50 cents per hour. One year, during spring fire season, the crews were so busy that I was allowed to take a week off school to man the tower.

On Easter Sunday in 1951 or 1952, we had a very large fire in the Taum Sauk area. Several fire crews were sent to the area. I was on a crew led by Taum Sauk Towerman Walter Holland, Jr. when we tied our fire line into a burned-out area our portion of the fire was under control. I was a few yards behind the crew mopping up and checking the fire line. One of the rules is to stay on the fire line always. Junior and the rest of the crew continued along the fire line and cut across the burn to the Jeeps. When I continued along the fire line, I did not know the crew had cut across the burn, so I continued walking, knowing I would eventually come to the Jeeps. When I didn't show up at the vehicles—Jim as lost!! The fire crews were searching, the airplane was sent to search, my Mom was on the Vulcan tower radio listening to the proceedings. When I finally came to the Jeeps, everyone wanted to know where I had been. I said I was just walking the fire line following the rules.

In the summertime from 1945 to 1949, I would go to work with my Dad almost every day. Most days were spent at the tower doing tower site improvement. The Sam A. Baker District office was in Piedmont, MO. The district maintenance shop was in Sam A. Baker Park at Mudlick Tower. The Conservation Commission was very good at preventive maintenance on their vehicles and equipment. Frequently we would go to Piedmont, or the maintenance shop, for meetings or to work on equipment. The summertime was used to get ready for fire seasons.

The State Maintenance Shop was in the Meramec State Park at Sullivan, MO. Each vehicle was required to be inspected each year. The first time I was in Sullivan was for a vehicle inspection. Route 66 was being replaced with I-44.

The Conservation Commission had a program called Timber Stand Improvement. Landowners with large tracks of land could sign up for this program. Periodically the towermen would inspect the land to check for trespass, or timber being cut. I remember in some areas, we picked huckleberries (wild blueberries, for the uninformed). There are very few things better than a huckleberry cobbler.

In the 1940s, deer and turkey were scarce. It was rare to see either a turkey or a deer. There was no deer season or turkey season for hunting. After the Conservation Commission started the program to replenish the deer and turkey, after a few years, they were more plentiful and hunting seasons were started. Now there are too many deer. They are very destructive, especially in the city suburbs. Turkey is also plentiful. Huckleberries are a thing of the past. The deer and turkey eat the berries and the bushes before the berries get ripe.

My Dad was a rural mail carrier before he went to work for the Conservation Commission in 1945. He delivered mail in a 1928 Model A Ford Coupe. During WW2 practically, everything was rationed. Since the mail was a priority, my Dad got ration stamps for gasoline, tires, oil, etc. for the Model A Ford. We were able to visit my grandparents James Andrew and Nellie Ruble at Brunot, MO on Sundays. This was my first experience with cars.

I have always been infatuated with cars and trucks. I would go with my Dad on the mail route to get to set in his lap and drive the Model A Ford. After he went to work for the Commission in 1945, I would go to the tower and stay all day just to get to drive part way to and from the tower.

There was not much room for furniture in the cab of the tower. There was a small kerosene heater for cool days, a chair made of 1" boards, the stand in the center and the suspended cabinet over the stand in the center for the radio equipment. In the ceiling of the cab was a small access hole to a small attic space. One of our pastimes was to scare the flying squirrels out of the attic and watch them sail to the ground. The standby fire crew would sometimes play cards in the tower cab. There was not much free time during fire season.

The focal point of any lookout tower, beside the communication radio, was the Osborne Fire Finder. It was located on top of the stand in the middle of the cab. Every tower was equipped with an Osborne Fire Finder. The base sits on two metal round bars so it can be adjusted latterly. The base is a 360-degree metal circle. Around the edge of the circle is the number 0 degree-360 degree. A rotating circular bar is rotated around the base to acquire a reading. Affixed to this rotating bar are two sight bars. One has a slit in the side, and the other has crosshairs. Over the center of the base is a topog map with the tower location in the center of the map. A reading (degree) is acquired by sighting through the sites while turning the rotating bar. The fire or smoke is sighted in the cross-hair site. The reading or degree was related to the Piedmont Headquarters. In the Headquarters office was a large board covered with a map of the Sam A Baker District. Each tower in the district had a 360-degree decal around the tower location. A weighted string with a pin attached was pulled out of the board and placed over the degree reading of the tower, reporting the reading. Another tower, able to see the fire or smoke, would have a reading and where the strings from each tower location crossed, located the fire. A very simple and accurate method of locating a fire.

When the towers were determined to be obsolete, they were abandoned. The towers were vandalized, windows were broken, furniture including fire finders was thrown out the windows. When I realized this had occurred, I asked Junior Green, the Vulcan towerman at the time, if he knew anything about the fire finder. He was able to retrieve, out of the woods, the base of the fire finder. The rotating ring, the sites, the map were not found. I kept the base stored in my garage for years.

Fast forward to 2016—my son, James Alan Ruble, a Mining Engineer who graduated from Missouri S & T in Rolla, MO, asked if he could have the fire finder base. About 6 months later, I got the surprise of my life. Alan had restored the fire finder. He made a wood base containing the metal rods, cleaned and painted the metal base, handmade the rotating ring with both the sights and mounted a topog map with the Vulcan tower in the center. I am the proud owner of the original restored Osborne fire finder, that was installed in the Vulcan tower in 1939. It is one of my prized possessions.

From 1945 to 1949, we lived in Happy Hollow (Holler) in Annapolis, MO. We traveled 10 miles to the tower each day. 1949 brought a change in our family life. I was 14 years old and graduated from the 8th grade, my sister, Helen, graduated from high school and left for college in Cape Girardeau in the fall. We moved to a new house at the Vulcan Tower in June 1949.

Howard Mondy, a carpenter for the Conservation Commission and a small crew of men, including my Dad, built a new house, two car-garage, chicken house, a barn and a three-hole outhouse (toilet). They did not drill a well. A concrete in-ground cistern was built for water supply. The house had two bedrooms, a small room for a bathroom with no fixtures, a small hall, living room, kitchen-dining area combined and a full basement. There was a small concrete front porch with a cover and a small screened-in back porch.

When the tower and buildings were scheduled to be torn down or sold, a small committee of local citizens, including a senator from Missouri, was formed to meet with the Conservation Commission to preserve the tower and tower site. The Commission agreed to leave the tower standing, but the house and car shed were sold and moved to the town of Vulcan, MO.

Citizens Discuss Plans To

Residents of the southern Iron County community of Vulcan expressed their desire Saturday to keep the Vulcan fire tower operational and asked State Sen. Danny Staples to negotiate that point with the Missouri Department of Conservation's Forestry Division in Jefferson City.

Meeting with residents at the Vulcan Community Center, Staples told them that the number of fire towers has been reduced over the years because of changing fire protection methods and educational programs that have decreased the number of forest fires.

"Back in the early '50s, every spring people burned the woods," he said. "They're not doing that anymore. Anytime a fire gets out now, it's because of lightning or someone's negligence."

Staples said Conservation "doesn't need the towers like they used to" and although the department is "not going to remove them all, they don't need as many" as they once did. He indicated that Conservation has long-range plans to tear down the Vulcan towerman's house and eventually the tower itself.

"Jerry Presley (head of the Forestry Division) told me they were going to dismantle the tower and the house in maybe two or three years," Staples said. "The house will go first." He added that Conservation is usually "pretty liberal" about donating or leasing abandoned property to nearby communities if an agreement can be reached on maintaining and insuring it.

Such an agreement would be necessary partly because of the problem of liability. "They don't want to leave the tower up there and have the possibility of a lawsuit if somebody's child fell off of it or maybe somebody intoxicated falls off," the senator said.

Residents told Staples that their top priority was keeping the tower manned and operating as it is now. "They see fires before the fire department ever does," one woman noted. Closing the tower would also mean the community would lose a family. "Our first priority is to keep that family here," said another resident.

Staples was to meet with Conservation Department officials Wednesday to negotiate the future of the tower, which some residents would like to see retained as an historical site or picnic area. The senator said he would begin the talks by asking for the situation to be left as is, with a full-time towerman on duty and a house at the site for he and his family to live in.

If Conservation refuses that suggestion, Staples said he would ask that the house and tower be donated to the Vulcan Community Center. Should that proposal be rejected, he will ask for the tower alone. If that fails, a long-term lease for a minimal fee (like $1 a year) will be proposed. The last resort would be a delegation of people from the Vulcan area going to Jefferson City to make their point in person.

Staples said he would propose that the properties be turned over to the Vulcan Community Center, but be allowed to revert back to the Conservation Department "if you don't want them any longer." Residents seemed agreeable to a long-term lease as long as the fee was minimal.

Jim Ruble, whose father manned the tower from 1945-55, said he had written to the Conservation Commission and been informed of the department's plans to tear down the house and eventually the tower. "Of course, the citizens of Vulcan don't want to see that," he said, adding that lack of use was the apparent reason for Conservation's plans.

"Fire control is different now with advancements like airplane detection, CB radios, blacktop roads and citizen interest. Towers are not needed as close together now. They were once used exclusively to plot the fires, to determine where they were and to have crews in various localities to fight the fires. But

Save Vulcan Tower

fires aren't nearly as prevalent now. And the towers aren't needed by Conservation like they were in the '40s and '50s," he said.

"We want to get ahead of the game," Ruble said in reference to efforts to save the Vulcan tower, "We don't want to get to the point where one day it's not here."

THE FATE OF THE VULCAN FIRE TOWER was a topic of concern Saturday as Vulcan residents met with State Sen. Danny Staples about the Conservation Department's long-range plans to close and dismantle the tower. Staples (below center) talked with an informal gathering of citizens at the tower site that included (from left) former resident Bill Davis, Jim Ruble, Guy Stevenson, Bill Lee and Kenny Sutton before holding a town meeting at the Vulcan Community Center to discuss possible alternatives. If Conservation cannot be convinced to keep the tower open and operating, some local citizens would like to see it retained as an historical site or picnic area.

After moving to the new house at the tower, we would not use the cistern water for drinking, so we hauled water from my Uncle Ralph Lewis's spring on Funk Branch about 3 miles from the tower. A pitcher pump was installed at the sink in the kitchen to pump water from the cistern for water other than drinking or cooking.

The REA electric did not install electric lines to the house for about 6-8 months. We used kerosene and Aladdin lamps and a battery-powered radio until electric lines were installed.

I always told people that in Annapolis we had 4 rooms and a path – four rooms in the house and a path to the outhouse (toilet). At the tower, we had 5 rooms and a path. The three-hole outhouse was built on a concrete pit. Lime was used to control the waste. Mail order catalogs were commonly used in outhouses. We did use factory toilet paper.

A coal furnace was installed in the basement of the house. Since we lived on top of Mann Mountain in the middle of the woods, we used wood in the furnace instead of buying coal. We would cut down a tree with a crosscut saw and trim it with an ax. No chain saws in the '50s. We cut all our wood with the cross-cut saw. We had a small woodshed built in an inside corner of the car shed—cut lots of wood.

For several years before moving to the tower in 1949, I had a dog named Boots and a cat named Henry. I don't remember what happened to Henry, but we took Boots with us to the tower. About a month after we moved to the tower, Boots was sick one day and the next day she disappeared.

My Dad was not a big hunter, so we did not go hunting very much when we lived in Annapolis. My hunting started with squirrel hunting after we moved to the tower in 1949. I started still hunting with a single shot 16-gauge shotgun with a 32-inch barrel. We lived in the middle of the woods, so any direction was a good hunting area, especially in the evenings. I would walk down an old log road west of the tower still hunting. I killed a lot of squirrels. My Mom cooked them different ways, mostly fried especially if they were young squirrels and the old ones with dumplings. Mom was an excellent cook and housekeeper. One evening I saw two squirrels in the same oak tree. There was a dead limb out to the left, one squirrel was on the dead limb, and the other was on the trunk. I watched until they were both on the dead limb going toward each other. I shot, and one squirrel fell to the ground, and the other went inside the tree. A few minutes later, I heard something fall inside the tree. I killed two squirrels with one shot. In the evenings, I would walk down the tower road hunting for rabbits. I killed a lot of rabbits along this road.

Shortly after we moved to the tower, I got a dog from one of my cousins. King was a cur dog and resembled a fox with short hair. He was medium brown, small, ears stood up. King was an excellent squirrel dog. He did not want to go hunting for a long time like a traditional dog, where the dog trees a squirrel, you kill the squirrel and go on to the tree and kill more squirrels. King would lay in the yard, and he would get up and go to the edge of the yard, look and listen in a certain direction and go directly to a tree and tree the squirrel. Sometimes the squirrel would run from tree to tree, and he would stay with him until he treed the squirrel. He would do this several times a day, whoever was available, my Dad, my Mom or myself would go kill the squirrel. We would return to the house and clean the squirrel. After a drink of water and a short rest, King was ready for another squirrel. I had another dog during this time. Smokey was a hound mix. He was not worth a dime for hunting or anything else, but he was a good dog and a good companion for King.

We had a white cat named Minnie Pearl. Minnie Pearl would sometimes go with us to kill a squirrel that King had treed. Smokey would go sometimes. He was a little lazy. One time my Mom went to kill a squirrel, and Minnie Pearl went along. When my Mom shot the squirrel, it lodged in a fork of the tree. Minnie Pearl climbed up the tree and dislodged the squirrel. I have a certificate, a story and a medal from Puss and Boots cat food company awarded to Minnie Pearl for this event. She also got cat food for a year.

My Dad was a good fisherman. The tower was only a few miles from Black River. My Uncle Issom Lewis owned property on Black River. There was a big spring with the water bubbling up through the sand and gravel. The spring branch ran into Black River along a rock bluff. There was a large hole of water at the bluff. My Dad used a level wind reel and rod that belonged to my grandfather James Andrew Ruble (it was one of the first two-reel and rods sold at Gene Fitz Store in Des Arc, MO.) I still have the reel and rod. He would stand on the sandbar across the river from the bluff and cast toward the bluff. Just before the bait would hit the bluff, he would stop the reel, and the bait would appear to be jumping into the deep hole of water. He caught a lot of large bass this way. His favorite bait was small frogs that we would catch in mud holes in the road leading to the river. Frequently, the family would camp for a day or two or just overnight near the big spring. My Mom was a great fish fryer. Fried fish (in an iron skillet), cornbread, some vegetables or slaw, fried potatoes, iced-tea and always a pie or cobbler. Good memories!

Before going to work at the Vulcan Tower, my Dad carried rural mail from the Annapolis Post Office in a Model A Ford Coupe. When he quit the mail route, he sold the Model A to a man that took over the mail route. We did not have a car when we moved to the tower. My Uncle Olin Ruble had a salvage yard and garage between Vulcan and Des Arc, MO. My Dad bought a 1940 Chevrolet 2-door sedan from Olin. Olin painted the car maroon, with new upholstery, new running boards, etc. The car was almost like new. I was 14 years old at that time. Until I was 16 years old, I could not legally drive, but I did drive to Annapolis and Vulcan when needed. The day I was 16 years old, I went to Vincent Sutton's Service Station in Annapolis and got my first driver's license – no test or anything. This was one of the biggest days or events in my life. I loved cars and driving them and still do. I put many, many miles on that 1940 Chevrolet, driving to school, on dates to the drive-in theaters, school functions, etc. I would put $1.00 worth of gas in the car at Elmer Kyle's Service Station and drive for a long time. The problem was a dollar was hard to get.

I worked part-time for 50 cents per hour on the tower and on the fire crew. That 1940 Chevrolet Sedan sparked my love for automobiles, especially Chevrolets. Over the years, I have owned several "old" Chevrolets and other brands as a hobby. In 1999, with the help of Les Schatz, I restored a 1941 Chevrolet Special Deluxe, 5 passenger Coupe to the original. This is my expensive toy. The 1940 and 1941 Chevrolets are almost identical. I have been a member of Vintage Chevrolet Club of America VCCA #1273 for over 50 years. I also belonged to the Rt. 66 Car Club for several years.

My Dad was a jack of all trades. When the tower road at Vulcan tower was improved, there were several areas that needed rock drilled and blasted. A portable compressor, a jackhammer drill and dynamite were used to break the rock. My Dad drilled and blasted the rock. In 1952, the Taum Sauk tower road was built. Marvin Holland, Construction Foreman for the Commission, supervised this construction. My Dad had the job of drilling and blasting the rock, and there was a lot of rock to be moved on Taum Sauk Mountain area. My Dad asked Marvin if he had any job that I could do. Marvin asked if I could drive a truck. My Dad said I could drive anything on wheels. I worked all summer driving a 1947 Ford dump truck hauling chat from the old railroad bed that was abandoned when the Missouri Pacific Railroad built a new railroad to eliminate the Tip Top grade that required two engines to pull a train over the hill. This was my first real job. Before this, I worked in the summers for my Uncle Ralph Lewis and brother-in-law Paul Dahlke on their farms and on the Vulcan tower and the fire crew.

I have mentioned my Dad many times in these memories. I spent a lot of time with him, going with him on the mail route, on the fire crew and on the tower. My Dad was a fine role model and was always there for me.

My Mom (Myrtle Ruble), in very busy times, would make contacts and check for smokes when my Dad was out on fires. She was very flexible and patient by preparing meals at any time day or night. She was an outstanding cook and took good care of me and my Dad. She washed our clothes with a tub and washboard by hand. One time, while scrubbing on the washboard, she ran a sewing needle deep in her hand. She climbed the tower and called my Dad on the radio. He came home and took her to the doctor. She was a tough and gentle woman. She passed away in 2009, at the age of 101 years.

In May 1953, I graduated from Annapolis High School. I worked in St. Louis for an ice cream company, drove a truck, loaded props and lumber on railroad cars and several other jobs in the Vulcan area.

On October 14, 1953, I caught the Wallen Bus at Edmondson's Restaurant in Annapolis, went to St. Louis and enlisted in the United States Air Force. After spending nine weeks in basic training at Lackland AFB in San Antonio, Texas, I was assigned as a Finance Specialist in the main finance office at Lackland AFB. I was stationed at Lackland for 3 years. My last year, I was stationed at Keflavic International AFB in Keflavic Iceland. I was discharged in August 1957 and enrolled in the first Forestry School class at the University of Missouri in Columbia, MO. Attending school on the G.I. Bill with no part-time jobs available, I was unable to afford college.

We moved to Sullivan, MO. I was back working for the Missouri Conservation Commission, first at the Meramec State Nursery and then for Lee Fine, District Forester at Meramec District, as the Lonedell towerman. In January 1958, I went to work at the new Meramec Mining Company at Sullivan, MO. I worked in accounting, personnel and safety department for 13 years. In 1970, I went to work for the United States Department of Labor, Mine Safety and Health Administration as a Federal Mine Inspector in Rolla, MO. I worked for MSHA for 25 years, retiring on Civil Service retirement in January 1996.

Above is a picture of the sign at the trailhead of the 12-mile horse trail through Meramec CA (Meramec State Park) that was named after Avery Ruble. Alan Ruble was instrumental in having it named for his granddad.

Memories and Reflections, by Jim Ruble

Volume 1, Issue 1, February 2018

Kelleter Tower

Kelleter Tower's Ed Christopher – the "One & Only"

Information supplied by Frances (Christopher) Long and Eddie Christopher

Kelleter Tower had its roots in Africa. According to Ron Woodland, it was based on a design that had become common there. It would be one of the first towers in Missouri using treated wood and as a result, would stand the test of time. When it was finally pulled down by dozer (below), it would hit the ground and land largely undamaged except for the cab. Kelleter Tower pictures, along with the wooden tower at Macedonia, remain today "iconic" among the tower pictures in Missouri.

Kelleter Tower sat on 8.91 acres that the Missouri Conservation Commission bought. It was erected for the Commission by the CCC camp S78 directed by R.S. Scott. It was dedicated on October 31, 1941, at Meramec State Park Lodge to escape the rain. Dedication at the site occurred November 1, 1941, and included a large granite rock with a plaque (see below) honoring Mrs. Pauline J. Kelleter, the mother of the supervisor of the Clark National Forest. Frances Long has located this plaque which got separated from the rock at some point and hopes to reunite the two at the Meramec State Park Lodge by the other CCC camp plaques there. The present site owners, Jim and Kim Kilburn, have agreed to this plan and Frances hopes to complete this undertaking as a tribute to the fire tower history of the state.

At times a discussion of tower workers at a location can get confusing but not so at Kelleter. That is because Ed Christopher was "the one and only" from 1942 thru 1979 when he retired from the Missouri Conservation Commission in Sullivan, Mo.

The site included not only the tower but also structures for the family to live in. It had a cistern for water (5,000 gallons), a wooden building for a bathroom, kerosene lamps for lighting, and a wood furnace in the basement for heat. Also included were a small barn, a chicken house, a large garden spot, and a couple of cows and some chickens. In the mid-sixties, the house was remolded, and two bedrooms and a bath were added. Then, a few years later, it was decided to maintain it as a historical site, and pressure treated wood was installed pretty well throughout.

Working the tower was often a family effort. Eddie recalls that nobody was better at getting to a fire on the gravel back roads than his Dad. It was often quite a ride. Often lost is the fact that "manning" a tower could be "familying" a tower. Frances recalls the time her brother tripped coming down the tower and caught himself just before going over the railing. There was another way to get down.

I had heard the story for years that the elder Ed would bet people he could beat them down the tower. Frances confirmed the story. It seems one of the cables was very slick, and they all became skilled at just sliding down the cable. It was a simpler time. I recall being told the story that when the school bus turned around at High Hill Tower from Birch Tree, the bus door would open now and then to allow the kids to climb the tower. Like I said – it was a simpler time.

During the fire season, the day began with a check from the tower. This would be repeated during the day. If a fire was spotted, Ed would stop by the school to pick up the 7th and 8th-grade boys that had permission to help fight the fire.

Fire Fighting required equipment such as the following: vehicle, broom rakes, backpack sprayer, canteens, ax, saw, flashlights, maps, fire extinguishers, radios, backfire tools, and panama pumps. Heavy equipment might be used, and crews had to be organized and practice proper technique. Ed's son Eddie remembers, as several have mentioned to me, the bad fires of the early 1950s. Dryness combined with heat and winds pushed the fire index up and created unusual fires for Missouri. Whereas most fires here were "on the ground," these became "tree crown fires" which we see more commonly out west. Eddie recalls the tree roots caught fire and carried the fires right across the fire breaks.

When the dryness passed, there was always much to do. In addition to teaching people how to fight fires, there was erosion control to be done. Improvements were always being made to the Huzzah State Forest. Equipment had to be maintained, forms and reports filled out, forest cropland addressed, and health and safety issues noted. Neighbors would ask about fire control, ponds and fish management, land improvements, or advice on a piece of equipment. In the early years, Ed worked with the CCC boys putting a fence around what is now Lone Elk Park.

Then there was always the odd job. A bobcat, thought to be rabid, came at a neighbor and Ed was called to dispatch it. Another time he found himself in the middle of some cow rustling which ended up with a tussle and a shotgun fired at his jeep. When he retired, he was given the piece of the panel that was shot. See below.

My thanks to Frances and Eddie the information for this "slice of life" at Kelleter Tower.

Chris Polka – The Google Map Project

I grew up in suburban St. Louis and hadn't explored the beautiful Missouri Ozarks much at all until I attended the University of Missouri-Rolla. Even then, the fire towers were something I subconsciously saw from a distance but didn't otherwise pay much attention to.

As I was doing some exploring in 2011, on the way back from Clifty Creek Natural Area in Maries County, I saw a tower very near the road, with a picnic table and small gravel parking lot and decided to pull in and have a snack. This turned out to be the Freeburg Tower, owned by the Missouri Department of Conservation. Eating at the table in the shadow of this tower, I wondered why they hadn't blocked off the steps or put a fence around it. I surmised (correctly it turns out) that climbing was allowed.

To say this was the first fire tower I climbed is true, but isn't the whole truth. In fact, it was the first, second, third, and fourth tower I climbed, all on the same day. That's how many attempts it took me to scale the wooden stairs to the very top, each time ascending one or two flights more than the last. More to the point, this little hobby of finding and climbing towers didn't immediately pair well with my extreme fear of heights – a fear that still exists, but I've been able to mitigate with a few tricks. It was not a minor feat to climb to the top landing and sit there, wishing for an extra hand as I clutched my camera with one hand and the railing with the other in a death grip, hurriedly taking (crooked) pictures of the rolling hills surrounding the site. Soaked in sweat, I descended to earth and decided to look into these towers further.

I soon found Jim Lyon's tower list, laying out the majority of standing and historic towers of different agencies. Seeking them out consumed a considerable number of fair weather weekends over the next year or two. Despite being employed as a "technology guy," the hunt itself was rather primitive. I didn't own either a GPS or a smartphone at the time. So a Saturday tower hunt consisted of laying out the MoDOT highway map and marking in pen the towers in the area to be searched. Working from Jim's list, I'd translate each pair or coordinates, bring it up on the Google Maps, and then hand-draw any minor roads, turns, or features to help navigate to each site. Finding the towers in this way really hones the geo-senses. Despite poking above the tree line (usually), towers aren't always easy to see from the road. Often the hunt involves looking for small gravel turn-offs, gates, or other markers that subtly hint a tower's presence. A hike up to a mile or more might ensue from there, though plenty of towers are right next to paved roads as well.

I still have the original paper map in the car and refer to it often. In fact, it helped me appreciate the spatial relationships between towers. This led me to begin pinning the towers in a Google map for easier online reference. About this time, I emailed Bob Frakes, featured in a River Hills Traveler article a year prior. Bob happily shared his knowledge with me, and we've swapped photos and tower stories over the years since.

While my original "finish line" was finding all the standing Missouri towers (which has since been completed), Bob sought to fill in the complete history by researching towers that have since been removed, as well as mysteries that appeared in such esoteric places as telephone maps and other publications. I have to admit, the search for a set of footings deep in the woods is almost as intriguing as walking up to a standing tower (although the view at the end is rarely as good). And going over the topography with a fine-toothed comb has actually uncovered several standing towers – most privately owned- that we didn't know existed at the beginning of this journey. Zooming in on Google Maps satellite view and seeing the unmistakable shadow cast by a previously unknown tower is the Ozarks equivalent of a hunt for private treasure.

As we began filling in more information, we broke the towers into layers – climbable, standing, historical, mystery—and have linked each to personal photos, historic document scans, notes about our visits, and other information. I'm glad to see my original work in seeking out the standing towers lives on as part of this ongoing project. Anyone is welcome to visit the site. The most direct way is going to http://tinyurl.com/mofiretowers, but it's listed on the FFLA site and is findable in a Google search as well.

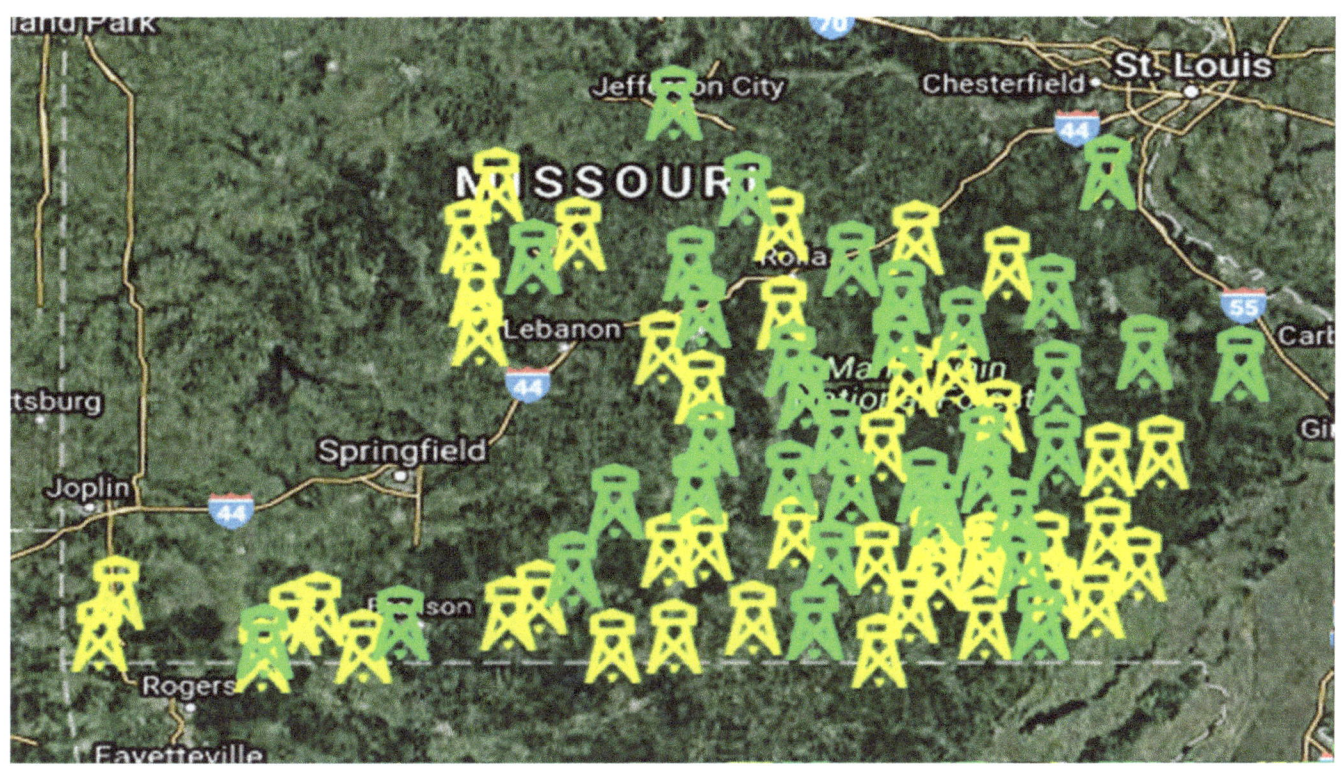

Panther Hill Tales

By Charley Santhuff / Retired MDC District Forester

The Panther Hill Towerman's wife and young child were home when the house seemed to literally explode. A lightning bolt had run in on the electric line blowing the fuse box to bits and destroying the closet where it was located. Aluminum-based joint tape had been used on the sheetrock, and it was peeled from the joints and hanging throughout the rooms like giant cobwebs. Electrical smoke was thick, but luckily no injuries were sustained by the family, and the house was not set on fire. This was my earliest recollection of the tower site. Located on the higher elevations increased the likelihood of lightning strikes at the sites. Once experienced, any thunderstorm was cause for uneasiness. The tower structure was adequately grounded but was usually vacated if lightning was in the area.

Panther Hill is located in west-central Reynolds County, on the head of Dry Valley. It was a mile from our farm, and it overlooked the valley like a guarding sentinel. My dad worked hourly at the tower for many years, and his first association with the tower was using his team of mules to skid a long pole to the site. It was lashed to a shorter and pruned tree, and spikes were driven in for climbing. Charlie Kirk was the District Forester. Charlie was Chief Forester for Pioneer Forest later in his career. A sixty-five-foot wooden tower replaced the pole in 1939-40. The access road to the tower was built by CCC personnel and Marvin Holland, who was the Forestry Division's construction foreman. Marvin told me in later years that was the first road he ever built. Road construction was halted before the project was completed and county roads provided the remaining access.

Panther Hill was constructed of wood since steel was not available due to the war effort. I know the wood for the Hunter Tower was obtained from the Millman Lumber Company located at Round Springs. The material for Panther Hill likely came from the same company. Panther Hill was unique in that it had a catwalk around the cab. As a kid, it was an ordeal to climb the last flight of stairs up through the catwalk floor and make my way around to the cab door. The railing around the catwalk seemed awfully low, and it didn't get any better with my age. The tower had guy wires of one-inch cable attached to each leg about fifty feet up the tower. The cables were attached to concrete deadmen. The tower was very stable in high winds, although a flashlight would roll around on the fire finder stand on the worst of days.

As standard practice, the tower site soon consisted of a dwelling, small barn, chicken house, garage, privy and a cistern system that caught runoff from the residence roof. These had to be cleaned periodically and in later years water was hauled to the site rather than relying on rainfall and dirty roofs. Tower sites were maintained to high standards and presented a good image for the Forestry Division. Annual inspections were made of all improvements, inside and out, which was a relief for the towerman's wife when it was completed. Housekeeping quality was noted. Maintenance of the wooden towers was not for the faint-hearted. They had to be treated with wood preservatives periodically, and this required climbing on the wood beamstop to bottom. Many of the beams in the lower part of the tower were large, perhaps 14 x 16 inches, with smaller beams as the height increased. Galvanized three quarter inch bolts were used for joints and splices. These had to be checked for tightness regularly.

In the early '70s, the wooden tower was replaced by a steel tower that had initially been located at Eminence. It was a 90-foot tower and had been built by the CCC personnel out of the Deer Run Camp. When the tower was moved to Panther Hill, the names of the CCC boys who initially erected it were discovered on the bottom surface of the cab sun shades. Written in lead pencil, they survived the years quite well.

Panther Hill "crossed" with nearby towers at Deer Run, Stegall, Coot Mountain, Himont, and Shannondale. The towermen were Gene Knuckles, Chester Sulser, Bill Reeves, and Bill Morey. Towermen were an important part of the community if they were well suited to the job. Panther Hill had the only telephone in the vicinity, and for many years local residents would ask to use the phone in emergencies. Towermen also had the only four-wheel drive vehicles and would assist neighbors in emergencies when roads were snow and ice covered. Wildfire prevention and conservation programs were accepted in rural areas largely due to the

PR efforts of the towerman. They were friends with the local people and could be counted on for help if needed.

Originally, phone lines were constructed to tower sites for fire reporting. Eventually, towers were equipped with military surplus #610, low band radios, as were vehicles. The tower sets had a telephone-like microphone with a toggle switch in the handle for transmitting. These early radios were powered by batteries that were located in wooden boxes on the lowest band of the tower. Power was provided to the cab with a cable up the tower leg. Locating the batteries near the ground saved carrying them up the tower steps! Each tower was assigned a three-digit radio call number with the towerman using the last two digits if he was in his vehicle. Panther Hill was 154, and the towerman was 54. The district headquarters was 5. The use of call numbers and the "10" codes saved time and allowed several districts to share the same radio frequency.

It was a common practice for high school age boys to work as hourly firefighters. I worked after school and weekends mostly and sometimes stayed on the tower while the crew checked smokes and took suppression action if needed. If I went with the crew, I was often the youngest and hopefully strongest crew member who got the honor of carrying the backpack pump. Not fun! Normally, a fire crew was limited to four members, as that was all that could fit in a jeep. The first two or three crew members would construct the fire line with broom rakes while the fourth man backfired the line. If volunteers were available, they would watch for breakovers. A backpack pump was valuable to get small breakovers before they got too big to handle. Backfiring was done with a broom rake with tines loaded with burning leaves, which were shaken off to start the backfire. An experienced back fireman could use a rake all day without ruining the tines with too much heat. Big Chief brand rakes were prone to the tines slipping until one side of the rake would have some tines several inches longer than the other side. Not good! One dozer plow unit was stationed at the Ellington Headquarters, and the next closest plow was at Garwood. The Ellington dozer was run by Wilmer Heiskell and later by Doug Youngblood. It was a military surplus Allis Chalmers HD 5 with a trailer type plow that initially required someone to ride the plow to adjust the plowing depth. A very dangerous job! It was soon modified so the tractor operator could pump the hydraulic system to regulate the plow. The plow unit was transported on a military surplus GMC tractor-trailer unit that was underpowered and difficult to get to fires because of its length. Peck Ranch was part of the Deer Run District and fires were common. The trailer encountered a gate too narrow, and the trailer won. Someone had some fence to repair. In spite of its shortcomings, the use of military surplus was a godsend for firefighting. Sure beat a broom rake!

The Panther Hill crew, like others, had busy and slow days. Some days we might work active fires all day and well into the night. Other days, no fires. Aerial detection had been used on districts since the 1940s. Deer Run had a small plane assigned to the district and piloted by Bob Larkin, a district employee. The plane was used for detection, but also aiding suppression efforts by guiding crews to fires and detecting breakovers and spot fires. The aircraft was used to drop equipment repair parts in a tow sack if necessary. The ground crews did not have radios except in vehicles, and the pilot had several antics he performed to get the ground crew's attention if need be. The plane frequently stayed airborne so late in fire season that the landing strip had to be marked by the headlights of vehicles. My senior year in high school I manned the Deer Run Tower at night on the weekends. We were having several night fires, and catching them before the fire danger got high the next day was important. Deer Run, Stegall, and Hunter were manned all night if fire danger was high. One night, Hunter reported fires on Beaver Dam Creek in Ripley County. By dawn, the glow could be seen by Deer Run. The fires were set by horseback, and an estimated 100 sets were made over several miles. It took all the district resources to work on the fires. We had a slow day on the north end of the district, and the Panther Hill crew was dispatched to the Beaver Dam fire the next day. I don't know the acreage burned, but it was considerable. In March of 1951, the Deer Run District reported 108 fires burned 23,015 acres. Eminence District reported 69 fires burned 25,686 acres. Fires were a problem in the Ozarks.

In the late 50s and early 60s, the Cold War fear was rampant. The federal government decided that fire towers could be helpful to identify aircraft flying over America. They furnished each tower a booklet of airplane descriptions complete with pictures of U.S. and foreign aircraft. They also supplied a set of high-quality binoculars for each tower. When a plane was observed and identified the information was to be called in by phone to some branch of the government. We tried to report a plane a few times on a slow day, but never accomplished the report. I guess our communication system in the Ozarks just wasn't up to the task. The booklet provided some reading material, and the binoculars were great.

As wildfire prevention began to be effective the residences at towers became a burden on budgets. Communications had improved to allow quick reporting of fires by the public. Telephone lines had reached most areas of the Ozarks. By the 1970s the buildings at selected tower sites were removed, and by the 90s few sites were still sporting a residence. The trend to eliminate fire towers continues, and hopefully, some will always remain to remind us of the past when one-third of the Ozarks burned annually. When Panther Hill is gone, part of me goes with it.

Jim Parker

Jim Parker – The M.D.C.'s "Go-To Guy"

Jim Parker at Indian Trail Tower, June 2012.

Matt Bevin once observed, "While it may seem small, the ripple effect of small things is extraordinary." Maybe that thought should have been on my mind a few years ago when I stopped by the M.D.C. office in Rolla, Missouri. Making that visit had been on my "to do" list for some time. I wanted to see if the footings for the lookout tower that once stood there could still be found.

Jim Parker

I was greeted cordially as I walked into the Conservation Office. Most of the employees were at work on plans for the CWD program, as deer season was to open the next day. When I explained my reason for being there, I was told that the footings for the lookout tower that had once stood at the office site most likely had been removed years ago. But I was shown a picture of the tower itself that they had hanging on the wall. One fellow, Doug Gall offered to take the picture down and make a copy of it for me. Doug was obviously a veteran MDC employee, and when I mentioned my interest in lookout towers, he perked right up. We spent a few minutes checking out the large area map in the dispatch room and then doing some tower talking. We wound down our conversation by exchanging email addresses for future tower talking and then I was on my way. Just as I was almost out the door, Doug added one more tidbit of information. He told me that I needed to call and talk to a man by the name of Jim Parker. In Doug's words, Jim could "answer all kinds of questions." As noted in the dedication section of this book, Douglas Gall passed away in February 2017. I am very thankful that I got to know him and for all the help he gave me. He was a good tower friend.

Soon after Doug's last minute suggestion, I called Jim Parker. Doug's idea soon proved to be very worthwhile. Since then, Jim and I have had many good, long phone conversations and he surely has answered many a tower question. As work on my book began to make some progress, I felt sure that I wanted to include a piece on Parker in my book. After nearly a year's worth of phone calls with Jim, we, at last, got to talk face to face. On November 12, 2018, my wife and I made a trip to Montauk State Park, located a few miles west of Salem, Mo. I was able to travel from there to just north of Rolla for a one-on-one interview with Jim. Good ole Missouri hospitality was on full display while visiting with the Parker family and I thank them for it all. The only thing that surpassed the cornbread, ham & bean dinner that day was the company.

Jim's M.D.C. story is another study in the "small beginnings" principle. Jim was born and raised on a farm north of Rolla. After graduating high school, he knew that the farm could support a certain way of life for him, but he also felt like he needed to check out other options for a livelihood. Through a visit to the Rolla unemployment office, Jim found out that there were temporary job openings at the local Conservation Commission headquarters. The office was located close to where he lived, so Jim stopped in to see about going to work there. I myself feel like it must have been his destiny. This was January of 1959, and Jim would indeed be hired to go to work for the Commission, filling the position of firefighter crew leader, as well as temporary towerman. He was issued a truck to drive and his own firefighting tools and equipment. He was 20 years old.

As with many others who filled similar positions, it wasn't very long before, in Jim's words, "smoke got in the blood." I asked Jim what his favorite job was, out of all that he did, and firefighting was his quick answer. Group effort and teamwork among firefighters was an absolute necessity. And the level of camaraderie and teamwork among the men he worked with was outstanding. Jim realized the value of these relationships at the time, but the memories of his fellow employees and their dedication to the job and to each other have grown even more precious as years have passed by. There was also a great deal of satisfaction for him in protecting forestlands, animals, and sometimes even people's homes. Jim noted that although there were "strategies" to be used in fighting wildfires, each fire was unique, so that most of the time, you just had to "learn as you go." He remembers that volunteers and temporary firefighters played an important role during the height of fire season. "Temps," as they were called, were paid 75 cents an hour. Often U.M.R. (now M.S.&T.) students were recruited for these jobs. While interviewing Jim, I also spent quite a lot of time taking notes on the use of "dozers." They were a critical tool, when available, in the suppression of wildfires. You'll find much about that in the chapter on "Dozers."

One of Jim's most memorable jobs with MDC would become the job of building towers, as well as taking towers down. He noted again, as with firefighting, there was no training offered, nor required. The training was "on the job" training. Tower building and dismantling was tedious and dangerous work. With heights of as much as 120 feet off the ground, and with no safety harness or nets, Jim said that some men were simply not able to handle the conditions. Some might have been able to work up as far as a few levels, but then had to pivot to another area of the job. Jim said that he was really scared on his first tower job. But soon, his desire to do the work overcame his fears. Regardless, those who elected to be involved in erecting the tower did the job by slowly raising one beam, one leg, one brace, one bolt at a time. The wooden towers, previous to steel towers, were assembled in a different manner. They were laid out and assembled on the ground before raising. Necessary bolt holes were pre-drilled, and then pieces were raised by A-frame with belts and braces attached as the work progressed. (More information is included in the "Wooden Tower" section.)

Jim's first tower building job would be the Goodman Tower in June of 1959. Over the next ten years, Jim would help build towers at Elk Horn, Powell, Lanagan, Joplin, Neosho, Marshfield, Phillipsburg, Squires, Norwood, Asher, Vichy, Freeburg, Dixon, Potosi, August A. Busch, Sunridge, Bloomfield and Tywappidy. Information on the Goodman Tower can be found in the "Towers Moved" chapter.

I asked Jim about any serious injuries that he might recall happening during tower jobs. Previous discussions with other employees failed to mention anyone getting seriously hurt. The only injury that Jim could recall was once when a fellow managed to get a few broken ribs. Jim did say that after the use of hard hats was in practice, his crew was in the process of dismantling a tower when one of the tower legs slipped and barely clipped the bill of Jim's hard hat, knocking it off his head. He was thankful that he hadn't been leaning forward at the time. Hard hats became required equipment in later years. A small nut, bolt or any tool dropped from high up could become a lethal weapon for those working below. Other safety equipment like ropes were considered but proved to be impractical as men were often in more danger from entanglement than they were from performing their duties. Regardless, Jim said that experience and teamwork were your greatest tools when it came to tower work.

I was curious about the process used in taking a tower down and asked Jim if it was the same as building a tower, except in reverse. I found out that it was not. Jim then proceeded to methodically describe all the many steps of dismantling a tower, piece by piece, from the top. After about ten minutes, I managed to slyly distract him from his detailed description and move onto another topic. He explained that lowering steel tower pieces could be as dangerous and tricky as raising them up on a gin pole. Many of the tower takedowns involved plans to move and then rebuild the tower at another location. In this case, much care had to be taken to make sure there was no damage done to the tower pieces. One exception he noted was a Michigan lookout tower that he and a crew had gone there to dismantle and move back to Missouri. It had been purchased by MDC for just a few dollars. But MDC had the responsibility of dismantling, loading, and then moving it. The Michigan tower was located where the soil was very sandy. Jim remembers that this made the job a little easier for the crew because if you dropped the tower pieces just right, they would land in the sand undamaged. Taking the Michigan tower down was only part of the job. Traveling back to Missouri, through cities and across bridges, hauling the dismantled tower was a huge challenge in itself. Jim said it was quite a journey.

Jim and I talked some about the concrete footings for the towers and how they were constructed. By nature, tower locations were often remote. A concrete truck was not always a possibility and was practically unheard of in early tower building days. Put-put (gasoline powered) cement mixers were used back then. In extremely remote areas, the materials for the concrete had to be transported by wagons and then mixed in troughs at the job site. The placement area for the footings had to be fairly large, large enough to accommodate the concrete forms. In Missouri terrain, that often meant the use of dynamite because of the amount of solid rock, mostly limestone. After the footings were secure, the concrete forms were then removed, cleaned, oiled and stored away for future use.

In 1960, Jim became the Vichy Towerman. The term "towerman" can be a little misleading. Acting as a fire lookout was only a small part of the job. From the Conservation Commission operation manual, a towerman's other duties were: act as a crew leader on fires when so directed by the District Forester, secure extra labor during periods of high fire danger, become familiar with the area, be responsible for the maintenance of the vehicles and tools, maintain the site and buildings, make contact with local people to share ideas and receive the public courteously. In addition, there were the deer and turkey check stations to help man when in season. And, of course, the tower up and down jobs never stopped.

In 1967, Jim would take a desk job for a short period of time. He took the job hoping it would lead to another job opportunity, which he would soon see materialize. Not long after, Jim was named as Forest Assistant of the South Gasconade District, a position that he held until his retirement in September 1998. In addition to fire control and supervisory responsibilities over the southern part of the district, this appointment would also include being "commissioned" to be available to assist conservation agents when and if needed in the area of law enforcement.

Whether by phone or in person, I always found Jim more than ready to tower talk. His memories are a beautiful reflection of a special time and a special place in the history of the Missouri Department of Conservation and its many dedicated employees. Jim remains filled with pride and satisfaction when it pertains to his years with the "Department," and I have found that to be true of all of the conservation employees that I have had the privilege of getting to know. Each one of them has played an important part in making Missouri's conservation story a successful one. And as far as Jim Parker is concerned, I believe Jim Sorenson's description of him was spot-on. He said, "Jim Parker is the #1 Go-To Guy on the #1 Tower Up & Tower Down Crew in Missouri." Good job, Buddy.

Jim Parker and Charlie Younger in 1980

Jim Parker and Wayne Peplow 4/2/63

Lawrence Buchheit

Lawrence Buchheit – Perry Tower Talk

As I write fire lookout articles here and there, I always find the feedback a great chance to learn and make friends. After one of my River Hill Traveler articles, I received a contact from Lawrence Buchheit of Apple Creek. Lawrence worked for the Missouri Department of Conservation from 1970 – 2001. He started there as the tower man at the Perry Tower south of Perryville. Lawrence invited me for a "tower tour" and talk. He was able to get a key, so we were also able to check out the cab . You could see Cottoner Mountain and the location where the Coffman Tower stood at one time. Knob Lick Tower was off the west and on a clear day he said you could even see the bridge at Chester and Bald Knob Cross. Bald Knob Cross is almost 40 miles away as the crow flies. He noted that early on fighter jets used the area for what seemed to be low-level training and on occasion, the fighter pilot appeared to be lower than the cab of the tower.

He is also a local historian and my first questions involved the area. He noted Old Appleton was 1st Apple Creek then changed to Appleton and then Old Appleton today. At that time Schnurbusch became Apple Creek. Missouri already had an Appleton so that name had caused confusion. He mentioned how the area had served as the capital for the five local Shawnee Nations and that Lewis & Clark had stopped there on their way from St. Louis on their journey of discovery. I enjoyed the lesson and looking at the maps he shared with me.

Lawrence wanted to make one point with an exclamation point – DON'T FORGET THE FAMILIES! He noted that the conservation work done required a family effort and at times sacrifice. He might be working long days and well into the night for several days at a time, working on different fires. There were school and family functions that he simply could not make on occasion. It was often a family effort.

My first questions involved his work as a tower man. Some have the impression a tower worker spent all their time in the cab of a tower. Towers were used in medium to high fire danger periods. When the "burn index" (winds over 7 m.p.h. and humidity less than 40%) was high, the towers were used to "get the jump" on fires. Being fast to the fire was everything. A crew that got to a fire when it was small had a small problem. Part of this equation was the fire finder. By aiming and "taking a shot" on the smoke, a worker could relay readings quickly to other towers or to a dispatch board. These numbers could be translated into an exact location to speed up the arrival of help. If it was a small fire, the worker might go themselves to put the fire out. Tower workers also knew the area. Even without several "shots," it could be evident to a tower worker where the problem was located. Early on these workers were paid by the month which could lead to some long days. Lawrence recalled that a report had to try and locate a source. On one occasion the fire traced back to a burned out house. It seemed the property owners had finally got their indoor plumbing just the way they wanted it and had a ceremonial "goodbye" burning party for the privy.

When the fire index dropped, there was always litter to be removed, mowing to get done, and T.S.I. This involved Timber Stand Improvement. The timber was cruised. This was done to determine what was there and how it could be best managed. For example: soil determines timber, White Oaks on the north slope, Red Oaks on the south slope, and Hickory on either. By replacing random and unorganized growth with management, the usefulness of the forest could be greatly improved.

The use of the towers changed over the years. As more areas were brought into the MDC for hunting and fishing, this meant more areas to cover. Many rural districts took over the work of firefighting. Cell phones made fire reports by the public easier, and the public itself became more fire knowledgeable. Trash pick-up replaced trash burning resulting in fewer fires. The towers became used less and less, although some are still "active" and used in the dry times. Some were abused at times by some who didn't realize the part they had played in Missouri's conservation success story.

We also discussed the firefighting itself. Lawrence pointed out that the "fire triangle" was heat, air, and fuel. Fires he sighted were almost always "on the ground" not in the crown on the trees. However, hollow trees would burn, fall and help spread the fire. A white smoke indicated leaves and grass burning. One fire season was February to May after the trees leafed out and the rains came. Another was from the first frost to December or January. Strong winds would push the fire fast in a narrow track with a hot fire head. In lesser winds, the fire would move more slowly and spread out wider.

Fires were often fought by setting a backfire. A break line would be established by rake, road or other means and small fires set to burn back and remove the fuel part of the equation. This required strategy and surveillance. Fires racing up a slope were often fought when they crossed over the ridge. Blowers were used in place of rakes at times and water was used by backpack or truck tank. Eighty gallons of water from a truck would last about a mile. If a local source of water could be found, pumps could be used to tap the water.

Observation was important to planning, and at times a small plane was used as eyes in the sky. Constant checking insured no flare-ups popped up to spoil the work done.

At times on big fires, a "Dozer" was called in. Lawrence liked the John Deere 450, but there were several makes and models. Different firefighters had their own favorites. The Dozer could dig a firebreak fast, doing the work of many men. If the terrain was right, it was the right tool for the job.

In the picture of Lawrence at Perry Tower, you can see a feature I have found common to the forestry workers – contented pride. Pride in the job they did over the last century in making Missouri a Conservation success story that stands out among the 50 states.

Interview with Lawrence Buchheit

Glenn Skinner – Knob Lick Fire Warden

By Jack Skinner

Glenn Skinner's ancestors came from Scotland in the 1870s. They settled in and around the Knob Lick/Syenite/Brightstone area. They were farmers and stone masons. This area contained a lot of granite which was used to build houses and pave streets, such as South Broadway, in St. Louis.

However, in 1911 Glenn's Family moved to Red Granite, Wisconsin to work the granite there. That's where Glenn was born on November 12, 1912. About six years later, the family moved back to Knob Lick. Knob Lick was a bustling, little community about that time. It boasted several churches, four grocery stores, barber shops, a lodge hall, and later a rock crusher. This then is the world Glenn grew up into. Several trains per day rolled through Knob Lick. These were not the passenger trains, though one regular train pulled a coach at the end. One of these went South in the morning, and another went North in the evening to provide local passenger service.

Glenn married Anna Ward on September 1, 1934. Work was hard to find in the Depression, so he moved to St. Louis. It was there, on November 28, 1935, that their only son, Jack Skinner, was born. When the War started, Glenn moved his family down to Fredericktown where he got a job driving a Sinclair Oil truck. He worked there until 1943 when he was drafted into the military, selecting to serve in the Navy. Glenn, along with his three brothers, all served in W.W. II. Glenn, being in the Navy, served in the Pacific Theater.

After the war, Glenn worked at different jobs until around 1963 when he went to work for the Missouri Forestry Commission. At the time, he lived in Fredericktown, Missouri. He started out on a job in Bollinger County, and he and one other worker built a forestry tower on County road "J." A short time later, the tower position at Knob Lick became available and Glenn bid and got that duty. Now he was back in familiar territory, so, in 1965, he and his wife Anna, moved to a little farmhouse just outside Knob Lick, to be closer to the tower.

During the higher part of the fire season, Glenn might spot as many as seven fires a day from his perch atop the tower on Knob Lick Mountain. When it was the high fire season, Glenn would take his lunch with him, because he would be on duty all day, either, in the tower, looking for fires, or actually out fighting them. Glenn would spend 14 years here, looking for fires from the eight-foot square house atop the 110-foot tall tower.

During July, a fire might move slowly because everything is green by that time. But, in April and November, the fire Rangers were busy all the time.

Glenn would use landmarks, such as, '… that's farmer Jones; he must be burning a brush pile.' If there was smoke in an uninhabited area, then it had the possibility of being a wildfire.

The fire would be located this way: In the middle of the house on top of the tower, there was a table. On top of this table was a round, topographic map of the area. It was orientated to the lay of the land surrounding the tower. Around the frame of this map was a track. In the middle, there was a flat, metal, horizontal piece. On one end was a vertical, tall, flat metal piece with a thin slit in it. On the opposite side of the horizontal strip of metal was a vertical rectangular frame with a crosshair in it. These sights could be rotated 360° around the track on the map frame. This functioned similarly to the front and rear sights on a rifle.

When the smoke from a fire was spotted, the worker would line up the "sights" on the fire. Then, he would look down at the map and could tell that the fire was somewhere along that line on the map. A second tower, such as the one on Stono Mountain, would also sight on the fire. This is like forming an imaginary baseline of a triangle between the two towers. Then, with radio communication, the two fire Rangers would locate the grid coordinates on the map where their two imaginary lines crossed. That would be the exact location of the fire. This is a method known as the triangulation.

After locating the fire, Glenn would look at the map for roads or trails to find the best way to get to the fire. Sometimes, he would stop in Knob Lick and pick up some volunteers to help fight the fire if it was a big one. The previous fire Ranger told Glenn that, a couple of times when he did this, he found out later that some of the boys had set some fires just so they could get some work. So, Glenn had to be careful about the workers he selected. Living in Knob Lick helped him to know the volunteers better.

One of the main instruments used to fight these forest fires was a metal rake. Glenn would go around the fire, sweeping the fire back on itself and clearing a path of dead leaves and sticks that would fuel the fire. They could also use backpacks, containing water, and spray the fire area. If it was a very large fire, he would call for backup, and the District Forestry would send in more men and maybe even a bulldozer to clear a fire break. Sometimes, if the wind was right, they could even start a backfire, letting it burn back to the original fire and creating a much wider fire break to stop the advancing fire.

During the season when fires were less prevalent, Glenn would work on building or repairing picnic tables, fire pits, and nature trails. On the Knob Lick Mountain, he was given the use of several high school boys in a work program one summer. Glenn mapped out a trail along one side of the mountain. The boys carried chat in wheelbarrows and spread it along the trail which looped around and came back to the top of the mountain. Along the trail, Glenn identified several trees and put plaques on them, telling the name of the tree and some incidentals about that kind of tree. The Conservation printed a little map handout so the visitor could follow the trail and see where these trees were located.

The tower at Knob Lick sits atop a 1,333-foot tall mountain. It gets its name from the early observations of animals coming to lick some natural salt rocks on the mountain.

Glenn worked longer than any other warden in the Knob Lick District. He retired in 1977. He then moved to Farmington, Missouri which is 10 miles north of Knob Lick.

The 80-acre Knob, Lick Tower site, is administered for public recreation by the Missouri Department of Conservation. The tower's upper levels have been made inaccessible for safety concerns.

By the 1980's the towers were being decommissioned. Aircraft were employed in the danger seasons. Then, by the 1990s, even this was no longer necessary. The rural population had increased to the point that no fire burned very long before someone discovered it and called in the alarm.

On November 14, 1997, Glenn Skinner passed away. Then, in 2004, the Forestry Commission received a grant to preserve the tower site. Most of the towers were torn down or sold to private individuals. A few were designated for preservation, such as Knob Lick Tower. The Commission had received a grant to upgrade the Knob Lick Mountain and Tower for handicapped people. At that time, the Commission decided to dedicate the tower at Knob Lick to Glenn Skinner for his service to the Commission and the community.

Glenn would have been so proud and honored with this dedication. He had always loved the outdoors, and this became a dream job for him.

The tower sits there today, waiting for visitors to climb it. A viewing platform has been built about two-thirds of the way to the top. A wire cage has been built around this platform for safety. The remaining top part of the tower is still there but has been blocked off to climbers.

In addition, handicap parking areas have been built, along with a paved sidewalk out to the southern face of the mountain where there is a bench and a picnic table to enjoy while one takes in the spectacular view.

At the time of World War II, Knob Lick was still a bustling, little community. Railroading was still king, and with the addition of troop trains, it was common to see special trains passing through town. But the war took twenty-two of its citizens to the military, all came back except one. Other able-bodied men left for the city to work in arms factories or some business that supported the war effort. When the war was over, some stayed on in the "bright lights" of another world they had experienced.

And so, the little town of Knob Lick began to decline in numbers. The rock quarries closed about the time the war ended. The railroads left completely in the 1970s. The school finally closed and consolidated in the 1990s, and now there is only one store left. No longer do kids look out of the school windows at that sentinel atop the mountain that gave the town its name.

But, thanks to the Missouri Department of Conservation, that beacon of a tower still stands there, still watching over its little town, down below. And, not only the town but all the surrounding countryside as well. For, though the town's population diminished, the population of the surrounding farmlands has increased. More and more people have settled on the mini-farms in the country. A four-lane highway, of almost interstate status, passes between the mountain and its town. And, if you should find yourself traveling down 67 highway between Fredericktown and Farmington, stop off, drive up to the top of that mountain with the tower on it and take in that spectacular view, either from the platform on the tower or the south face of the mountain, where there's a bench to just sit and take in the grandeur of God's creation.

Because, some things never change: the view of Stono Mountain to the west, the range of the St. Francois Mountains to the west and south, the city of Farmington to the north, the rolling farmlands to the east. And, just along the edge to the south glade of rock, there is a little old twisted and spindly tree with a carpet of thick moss around it. The tree is not much larger than my arm although it has been there since long before I was born, eking out its existence on a bed of solid granite. Sometimes I go there and sit on that soft cushion of moss, beneath the shade of the tiny tress, and look out over the southern view. I think of the countless people, even back to the Native Americans of the area that have taken that view and marveled at its creator as well as that tree and that tower that continue to watch over the countryside and the little town below.

I also think of my Dad, Glenn Skinner and how he spent all those years watching over the same scene and guarding it against the destruction that fires might bring. I feel a closeness to him, to the tower that knew him, and to the mountain that he loved.

Jack W. Skinner

Jack Skinner enjoying a visit to the Glen Skinner Memorial Lookout Tower dedicated to his Dad who worked the tower for many years.

The Knob Lick View

Jerry Presley

Former MDC Director Jerry Presley honored – Conservationist from Low Wassie

(The preceding article and photo appeared in the Nov. 15, 2018 edition of the Current Local, a weekly newspaper in Carter County)

A name which speaks of the outdoors – With a little help from his great-grandchildren, retired Missouri Department of Conservation Director Jerry Presley (right) unveils the new sign for Twin Pines Conservation Center's education building, located near his childhood home of Low Wassie. Presley was honored last Wednesday at the center by current MDC Director Sarah Parker Pauley and Conservation Commissioner Don Bedell, among others.

"He's just a Shannon County boy who could always relate." It's an apt description for Jerry J. Presley, the now 87-year-old Low Wassie boy who, according to Missouri Department of Conservation (MDC) chief Sara Parker Pauley, has "done more to enlarge public engagement than any director." Pauley's praise came Thursday during a ceremony honoring Presley at Twin Pines Conservation Education Center near Winona.

There, five miles from his boyhood home, the former MDC director – who has always emphasized the importance of learning – saw his name given to the Center's educational building.

It's the sort of "local boy makes good" story that we all love to hear. Making it better is the undeniable feeling one has in Jerry's presence that he is still a local boy. When talking to Jerry, you find yourself spoken to directly, confidingly. There's no swagger, but instead, a disarming modesty which leaves the impression that here is a man who wants to hear what you have to say and will consider it. It's a personality which proved itself equally adept at working with staff members in Neosho, legislators in Jefferson City, and forest arsonists in Camden County. "The important thing is getting along with people," Presley insists. "And being willing to compromise once in a while."

Educated in Forestry at the University of Missouri-Columbia, Presley's 39-year career with MDC began as an assistant forester at Ellington in 1958, then stair-stepped to Neosho, Lake of the Ozarks, and Eminence. The jobs of the day were a newly-fledged timber management program the was "just getting ramped up" and fire suppression. "It had been open range for years," Presley points out. "People believed if you burned the woods every year, you'd have more grass, and get rid of ticks, chiggers and snakes." In 1977 he was named State Forester and in 1986, Deputy Director. In 1988 Presley took the department's reins from Larry Gale.

As Director, his unassuming manner was immediately evident. Asked by a senator what he intended to do with the department, Presley responded, "I'm not going to make any changes; we have a wonderful organization, and we are going to do everything we can to enhance it." And, enhance he did.

During Thursday's ceremony at Twin Pines, Director Pauley enumerated just a few shining examples of Presley's legacy:

Stream Teams began cleaning up local waterways in 1989; now there are 3,000 teams in the state;

- 1992 saw the advent of Free Fishing Day; Missouri is now home to over one million anglers;
- In 1993, Share the Harvest gave hunters a way to contribute to the state's hungry: last year over 200,000 lbs. of venison was donated;
- Youth-only deer hunts were inaugurated in 1994 when 56 young hunters tagged a total of 21 deer: this year, youngsters harvested 14,000 deer statewide .

"I found a lot of legislators like to hunt and fish," Presley recalls, adding that he took a number of them into the woods. "They're wonderful people, and I have great respect for them." But a challenge he faced early in his tenure was maintaining the still-new conservation sales tax. It was here that Presley's ability to forge bonds with legislators paid dividends. "We had some freshman legislators that would have taken money away from us, but [their bills] didn't get out of committee."

Presley's belief in conservation was sincere, formed by example and the scarcity of wildlife during his youth. He points to the influence of his maternal grandmother in particular. As a sophomore at Winona High School, Presley relates walking to school one morning when, "I looked up, and there was a doe deer with a fawn-that was the first deer I had ever seen, and I was in the woods constantly squirrel hunting. I ran all the way back to the house to tell my grandmother, I was so excited. She told me, 'You'll probably want to tell all your buddies that you saw a deer, but don't do it—they'll all be here trying to kill it.' She was a great conservationist."

As a high school senior walking home from ball practice he had another revelation-this time his first glimpse of strutting turkeys. "I saw three big birds come out in the road, and I thought, 'My God, what is that?'" And then one of them got about twice as large. His grandmother gave him the same cautionary instructions about telling his friends, then chastised Presley's uncle: "Lemro, why do you have to feel like you have to kill every bird in the world?"

Retiring from MDC in 1997, Presley has remained active, working at Bass Pro Shops in public relations for six years, then serving seven years with the Missouri Forest Products Association mediating contract disputes. He also serves on the Board of Directors of the Conservation Federation of Missouri and sits on MU's advisory council for its School of Natural Resources.

Presley and his wife of 63 years, Bonnie, now spend much of their time at their home in Van Buren, close to the Current River and the fishing he loves. Meanwhile, his legacy and that of conservation leaders like him-endow us in every vision of a fawn in train, in every gobblers' strut.

Kerwin Hafner

Forestry Veteran to Retire by Lynn Barnickol was first published in the November 1987 edition of the Conservation Currents, and it appears here courtesy of the Missouri Department of Conservation.

Forestry Veteran to Retire

Kerwin F. Hafner, a 37-year veteran with the Forestry Division, recently has announced his retirement which will be effective Jan. 31, 1988.

Because his father was a conservation agent for many years, going to work for the Conservation Department probably felt natural to Kerwin. July 1950 found Kerwin as the crew leader for the Deer Run State Forest boundary survey crew. Edwin C. Glaser, a former forester on the Deer Run Fire Protection District, was one of Kerwin's first supervisors.

Survey tools of chain and staff compass were later traded for broom rake fire tools during the drought years of the early '50s. During that time, Kerwin was reassigned as assistant district forester of the Deer Run Fire Protection District headquartered at Ellington.

In 1954 he was promoted and transferred to Van Buren Farm Forestry Project, which included three heavily timbered counties. He prepared forest management plans, planted trees, marked and sold timber on privately owned lands, and did forest crop land work in two additional counties.

"I requested a transfer from Van Buren to the Ironton Farm Forestry Project in 1956 hoping for a more urban setting," says Kerwin. Later in 1956 Kerwin was transferred to the

Pat Hutchison, district forester in the Clearwater Forest District—Piedmont, reads excerpts from Kerwin Hafner's 1950s activity reports. Investigating timber theft was high on the list of priorities 37 years ago when Kerwin began his career with the Forestry Division on Deer Run State Forest.

Lake Ozark Fire Protection District for a six-year tour of duty.

Kerwin spent four years on the Mokane Farm Forest Project before transferring to the Central Office as the forest crop land supervisor and fire staff assistant in 1963. "Although both program supervisors were outstanding," Kerwin emphasizes that, "having one supervisor is enough."

In 1965 Kerwin was promoted to assistant state forester where he has remained.

During 1978 the Outstanding Service in Fire Management Award was presented to Kerwin at the Northeastern National Association of State Foresters meeting. The award was made for Kerwin's leadership ability in dealing with forest fire problems in Missouri and on a national level. —Lynn Barnickol

Kerwin related to me—When my father raised his "right" hand to be hired into a new classification (Conservation Agent) MDC received an early shot of forestry effort. On July 1st, 1950, I steered my 1940 Dodge into the new country of a Forestry Division and the people who manned it.

A reluctant legislature had listened to newly appointed State Forester George O. White and found enough money for a few personnel. Some of these people climbed towers and gazed into the future. Why has a private land forester sell his client on a timber rotation and have it "burn" three years out of five? We must have a total forest fire program! Such an effort requires fire detection and a network of affordable development of our highest hills. This required a 100-foot tower, one bedroom house (no bath), and a two car garage and a well-worn lawn mower for exercise. This field of vision could start out something less than perfect but must reach 100% soon after. This would allow a half a million acres of privately owned forest cropland to be PROTECTED.

The 1946 "Legislature Bill" also took care of out of date Grandma practices. Loggers were required to provide locations where timber had been harvested. Whenever they did not want it known they would just sell on "Grandma's forty."

When I mentioned Kerwin's name, Lawrence Buchheit recalled working with him at Gutherie, and highlighted the "drift pin/punch/spud bar" terminology snafu noted in the Glossary. Lawrence noted he went to Gutherie to help install a Lookout Tower. On the third day of construction, Kerwin made a visit to the job site. Guess we were around 60 feet or so of completion on a 125-foot tower. There was a 100-foot crane on site to raise the material to working level. At working level, long pieces of timber were laid from side to side for a platform to work from. Also on the platform was a piece of plywood 4' by 4' to keep needed tools. The crane had just raised a piece of steel to our working level, and Kerwin told me to get him a "drift pin." I looked at this piece of plywood that had probably 25 different tools on it trying to figure out just what is a "drift pin." About a minute later Kerwin again tells me, a little firmer to get him a "drift pin." I'm still trying to figure out what is a "drift pin." A third time he tells me with a raised voice to get him a "drift pin." I'm still trying to figure out what is a "drift pin" when he gets up and goes over and picks up what I call a punch. I told Kerwin if he needed a punch why he didn't call it a punch—only to be reminded this tool is called a drift pin, not a punch.

Jim Sorenson noted he had just started at the Lebanon District in 1967 and was fighting a big fire by himself. He heard rustling in the leaves uphill from his position and knew somebody was coming. Here came Kerwin, Assistant State Forester stationed in Jeff City, hurrying down the slope with boots, gloves and a rake. He said the two finally got the fire out and you can bet I was impressed to see a person of his status willing to give up his time off to help a new District Forester.

Ron "Woody" Woodland

I was urged often to contact Ron which I did a few years ago. We had several telephone "tower talks" and tentatively had a meeting set up for his favorite Bar-B-Que place in or near Sullivan. Sadly, Ron had an accident and passed away before we had a chance to meet. The following is from some notes I took during the phone talks, some ideas from audio recordings done years ago, and ideas from his daughter Laura Kampschroeder and Kathleen Boulay-Eaton (a clerk 3 for the department).

Ron was an accomplished writer who had written a number of articles for the MDC and others. I leaned on him several times to do a piece for the book. He came close to saying yes several times, but I could never get him to commit. He was willing to talk on the phone and meet down the road. I sure wish now I had been a little more persuasive. His writing skills showed in works of poetry he penned. His book of poetry is entitled "Acceptance." He also penned "Wild Daisies." Ron was a man of great faith and wrote articles each week in the local newspaper for his church.

Ron was in the USAF before joining the MDC. He was unsure of his future as a pilot as he could take off and fly just fine, but he could not do as well with the landings.

"Woody," as he was known, worked for the department from 1958-1997. Most of that was spent as a District Forester here and there. His first job was at Meramec in training and then he was transferred to Neosho as District Forester. He noted that when he arrived at Neosho, the area was in the midst of a long drought with a large number of subsequent fires. The day he arrived it began raining and the more it rained, the more his reputation grew!

He recalled 1962 as a bad year for fires, but he noted the Neosho crew could work towers and drive dozers and everything in between. He said when the tower workers left the towers, others would just pick up the slack. Ron noted that dust from Oklahoma would blow in and make observations from the towers very difficult. Neosho had "blanket agreements" with the surrounding areas and fire detection and suppression would at times cross state boundaries.

In 1967 he was transferred back to Meramec as District Forester. He noted how education became a big part of his job. Presentations were made to local schools. Smokey Bear materials were distributed. So successful were these efforts that he noted he "almost worked himself out of a job." He was especially proud of one presentation made at a school. A week later a fire broke out at the house of two students, and after they became separated from their parents, they were saved when they put Smokey's advice to use and crawled close to the ground to avoid the smoke. Speaking of house fires, Woody noted one occasion when a tower worker crossed out a fire that turned out to be his own home.

Woody noted to me the fact that you learned to become your own weather forecaster and became skilled at anticipating even the time of day that fires were more likely to spring up. He also recalled various experiments that took place using planes to drop water on a fire. In a drop he noted, 50% of the water was lost before it hit the ground. Experiments were done to use additives to thicken the water which became a precursor to various water drop efforts out west.

Woody said he learned to do high steel "on the job." He helped put the Elkhorn steel tower up to replace the 70' wood tower nearby. He said he did well until the level of the steel tower grew above the wooden and he could "look down" at the wooden structure. It was then he realized how "up in the air" he was. He noted putting a tower up was "interesting" but taking one down was even more so. As you took this or that down things got loose and "on the move." When taking the Beaufort Tower down, the cab (attached to a rope) was caught by the wind and blew out horizontal to the ground. One of the workers refused to do any more tower down work on the spot.

Kathleen Boulay-Eaton noted that when the repair shop at Meramec caught fire, Woody burned his hand getting a fairly new jeep out of the building. She also noted that Ron wore a pair of light buckskin shoes to work the first day, was sent off to a big fire, and had the shoes baptized by fire you might say.

Those around him note Woody as a man of faith who loved his family above all else. Lawrence Buchheit had also cautioned me when I interviewed him to "not forgot the families." Detection and suppression often did not recognize the clock and as Ron put it, "I should be home flying kites with the girls." The demands of conservation have been a common theme in my tower discussions.

His daughter Laura offered the following testimonial:

"From the very first night of my life, my father has protected me. That first night, Dad sat at the end of his bed and made sure I was breathing all night long. Just a few weeks before he passed away, Dad was explaining how to overcome a blind spot in my new, first-ever SUV. There are many instances in between: walking me home from elementary school during a sudden and unpredicted snowstorm, following in the family car as I traveled back to college on an icy day, teaching me to swallow pills, and making sure I could change a tire in case of an emergency.

Dad made sure he was an involved parent. He attended every function my sister, and I were a part of, he took us to church every Sunday and taught us to read the bulletin and hymnal so we could participate. He shared his love of books with us, reading aloud to us before bed every evening. Rudyard Kipling's "Just So Stories" and "White Fang" were among our favorites. Dad hooked me on reading by buying me my very own Nancy Drew books. I've loved mysteries ever since, and still own those books. He spoke at our schools every year during Fire Prevention Week and sometimes dressed as Smokey Bear. He taught us to love and respect nature. "Take nothing but pictures, leave nothing but footprints" was a motto shared with us early on. Dad taught us to fish, swim, and how to drive a boat safely. Hiking the trails in Rockwoods Reservation was a favorite family activity.

Our education was extremely important to our parents. Together they attended every conference and PTO meeting. Dad was a great help with homework. Even during fire season, tired as he must've been and smelling of smoke, he always took time to help me with fractions, and later Algebra and Geometry. Once, he and I came up with mnemonic devices to help me remember the name and location of every country in the world for a big test. I can still remember many of them. In junior high, one assignment was to collect and identify leaves. Dad took me to Meramec State Park, and we enjoyed a fall afternoon together. Not only could I identify trees by their leaves, but also by their bark. Dad taught me how to read a newspaper when I was about 10 years old. Together, we enjoyed discussing current events. Each year, the Post-Dispatch prints the 100 Neediest Cases. We had always been taught to help the less fortunate, and Dad and I would read the cases and decide which ones we could help. Once, I lamented about not being able to help all of them. Dad told me if I prayed for them that would be a way I could help all 100.

Not too many men like to shop, but having a wife whose hobby was shopping, and 2 daughters following in her footsteps, Dad became a good sport about it. We'd head to St. Louis for new clothes as seasons changed, and we outgrew what we had. Once, when I was older, Dad left an important football game on TV to take me to the mall to buy a new outfit for a special date. My favorite memory of those shopping trips, though, was Christmas shopping. We would sing Christmas carols all the way there. When we arrived, we would split up. Dad and I would shop for Mom, and my sister and mom would shop for Dad. And it was always, always so much fun!

Every kid thinks their dad is the strongest in the neighborhood or the world for that matter. I have no doubt that my dad actually was. He walked into burning forests, he caught arsonists, he played football in high school, took down a fire tower, flew in the Air Force, raced off into the night when a fire call came in and watched as his wife was given six months to live after a cancer diagnosis. But she was strong too, and so was their faith. She fought that demon for 21 years, and Dad was strong for us as Mom slipped away. He remained strong for 10 more years without her, for us. And at age 86, he endured 2 brain surgeries after being airlifted to St. Louis University Hospital. Yes, my dad was strong.

Dad was very involved in his community and church, and we learned by example. He was Sullivan's first ever Outstanding Citizen. An important contribution was his outreach to schools and community about protecting the environment, and being good stewards of the Earth. He also coached Little League, taught tennis lessons, volunteered at the Teen Community Center, was a member of Optimist Club, and was an elder and Sunday school leader at his beloved First Presbyterian Church, even filling the pulpit for vacationing ministers through the years. Dad wrote articles for the local newspaper, church newsletter, and the Conservationist magazine.

Our dad was a lifelong learner, taking a college course after his retirement. He also studied courses online and enjoyed learning about new technology. He could tell a story about his life experiences like nobody else! Family dinners had us begging for a story or a repeat of one of our favorites.

Dad tolerated cats, but he loved dogs. They always held a special place in his heart-from his Grandpa's beagles, his labs, and the sweet mixed breed that Mom left to take care of him. He always helped us find homes for the strays that would appear around our house.

The most important thing my Dad did was love my mother. Seeing their relationship taught my sister and me what to look for in our future husbands. If ever there was such a thing as soul mates, our parents were one another's. Our family laughed together, prayed together, and supported one another. It might seem too good to be true, but that's what our family was. And we knew we were loved and blessed.

Dad was many things to different people: husband, son, brother, father in law, son in law, uncle, forester, boss,

Woody doing the "Check Station Shuffle."

friend, elder, tennis partner, coach… But to me, he'll always be Dad-o, my hero, my Superman. He made a difference in his time here on Earth, leaving a legacy we will forever cherish. I'd say the world needs more men like my Dad."

Back in those days, "family" also included the conservation team that bonded in a manner that all note, but find hard to put into words at times. Woody encouraged this camaraderie telling Kathleen that whatever decisions she made, he would always back her up. He said he might not always agree, but would always back her up. Kathleen notes that during deer and turkey season everyone took turns at the check stations. Being a "people person," Woody enjoyed the visiting. He listened to all the hunters as they talked about their kills. Kathleen noted she was more "check em in and check em out." Woody also kept the District fire stats. This included the number of fires for the year, acres burned, etc. He was big on MDC history.

In the picture from Kathleen, Woody is standing next to Mike Reavis. She noted Woody and Mike were great pals and had some "interesting" experiences in one of the areas. It seems the Huzzah State Forest in Crawford County had a camping area just off where the Meramec River and Huzzah Creeks meet. It tended to attract at times a rowdy crowd trying to avoid the Rangers at the State Park. On the weekends guys would take turns monitoring the area, especially in the summer. It was not an easy job, but Woody took his turns like everyone. Somebody also worked the radio at HQ or home in case backup might be needed.

Kathleen also notes that one day, in the midst of a very hot, dry, and windy fire season there erupted a very nasty fire in Southern Washington County. Two people were kept at dispatch on such days because one "manned" the phones and the other dispatched. This was a Red Flag Day, and when people would call with a fire, they would just be put on a list, she explained. There was no more personnel to send, and all our area fire departments were in the same boat. The fire was so big and bad that one of the St. Louis news stations had sent a chopper to the scene to take video from the air. Our pilot radioed in that the chopper kept getting in his way and he couldn't see the fire well enough to let our guys on the ground know where the fire was at its worst. Kathleen says she called the news station and told the guy I was talking to that they had to get that chopper out of there. Woody was mad and when the chopper didn't leave he grabbed the phone and suggested where they could put the chopper. While it is unlikely that is where they parked it—it immediately disappeared!

I am sorry I didn't get the chance to "tower talk" with Woody in person, but I am thankful for the phone conversations I was able to enjoy. Thanks to Laura and Kathleen for all the help.

Steel Towers

There are no wooden towers that I know of still standing in Missouri. There are, however, around 65 or so steel ones. In fact, the steel tower at Deer Run is commonly cited as the state's oldest and is still up. Here are pictures from our visit in 2017.

The fact is that a properly constructed galvanized steel tower can stand for a long time when maintained. Over the next few pages, let me discuss that construction with some notes I have taken from Max Gorman, Jim Parker, and Jim Sorenson.

Much like a pyramid, it all starts with the base. Any errors made here will just compound themselves as the tower rises. According to Jim Parker, the footings at the Squires Tower were a little off, and that had to be dealt with all the way up in construction. This leads us to the footings, or the word piers to be correct.

These footings had to be placed at a specific distance from one another. I still carry around a note card that I got from Jim Lyon:

Aermotor Crow's Nest (center to center of pier)
40   8'4"
53   11'0"
66   13'8"
80   16'4"

Aermotor 7 by 7 Cab
46   13'11"
60   15'11"
73   18'0"
80   19'0"
86   20'0"
100 22'0"

On a historic site, you can just measure the distance between footings and estimate the tower size.

Once the distance between the footings was established for the tower size to be built, a large hole to hold footing forms had to be made. At times these were dug by hand. In rocky conditions, dynamite might be used. The four holes had to be larger than the piers so the forms could be removed, oiled, and stored.

The amount of concrete increased with the size of the tower. The forms and footings were beveled out at the bottom for added stability. For a 100 foot tower, the footings might be seven feet deep and require almost 100 cubic yards of concrete per footing. A truck would be used if possible to bring in the concrete, but if not possible a "putt-putt" mixer was used. The anchor bolts were set deep into the concrete with correct spacing so the anchor plates could be attached and work.

The footings would be set to dry and then the forms removed. With dry and correct footings, a tower could be put up by a crew in a week and a half for about $1,500—in the 1930s.

Steel pieces were then constructed upward. Unlike a wooden tower where a single pole served as a leg, steel tower legs were a series of pieces bolted together and supported with belts and braces. As the tower rose, steel had to be brought up to continue work. This was accomplished with the use of a "gin pole." This device held a pulley or block and tackle above the work area which brought the steel up to be used. This meant that the workers were often working with steel overhead. As each level was completed the gin pole would be "jumped" up to work ever higher. As the work grew higher, a number of concerns arose. If the ground was soft, a dropped tool could easily disappear in the mud or become a dangerous item.

To work at each level, boards were set between girders. These 2 by 12 boards would dip as the worker moved. At lower levels, the distance was greater and the dip more. As the work moved up and the distance between the girders shrank, the sway decreased, but the height increased. When pieces didn't line up, a drift pin or punch was used to line up the holes and a clamp attached. Then a bolt could be inserted and secured.

Risers and platforms would be added depending on the style. The cab was constructed from pieces. The blueprints for the cab alone were very intricate.

Steel Towers

The 100-foot steel towers cost under one thousand dollars in 1936. Including concrete foundations and erection, the total cost averages fourteen hundred dollars. A trained crew of 10 men can erect a tower in ten days after the foundations are ready, or 100 man days (KWTO 1936).

Below, you will find construction at Blue Slip and Marshfield. Notice the boards in use and the gin pole on the right leg of the Blue Slip construction.

Taking a tower down was just running the reel backward in a way. I asked Jim Parker about it one time, and he began at the cab with one disassemble point after another. I was amazed and let him go on for several minutes. I am convinced he could have noted every step all the way back to the footings. You had the same dangers as in construction: working on boards, steel up above, items dropped, etc.

The footings were seldom touched. Now and then the knobs were cleaved off, but for a tower documenter, if you look in the right place, the footing evidence can usually be found.

Now and then cranes were used to take the tower down in parts. You took the cab loose and lowered it and so forth. Cabs show up now and then that were taken off whole. More on that later as well.

Jim noted these sections tended to "scissor" and were not always easy to work with. Below is a picture of the top of the Seymour Tower being taken down.

When discussing the topic of "putting up" and " taking down," the question of safety pops into your mind almost as soon as you look at any picture. It was obviously a job with many inherent dangers.

I ask several of the "tower constructors" about this, and one answer I received was that hard hats and gloves were standard issue. It was pointed out, and I had never thought about it, the hard hats were maybe more for those below than those above.

I ask what is maybe obvious, what about safety harnesses? The answer was that as the years passed safety harnesses were at the sites more and more. They could be especially useful when a certain job required the use of both hands. However, as several workers did this and that they could also be counter-productive as the ropes tended to wrap around the legs of other workers. So, one answer I got was they were used "when required," with a wink.

Although there were "close call" stories, like a worker at Seymour almost blown off by a sudden gust of wind while holding a large sheet, nobody could actually remember any serious accidents. It seems experience, skill, and crew communication took care of most problems.

In the picture below, Les Carson "ground tests" a safety harness.

Safety also could utilize some simple ideas. Vehicles often had large numbers stenciled on the top. This may seem useless since they can't be viewed from ground level, but with the large numerals, they could be easily seen from a tower or even airplane. This vehicle was reportedly that of Vonnie Johnson who worked the Seymour Tower area. It was used often to haul workers used from the Fordland Honor Camp to help with various projects.

Windmill Towers – One of the most common steel towers across Missouri was the so-called "windmill tower." The name was derived from an Aermotor windmill that the company had been selling out west. When the need arose for forest lookout towers, they realized the windmill could be replaced by a platform to make a secondary or spot coverage tower. You can today find smaller and closely spaced footings denoting where these towers stood. You can even find one still up. More on that later.

On some models, like at Corn Creek, the platform even had a canvass "cab" to cover a fire finder, although these towers were most commonly used for eyeball observation during the dry season. The climb up involved a ladder that ran up one of the legs or side. Many found this climb "interesting."

Below is a picture of Jim Parker climbing the "windmill" tower at Rolla.

An Aermotor windmill that was the basis for the windmill towers

The Jay/Botkin Tower – (The following is reprinted with permission from the Reynolds County Courier. I did a five-part series on the towers of Reynolds County, and the paper concluded it with this sixth part. I dedicate it to Mary Botkin, who passed away in 2017.)

Several years ago (possibly as early as the 1970s) there was a 53-foot fire tower located just east of Hwy. TT near the Fletcher Mine and Mill entrance. This tower was known locally as "the Jay Tower." It is not known just how the tower earned that name. Centerville resident Dewayne Botkin remembers climbing the tower on more than one occasion as a youngster.

A time came that the Forest Service advertised the tower to be for sale and Merrell "Pete" Botkin (Dewayne's father) was the successful bidder – the only potential problem was that the new owner would have to remove the tower at his own expense.

"The tower was bolted to a concrete foundation on all four sides," Pete later told his son, Dewayne. Thus the first order of business was to undo each bolt.

"He then climbed the tower and attached a long cable to it, hooked the other end of the cable to his ¾-ton truck, put the truck into four-wheel drive and backed up to the tower," Dewayne continued. "He then took off fast , and when he came to the length of the cable, he told me the back of the truck came up off the ground about four feet and down came the tower.

Upon checking the tower, the elder Botkin found only one of the "handrails" was bent. He dismantled the tower on the spot and hauled it to Centerville where he reconstructed it in his backyard to which he then mounted a television antenna."

"As far as I know, he did all this by himself," Dewayne said. "He got the tower all put together except for the very top where the platform was and then got Ray Johnson to come in with a crane to lift the platform up for him."

With the coming of satellite television, the younger Botkin has had the useless antenna removed since he and his wife moved to Centerville in September 2000, but the tower still sits in the Botkin back yard, high above the housetops. Persons wanting to see it can do so easily when traveling through Centerville from north to south on Highway 21. As they pass the county courthouse, they only need to look off to the left over the top of Moody's convenience store . There, high above Botkin's second-story home, is the top half of Jay Tower standing tall over the town.

"We recently listed our place 'For Sale,' and the Jay Tower goes with the property," Dewayne said. "Those of you who knew Pete Botkin, know there is not much he couldn't do. I still miss him…"

This is the sixth section to what started as a five-part series in the Courier regarding the firetowers of Reynolds County. Thanks to Bob Frakes for sharing his research of the towers.

Update – The house & tower were recently sold to Justin Barton, so it now is the Jay/Botkin/Barton Tower I suppose.

Aermotor & I.D.M. – Moving on to the larger steel towers in Missouri is a simply complicated story of sorts. The maker of the "windmill" towers, the Aermotor Company made several models of larger steel towers. The International Derrick Company also made several "I.D.M." models. Some of these I.D.M. models were licensed clones of sorts of Aermotor models. As you can see, identifying towers can get to be a challenge so I will try to keep it simple.

Several Aermotor "LL" variations – In the case of the Tram Tower or the Roby Tower (originally) a person made their way to the cab, even at 100 feet, by climbing a steel ladder. This eliminated the risers and platforms (one version did have the platforms connected by ladders and not steps) . Other versions had a steel ladder running all the way up the inside or outside of the tower. This made the tower lighter, simpler, and less expensive. It also made the climb "interesting," especially in the darkness or bad weather. In fact, these models were so dangerous kits were made available to convert them to internal risers and platforms.

Aermotor LS-40 – Perhaps the most iconic tower in Missouri and one of the most common. The number of platforms could even give you the height, even at a distance.

3 platforms=22 feet
5 platroms=35 feet
6 platforms=42 feet
7 platforms=47 feet
9 platforms=60 feet
11 platforms=73 feet
12 platforms=80 feet

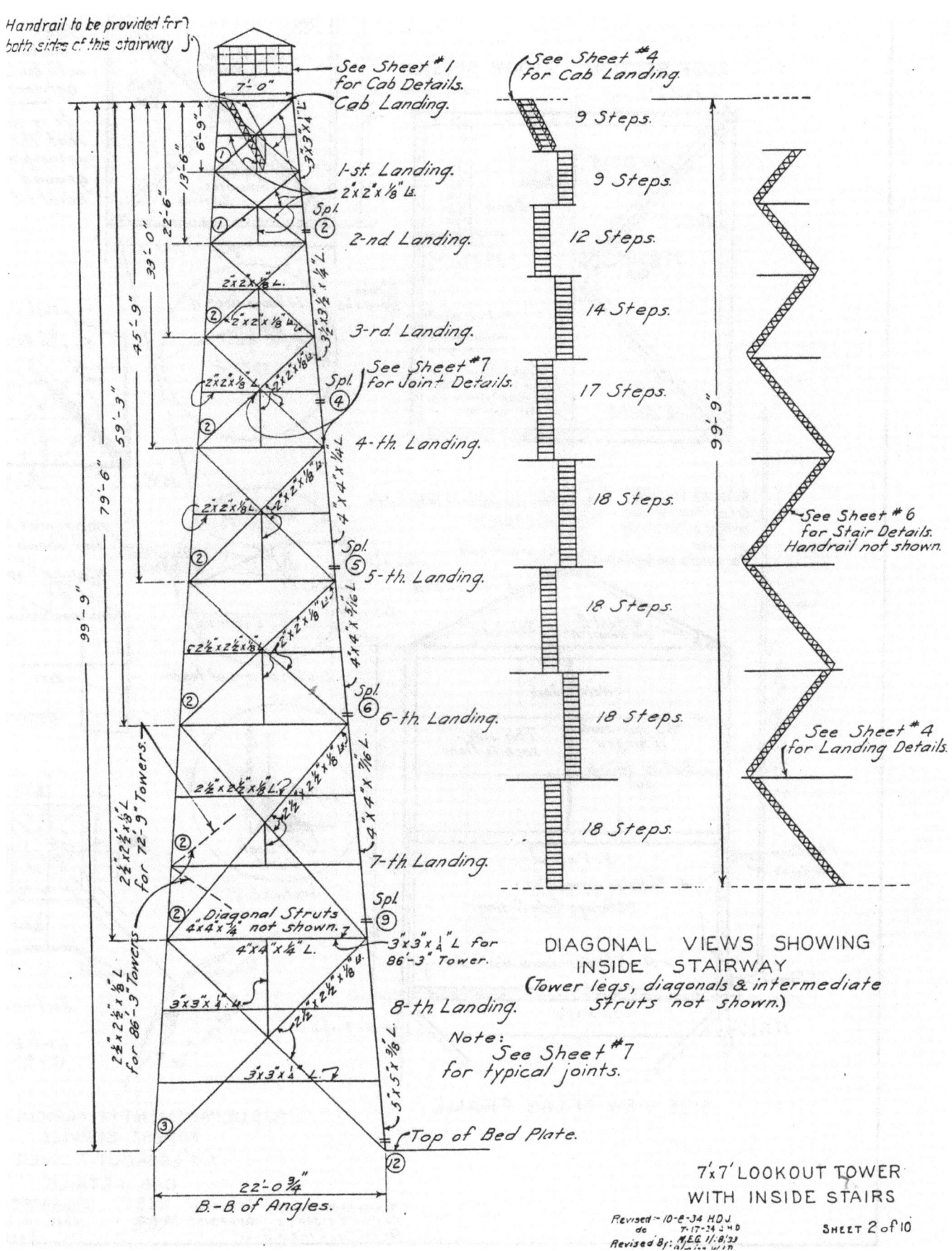

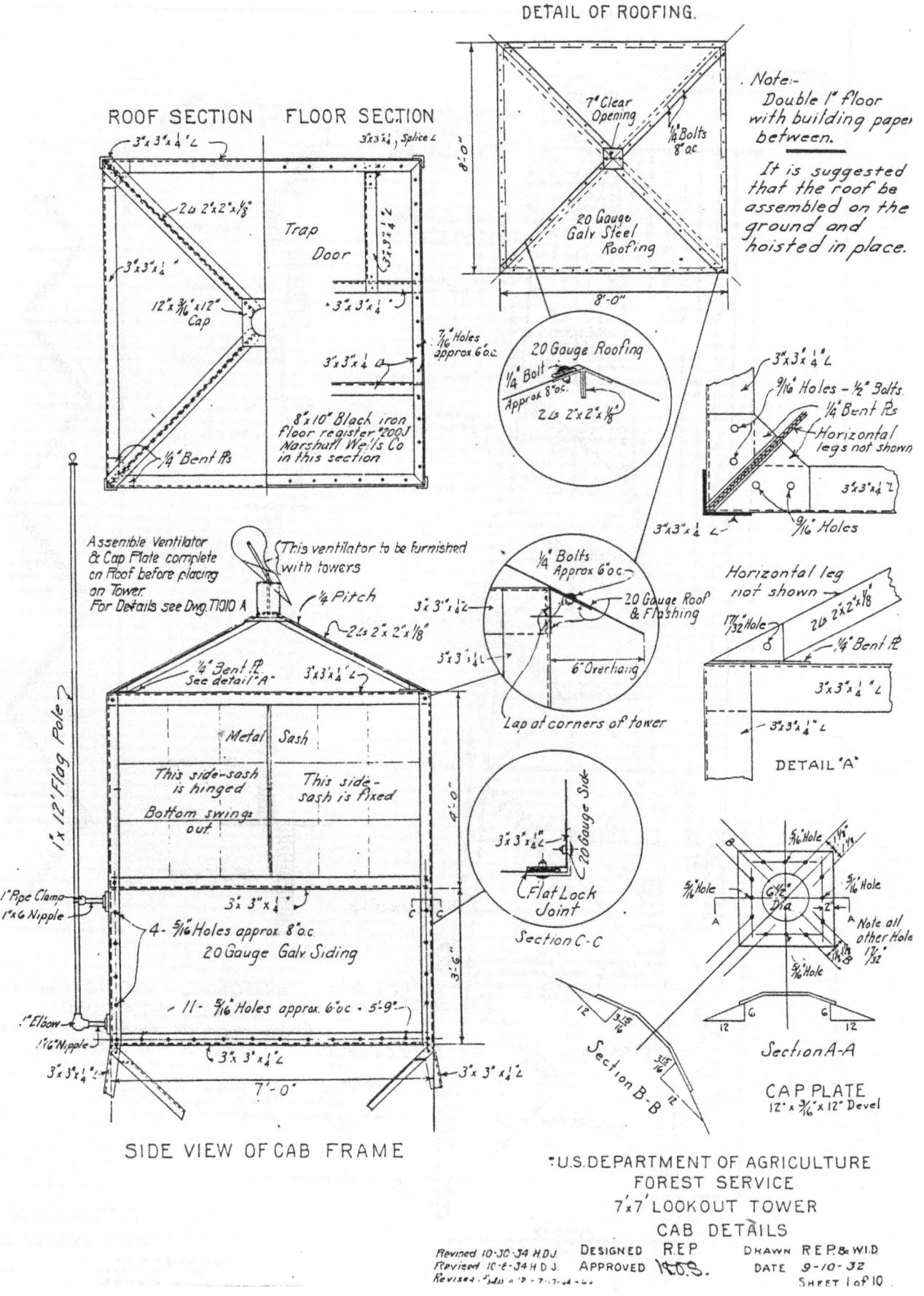

I often refer to these as "back and forth" towers as you climb a set of risers and then turn 180° to climb another set. The length of each riser is short which I appreciate as the years slip by. Max Gorman noted to me a feature of the LS-40, the unique "bounce" as you made your way up or down.

Pictured below is a classic LS-40, the Shannondale Tower.

Variations – Back in the day, you would find instead of stairs, ladders used to connect platforms or even used to go "all the way up." The advantage of this can be found in the following cost and weight figures (around 1930).

100-foot LX-24 Outside Ladder
Weight 8,400 Pounds/Cost $725

100 foot LX-25 Inside Ladder (Pictured on the next page)
Weight 12,500 Pounds/$1,000

LS-40 100 foot with Inside Stairway (Above).
Weight 16,500 pounds/$1,340

There was a temptation to save pounds and especially money by using ladders instead of steps. Climbing these in the dark while carrying equipment after a rain proved to be "interesting". Aermotor began selling "conversion kits" to change an LX-25 to a "conversion" LS-40. The Roby Tower is a conversion with the ladder out by the fence I am told.

Aermotor MC-39 – This type is what I call the "diagonal" with the risers running corner to corner. Here is a shot of the Twin Knobs Tower and you can clearly see the diagonal pattern. It also has an Aermotor tag on it – MC-39.

Now, the International Derrick Company made two versions of this, the Model 1933 and 1937. How do you tell an MC-39 from and I.D.M.1933 or I.D.M. 1937? If it is tagged or labeled with "Aermotor," it is likely an MC-39. If it is a diagonal tagged or labeled International Derrick Company, it is likely a 1933 or 1937. The length of cab or window style can also be a giveaway. I.D.M. 1937s had over half the cab given to the window. Coot Mountain is an I.D.M. 1937, below.

There were also a couple of examples of lookouts seen mostly out west. Jim Lyon told me that out west the height of the mountains often made tall towers unnecessary. The isolation also made living quarters a must. You can see these features at the Taum Sauk Tower below. The Old Baldy Tower was similar. You can see the insides of Baldy and Joe Donley.

Finally, the International Derrick Company, Carnage, and others made towers that were converted from oil derricks. A cab was set atop the derrick frame. There was no internal system for risers and platform leaving the worker to climb metal ladders. As with the metal ladder Aermotor "LL" designs, there were not popular with the workers. Climbing these at night with a radio and other equipment was often, again very "interesting." Most workers used a rope and pulley system to help ease the load with equipment. Here is an example from Caney II.

Tags or labels – I mentioned the tags or labels you find on some towers. The following demonstrates several examples. You have the Aermotor classic. You also see the Aermotor inverted. There are several examples here and there of the Aermotor tag showing upside down. The common consensus is the tag was attached at the factory and with the two holes being made toward an end to accommodate eye level, you had to think it out or get it upside down. At times, like at Blue Slip, you can actually find the Aermotor stencil on a beam. In this case, notice it is Aermotor in Broken Arrow, Oklahoma and not Chicago. A different vertical Aermotor tag is also labeled Broken Arrow. Finally, you see an International Derrick Company tag.

Stamps – You can also come across "stamps" that indicate where the steel came from. "Inland" is one you see often as in the Inland Steel Company in Chicago. You may also see "Carnegie" for the steelworks near Pittsburg. Andrew Carnegie sold his steel holdings, and it eventually became U.S. Steel. "Bethlehem" stands for Bethlehem, Pennsylvania and the steel works there.

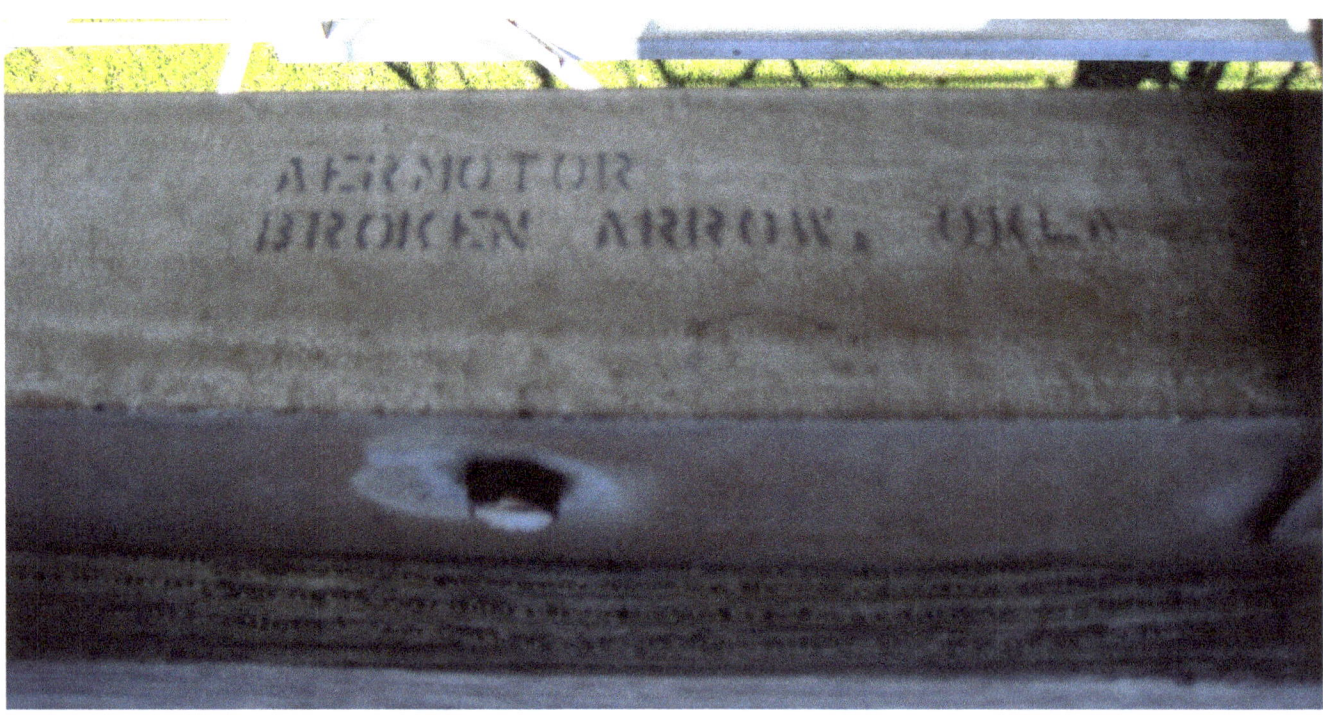

Firetowers

"Inland"

"Carnegie"

"Bethlehem"

Contribution to Book on Lookout Towers

By Jim Sorenson

Over the years, I have accumulated a fairly large library dealing with the various aspects of forest fire management. Most of these are volumes of some size and go into great detail on these subjects, especially suppression. At some point, the subject of detection comes up, and it is acknowledged as being important to the entire effort. However, it is the rare publication that then proceeds to discuss in any length, the details that contribute to its proper functioning. Two of these details are addressed here.

Fire Finders.

The earliest efforts to locate forest fires relied on climbing up a tree or standing on a high ridge top. These primitive methods were all that were available to early forest protection workers, but they were easily shown to be ineffective. The person could see smoke at some distance but had no accurate way to determine the distance and direction to the fire. Once he climbed down from the tree or left the ridge, he was once again at a loss to locate the fire. If he was a good woodsman, he could use his compass to take a bearing to the fire from the tree, estimate the route he would travel to the fire, and hope for the best. This limitation, coupled with the fact that he was probably the only person available to fight the fire when he arrived, led to many large fires in the early days.

As fire management capabilities advanced, it became common to build permanent or semi-permanent structures, lookout towers, from which it was possible to view a large area of terrain needing protection from fires. The tower replaced the tree but did nothing to correct the

problem of true fire location. Of course, in the earliest days, the person in the tower was also the person who had to attack the fire, so he still needed to take a compass reading and estimate how far he had to walk to the fire. Once the fire management program had developed to the point where additional resources could be sent to the fire, it became necessary to have a better way to pinpoint the fire's location. Direction and distance were still important, but difficult to accurately transmit to the incoming resources.

To correct this deficiency, a tool called a "fire finder" was developed. Early designs were adaptations of surveyors' alidades. The alidade, which was simply a straight-edge with a sighting device attached, was aimed at the fire, similar to aiming a rifle. A compass ring was provided, around which the alidade was turned to indicate a bearing to the fire. That information would be relayed to incoming crews via radio or telephone line to headquarters.

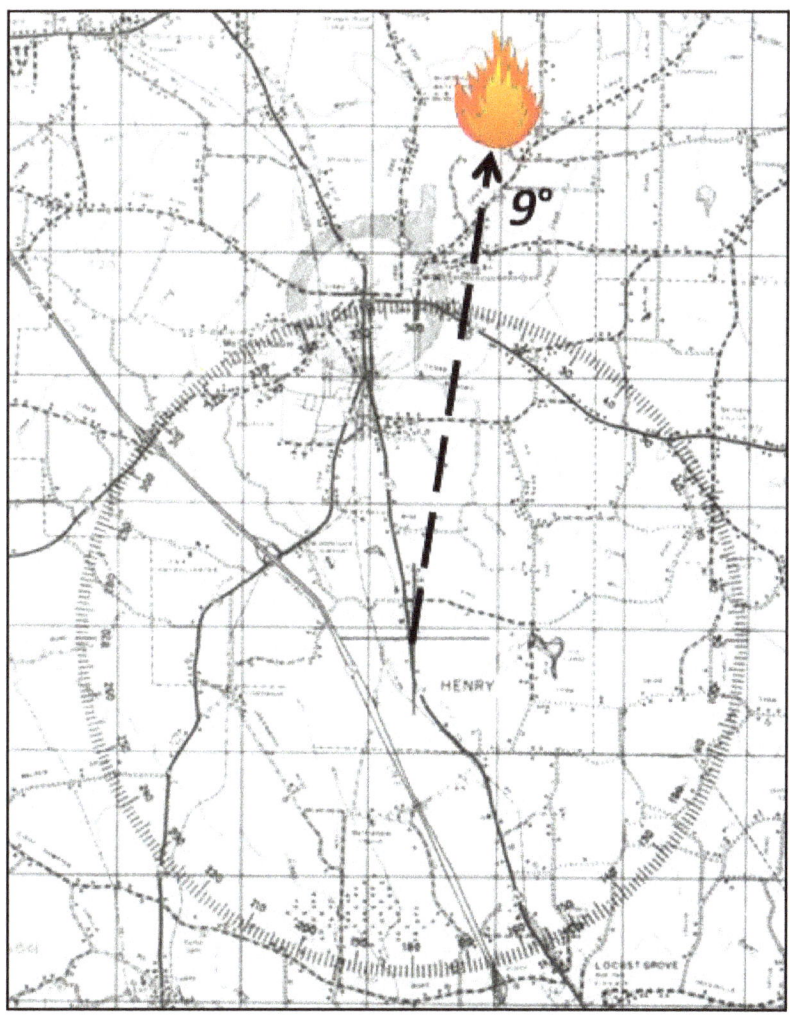

Later on, a good map of the protected area was attached to a flat surface, oriented to true North, and secured so it could not move. The fire was then sighted with the alidade, and a line on the map indicated the fire's location at some distance from the tower. It was now up to the judgment, (skill), of the towerman to estimate exactly where along that line the fire was burning. In some cases, there was no map involved, but this procedure worked fairly well, especially if the terrain was reasonably flat, and the towerman was well acquainted with the area. However, there was room for improvement, and further tinkering with the system resulted

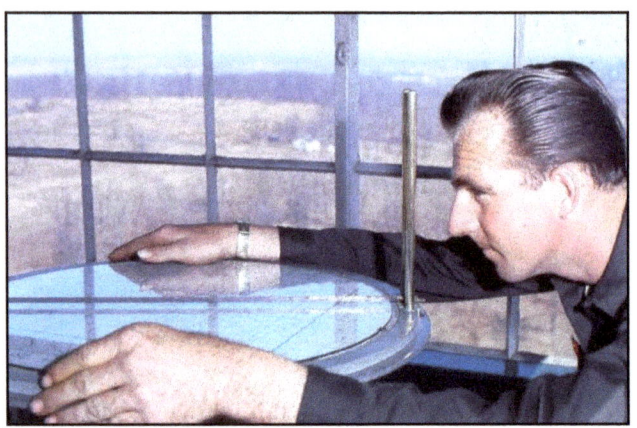

Photo by J. C. Sorenson

in the Osborne Fire Finder in the early 1900s. Its inventor, (W. B. Osborne), kept improving the design for a number of years, and it continues to be used wherever it has escaped vandalism and deterioration due to age.

The Osborne Fire Finder incorporated all of the technology available at the time into a unit that allowed very precise location for fires, especially when more than one tower could see the same fire. Instead of an opaque compass ring upon which the alidade rotated, it had a glass plate overlaying a properly oriented map of the coverage area. The precise location of the tower on the map coincided with the center of the compass ring. When a towerman took a reading on a fire, his line of sight passed directly over the map, giving him an accurate bearing to the fire. A vertically sliding "peep sight" allowed the towerman to depress his line of sight to give a better estimate of distance from the tower to the fire. It could also be used to determine the approximate size of a fire.

Lookout towers, and the resources to support them, including personnel to staff them, can add up quickly, so care must be exercised in their location. Terrain features and atmospheric conditions can limit visibility, so more towers may be necessary in one area than in another.

Dispatch Boards.

A properly constituted fire protection unit would have enough lookout towers to adequately cover the areas that might require fire suppression activities. Ideally, these towers would be so located as to allow more than one of them to see any given fire. This would allow fires to be "crossed out," meaning that their precise location could be determined, greatly reducing the time required to get suppression crews on site. Radio communications between towers allow the towermen to discuss the attributes of their co-located fires to assist management in decisions regarding proper resources to be sent.

The ability to "cross out" fires is only possible if a proper dispatch board is available to the fire management unit responsible for the area, so this task must be performed early in the development of the district.

The complexity of the dispatch board is determined by the anticipated fire load of the district. If it is anticipated that only one or two fires will occur on any given day, the board may just be a simple district map with a map showing the exact location of all towers covered with a sheet of glass or plastic on which azimuth lines can be drawn with a grease pencil when needed.

If a fairly heavy workload is expected on a regular basis, a more complex board may be needed, due to more fires to be crossed out by more towers, with extended suppression times. Some designs include strings, radiating outward from holes in the map from at each tower's azimuth circle. The end of each string is attached to a magnet that holds fast to an iron sheet under the map. The point where these strings meet indicates the location of the fire. That point is now marked on the glass/Plexiglas overlay, and the strings are free to be used for subsequent fires without cluttering up the map's surface if the fire load gets heavy.

Contribution to Book on Lookout Towers

Photo by J. C. Sorenson

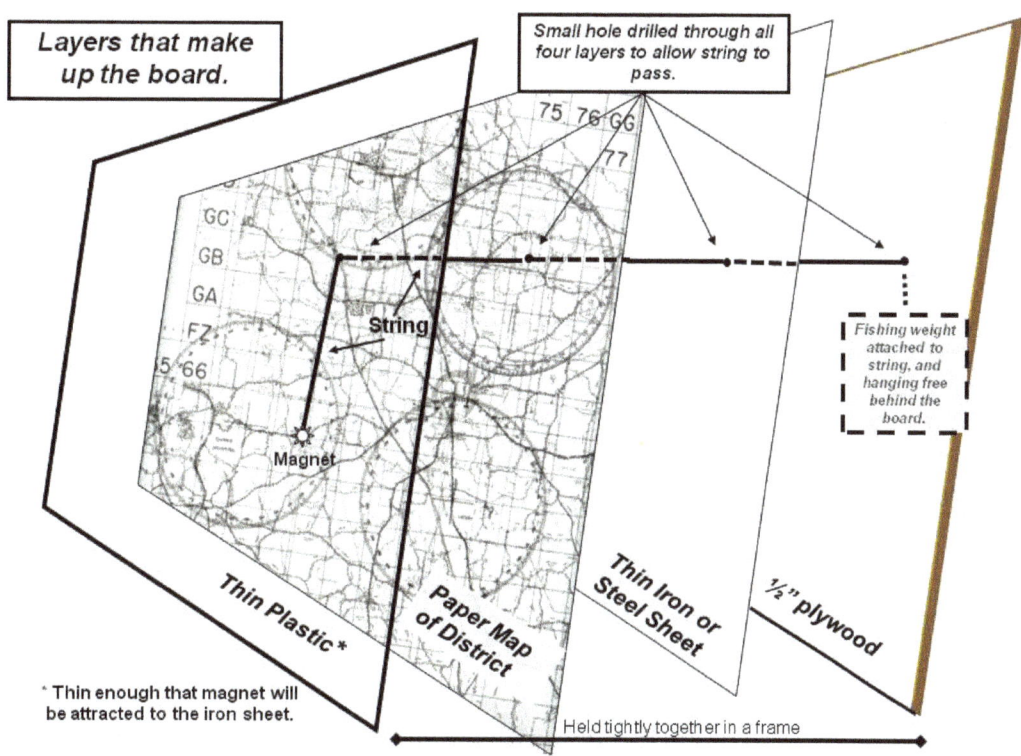

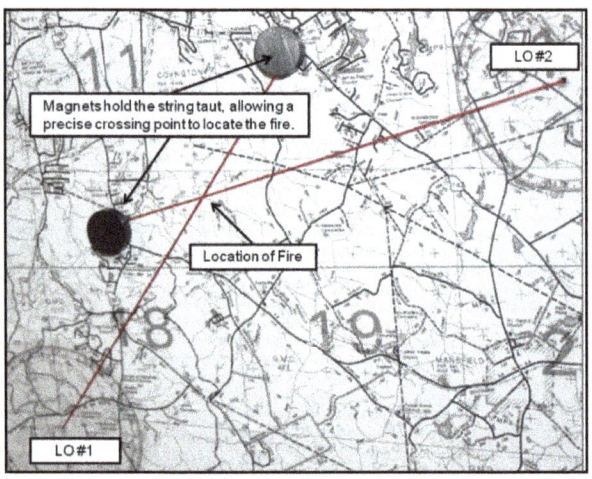 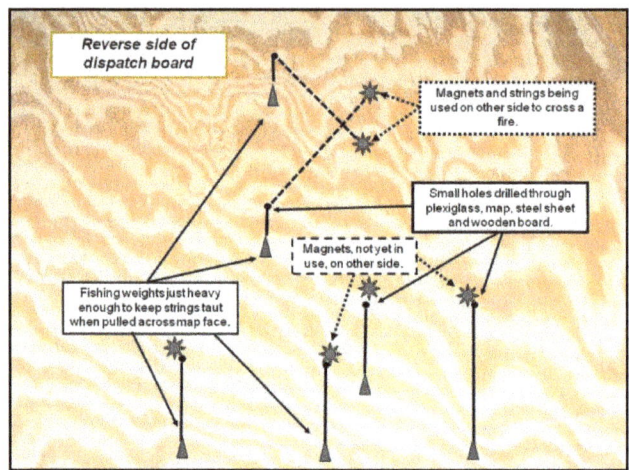

Once the precise location of the new fire has been determined it is up to the Dispatcher to make a number of critical decisions.

Depending on the current and anticipated fire activity, this person must decide if immediate action on this fire is even justified. In some cases, the fire may be in an area frequented by individuals who will simply reignite any fires that crews may extinguish, making efforts in that area futile. Depending on the fuels and terrain involved in this fire, a decision will have to be made regarding the types of resources and the size of the crew to send. Distances, alternate routes, and safe speeds for responding resources must be considered.

Regardless of the type and complexity of the dispatch board, one fact is of utmost importance, and that involves the base map to be used. If the protection area consists of principally uninhabited forest and/or rangeland, a topographic map may be best; but if the protection area includes considerable developed areas including towns and extensive road grids, county highway maps may prove more suitable. The area included must extend beyond the limits of the unit's protection responsibility so it can include some of the towers in

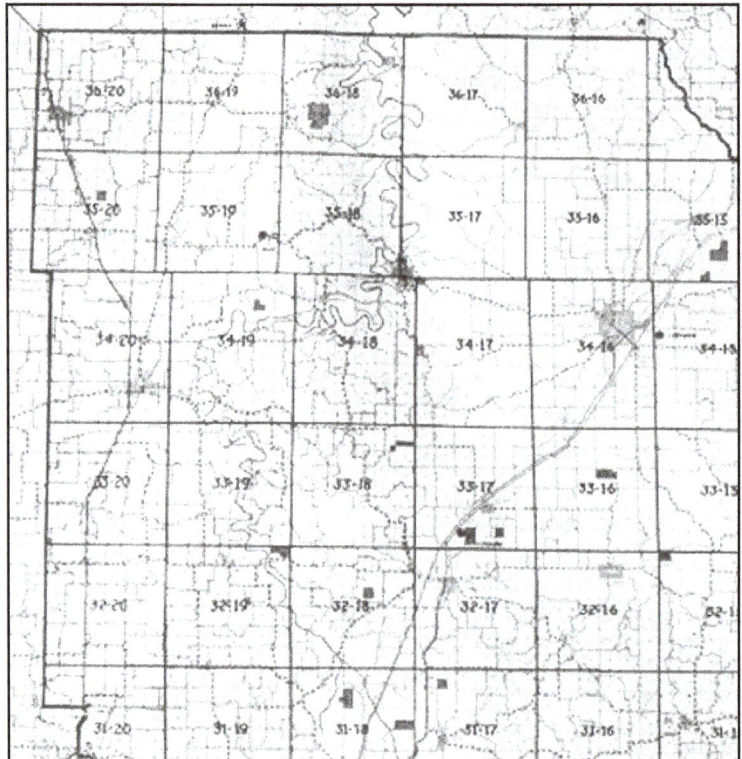

adjoining units. There will be times when it is necessary to cross out fires with those units, so their towers need to show on this board. The area being protected usually exceeds the area covered by one map, so it is necessary to carefully join adjacent maps to ensure that azimuth shots will be accurately carried from one map to another.

The source of maps used in making the dispatch board should be the same as the ones used in the lookouts and those issued to responding crews so everyone involved will have the same information. The only difference here is that the map underlying the fire finder glass in the tower will only need to cover the area seen from the tower, rather than the total responsibility area of the protection unit; and maps used by responding units will not show azimuth circles.

Experience has shown that some method of breaking the protection unit's large area into more quickly identified areas is needed, and every agency has developed its own system. The example shown here used the common "Section, Township, and Range" system to create units approximately six miles square which could be easily relayed to responding units, positioning them for more precise instructions as they get closer to the fire. Another agency may prefer a drastically different system, but some system will be required if dispatches are to be timely. Once such a "master map" is prepared, it can be taken to a printer and sufficient copies made of it to supply unit employees until changes are necessary.

Location of the dispatch board is an item that is often overlooked. This has a number of causes, but a common one is related to the fact that many units have fire seasons that do not extend over long periods of time in any given year. This often results in the job of dispatcher being only part of one employee's assignment. This places the dispatch board in a part of the office used by a number of personnel, and radio/telephone traffic can become difficult over the noise of other office operations. Dispatching, and location of the dispatch board, are best handled in less trafficked locations. However, the dispatcher should not be completely unaware of ongoing unit activities. This person must be able to monitor all radio traffic, in order to know about changes in conditions that may affect future dispatch decisions

Bucksnort

By Shari Wolford

We opened our original food stand during gun deer season in 1974. Mom, my sister, and I served out the window of my sister's mobile home. Hunters or anyone who was hungry could stop by and order food. We cleared $10 that year. Ten dollars in nine days! I guess we were crazy, but we opened for over 30 deer seasons. It was a lot of work with early and late hours. I shopped for weeks for groceries. Our income bought our kids Christmas gifts.

We decided we needed a cook shack and a better location. Dad had bought the entire Tram Tower in 1983. A couple days before one deer season we reassembled the cab of the tower. It would make a 7 by 7 kitchen. The weather was brutally cold and windy, but we were determined. Bucksnort was transported via skids. Its new location was one mile east of High Tower at a crossroads on the corner of our place.

Everyone could not believe three of us cooked in such a small space. Early on we had our three little kids playing, eating, and sleeping beneath our feet. We learned to zig and zag knowing who did what job. I always told the hunters that we had a pool table in the basement. We kept a campfire out front which was a welcome sight to cold hunters. Our seats were blocks of wood chunked off a log.

A few years later Dad thought we needed a shed to keep the hunters warm and dry. So, we built it! We set old electric poles and closed in all but the south side with pine lumber that Dad milled. The roof was old used metal. A neighbor loaned us a picnic table. Old church pews circled the fire ring. Dad and I used native rocks to make it. He riveted old metal to make the pipe and hood. Hunters always put their feet up on the ring. Many would nearly melt the soles off their boots before they knew it.

Bucksnort was everyone's meeting place. There were always deer hunting stories to listen to. It got mighty "windy" at times. Hunters came from many states and other countries. They were always anxious to sign and date our walls.

There was a flood one deer season. It almost got two hunters. They came to Bucksnort . One of them was on the verge of hypothermia. Our fire warmed him up, and he was okay.

A knock at our door one night after Bucksnort had closed was a friend who got lost. He had walked many miles. We took him back to his family's camp. Of course, they had been worried sick.

A U.S.F.S. map was displayed on the Bucksnort wall. It sure came in handy, especially for hunters new to our area. Many locals use names instead of road numbers most of the time. My family had made up names for certain areas and events that took place there.

Mom made hundreds of fruit turnovers. There would be orders for a dozen for the next day on top of her usual amount. I made so many gallons of chili. It was simmered on our heating stove and wood cook stove. All of us baked various desserts at night. One hunter ordered his favorite dessert, bought the whole pan full, and took it back to camp. We filled many a thermos of coffee and hot chocolate. Our menu also included sodas, chips, candy bars, burgers, chili, chili dogs, hotdogs, grilled cheese sandwiches, peanut butter and jelly sandwiches, breakfast sandwiches, and hash browns.

Bucksnort didn't have running water. Dirty dishes had to be packed home each night. We would be worn out with dishes and baking to do.

There were lots of laughs with the rubber hamburger we had. Many requests were made to serve it to certain hunters. Another funny thing was the metal five-gallon bucket we found and hung on the wall. It was for our tips. Lots of pictures were taken of our outhouse. One side of the seat said BUCKS and the other DOES. We heard more laughs and giggles when hunters saw our sign that read DEPRESSED DEER HUNTER RECOVERY AREA – SYMPATHY IS FREE.

Everyone misses Bucksnort so much, and that includes our family. I'm afraid health issues kept us from keeping our food stand open. We will forever treasure all the friendships we made over the years.

THANKS FOR THE MEMORIES!

Above is Everett Chaney acting silly.

Everett Chaney and Tram Tower

Not only were the towers on the move, the cabs ended up here and there also. One of the rewards of writing an article in the paper about forest lookout towers is the information feedback. I wrote some articles in the Eminence Current Wave and River Hills Traveler a few months ago. One dealt with High (Hill) Tower.

I received a call from Marguerite (Scoville) Barkley who had grown up at High Tower while her father, John Scoville was the tower man there. She had lots of good stories and information to share. She mentioned during one conversation that the top of the Tram Tower was used when the tower was purchased by Everett Chaney, as a gathering point for deer hunters - Bucksnort Foodstand. That rang a bell of sorts with me. I did recall reading a paper I have recounting Tram was sold on January 7, 1983, to Mr. Carl E. "Everett" Chaney of Birch Tree. The story recounted the unusual "ladder" design of Tram and the fact that Everett planned to reassemble the cab at "his place." I took that to mean Birch Tree itself.

By coincidence, I came across several other tower cabs still up here and there and became curious. I called Marguerite asking where in Birch Tree, and she corrected me that the cab sat, and still sits only one mile east of High Tower at the "crossroads." She mentioned that Betty Chaney might still live there or one of Everett's daughters, Dana or Shari. She had no phone number but knew Dana worked at a market in Mountain View. I was able to reach Dana, and she told me her sister Shari Wolford lived at the site, and probably most of the papers and pictures were there. She was also helpful in providing a phone number.

I was able to reach Bill and Shari Wolford, and they were eager to help. In addition, Bill had worked in forestry and conservation, so he was able to answer many of my questions.

As I began working on "Bucksnort", I was constantly drawn by everyone to Everett. It was becoming obvious to me that the Everett Chaney story was as interesting as Bucksnort Foodstand. Everett, like John Scoville, had worked High Tower and lived at the site with the family. Shari Wolford recounted many tower tales similar to Marguerite Barkley. She remembered using the landings like doll houses and spending time in the cab on windy nights. She also mentioned sleeping or trying to in the living room with her sister and brother and the "always on" U.S.F.S. communication radio. She also mentioned the dog joined right in and became adept at scaling the tower steps with needed pill bottles or whatever. Like Marguerite, one could sense the fortune they felt at being able to experience a "special time, a special place".

Jim Voyles had worked with Everett in the Forest Service. When I ask him, he could remember three things about Everett: 1) He could do anything, 2) He would always help and never take a payback, and 3) He had that certain personality that brought out lots of smiles and laughter. Jim also recounted some of his favorite memories such as Everett's "mechanical woodworm." This was his sawmill and the mill itself his "piece of junk." Jim said Everett was an expert with woodworking and about things in general. The engine at the mill had a five-gallon bucket hanging on the wall by a nail and a glove that had been burned as a reminder to be careful. Jim said on one occasion they went in and fired the engine up only to spray acorns all over the building. It seems the chipmunks had been using the exhaust pipe for nut storage. Jim also said Everett was famous for his "lights out" tours of Turner Mill Cave.

Besides towering during the dry times, Everett had the usual Conservation/Forestry duties. He even journeyed west to fight some big fires out there now and then. Now, John Strange is retired U.S.F.S., and I use him as a great resource person now and then. He worked with Everett for a time. When I mentioned Everett's name John immediately said, "great guy and hydrology."

The U.S.F.S. had undertaken, in Everett's time, the job of determining from a quality and quantity standpoint the hydrology of its national forests. In the Winona area, this involved tracings and Everett became heavily involved in this process right up to his retirement in 1982. Out of this came studies as to how much water, where it went, where it emerged. This information would be essential in maintaining water quality.

For six and a half years, he worked with Tom Aley in this undertaking. Tom recalled Everett as "Never Rest" Chaney. He remembered one of Everett's timecards had 11 p.m. on it. Tom asked if he meant 11 a.m.? Now it seems one night as the waters at Rt. 19 and Hurricane Creek rose, "Never Rest" had driven his tractor 10 or 15 miles at night through high water to get several needed measurements.

Joyce Barrett (retired USFS secretary) and Elsie and Curt Patterson (also manned High Tower and lived there with his wife and son) remembered Everett as a "great and helpful guy" who was always the same and "nobody was friendlier." Everett and Betty's children, Gary and Shari along with Dan Scoville and Ken Coates found a cave that was named by the U.S.F.S. the "Everett Chaney Cave."

Everett also practiced "citizen conservation" and was recognized by the M.D.C. for 47 years of volunteer service. He had coordinated and participated in "turkey brood surveys" to assess the success of the department's turkey reintroduction efforts.

I have talked some about the road from my original tower article to Everett Chaney and Bucksnort Foodstand. Now, let's take a look back at Bucksnort. You may recall that as a tower hunter, I first became interested in the food stand because the cab of the Tram Tower had found a new usage. I have been surprised how many tower cabs have turned up here and there for a new life.

I suppose my first question had to be the name. The Wolfords told me their Pastor, Keith Hackworth and some of the men in the church had a "deer camp" called Bucksnort and the name was borrowed from them. They said at first their deer food stand was not called Bucksnort. In fact, the cab from Tram Tower was not a part of the food stand, at first. The food stand began around 1974, and Tram Lookout was purchased around 1983.

In its original form, the food stand had patrons sitting on stumps or in their cars among the shortleaf pines. The first few years, food was sold right out Dana's kitchen window. When my wife and I stopped by a few months ago, I wondered if it was the pine whisper or happy laughter I could hear? The food stand itself grew into a three-sided structure open to the south sun. The floor was soil, pine needles, with wood shavings and the heat was a fire ring. You may recognize the kitchen in the picture with a close look. It is the cab from the Tram Lookout that sat atop a very unusual "ladder not step" tower near Winona. In 1983 Everett had bought the tower and had plans for a new life for the cab. Everett took down the purchased tower and took it to his farm southeast of Birch Tree. The food stand idea was "all of us" says Shari Wolford.

For the next four decades what grew to be called Bucksnort Foodstand would serve coffee, chili(spicy), chili dogs, hot dogs, hash browns, sausage and cheese on a bun, hamburgers, and homemade fried pies to the hunter or would be hunter. Everett's wife, Betty made over 300 pies a season, and the girls made other desserts also. You see, many explain that at least some of the hunters never made it to the woods. Although many spent the entire day in the woods some, it seems, just came to enjoy the company. At times, the family and friends who helped would find themselves 12 orders behind. It seems everybody knew Everett and wanted his advice on the coming hunt. Shari remembers the first year they were open nine days, and she and Dana made $5 apiece!

Some remember one year a convict was on the loose which caused a little stir. Most felt however that the food stand, full of deer hunters, was probably the safest place in the state. Visitors were encouraged to sign the "guest book." This involved leaving names, messages, points of origin written on the walls. In many ways, the history of the food stand played itself out in these etchings.

Shari Wolford mentioned that it would have been great if I could have spent a few days "tower talking" with her Dad. Probably most of my questions could have been answered. That is for sure. I am sure it would have been a fun time also. Just the mention of Everett's name seems to bring a smile to everyone's face.

When my wife and I stopped by a few months ago, I was struck by what a peaceful place it was. You had the smell of pine and the whisper of the trees. Tram cab seemed to be at peace also. Happy to have worked 50 years atop Tram Lookout and happy to have been a part of so many happy times and content now to take a well-deserved rest.

Our U.S.F.S. Life

By Shari Wolford

My Dad, Everett Chaney, was employed with the United States Forestry Service very early in life. I can't remember him ever working anywhere else. Some tasks I remember him performing were timber management, planting pine seedlings, dozing ponds, meeting with school groups to share his knowledge, fighting fires, and managing High Tower. He also manned other towers on the Mark Twain Forest. Mom, Betty, often kept him company on the towers. Dad was crew boss on several huge fires out west. He would bring home his leftover rations for us kids. To this day I still use a G.I. can opener in my kitchen. Betty and Everett Chaney (right)

Dad was an unmatched asset for the Winona District. I tried to soak up his knowledge, but so wish I had learned much more. We not only lost a great man, but we also lost a wealth of information about our area and the past.

His last job on the district was a hydrologist. It was quite an accomplishment without a college education. He did water quality and dye tracing. Mom went with Dad and helped keep records of his findings.

Mom was a very good Mom. She loved to bake and had quite the sweet tooth. Her favorite dessert was pie, but her specialty to bake was always cookies. She loved sharing with family and friends. I will share her favorite -

Preheat oven to 350° -
Betty's Fruity Nutty Butter Cookies
¾ cup margarine
½ cup brown sugar
1 tbsp. sugar
Cream the three above together
1 large egg yolk
1 and a half tsp. vanilla
Add the egg and vanilla and combine
1 and ¾ cup all-purpose flour – add & combine

Add raisins and dried or candied fruit (chopped), coconut, nuts (chopped) or seeds. Drop dough by teaspoonfuls on parchment lined cookie sheet. Bake 7-9 minutes.

Mom was a seamstress, making tiny, even spaced stitches. She made my sister, and I summer outfits out of flour sacks. Our wedding dresses were her creations as well. We helped each other tack quilts. They weren't fancy but were pretty & useful.

Dad and Mom bought his parents' farm. We usually had twenty-some cows on the place. Most were named . Dad & Mom got very attached. That made it tough to send them to market. They were a lot of work, but it was very enjoyable watching them graze and seeing the calves romp and play.

The cows reaped the fruits of all our labor in the hayfields. Dad rode the baler to keep it set right as Mom baled hay. The rest of the family loaded square bales and put them in the barn.

Way back when and for many years we had long hay seasons. Many neighbors didn't have equipment, so our family helped them. It was hard, hot work but we still had fun. There was work the next day and back to the fields that evening.

Hogs brought in some of our income. Most of the time they were ornery and stubborn. It was never fun to castrate, notch ears, cut tusks, ring noses, or dock tails.

Dad was the first professional hog caller on the Eleven Point Game Refuge. He had a lot of practice on the farm. Dad and Mom's Dad helped run the refuge fences. Their farms were north and northeast of the refuge.

Our hogs ran free range when the forest service offered that option. Every night all our family would pile in our old flatbed truck, ride through the Mark Twain to the area where our hogs were, call them in to feed them and sing all the way, coming and going. I remember it snowing so hard and the flakes looked like bowls.

Dad was our Banner Community phone man. He strung wire across miles, attaching it up in trees. It was a chore to keep the lines up during windy weather. We all had the "ringy dingy" crank phones. Dada loaned phones to some families. Our phones all rang no matter whose call it was so everyone could listen to all the conversations. These phones were not connected to the modern phone system. There were probably 12 neighbors who Dad kept connected to each other.

Us kids always had a dog. Most of the time we had pet chickens. Four of our bantys were named Kenny, Rhonda, Hailey, and Peggy after our older cousins. They would lay upside down on our laps as we swung. My big gray Henny Penny laid her first egg in our house. She would sit on my lap at supper-time and drink bean soup out of my plate. Once she fell in a vat of used motor oil. What a mess to clean her up!

Mom loved her chickens as well. She sold and gave away eggs. I was her chicken doctor, doing whatever necessary to help ailing hens and roosters. There were spurs and toenails to trim. I also cut wing feathers shorter. This kept the chickens from flying out of their pens. Black snakes were a big problem. They would crawl in and steal chicks and eggs. One day we removed three big ones. Another day one tried to get away in a hole in the ground. I pinned it down, and it kept wrapping its tail around the hoe and up my arm. That huge one got away!

I guess I better tell my turkey story while I'm talking fowl. We had several large turkeys that roosted on the yard fence. My siblings and I got off the school bus by High Tower which was about fifty foot from our house. Those turkeys would run right up to the bus door. They always chose me to flog. My legs were scratched and bleeding every day. I'm still bumfuzzled as to why it was always me. Needless to say, I didn't shed any tears when either a varmit or a person stole them.

Entertainment was very different when we were kids. We had acorn fights hiding behind trees and mudball fights in the dark in our garden. We fished a lot & swam in the pond. Four of us older teens scrunched up in a dark, tiny, closet to tell ghost stories. Clothespins and playing cards on the spokes of our bicycles gave us "motors." Our stick horses were made with baling twine and sawmill strips. We cut shorter strips and used them to bat a jillion rocks. Taking friends on snipe hunts was always fun.

Mom and us kids played bad-mitten almost every day in the summer. My brother made boundary lines with large nails and string we unraveled from feed bags. Boy, we were in big trouble if we got our feet wound up and tore the string down. We played at the same time of the morning and quit to eat lunch at the same time. Everything halted when Mom's soap operas came on.

Men stood by at the tower during high fire danger. Some were full-time USFS employees and some part-time during fire season. We knew all of them. They would rake leaves in the area around the tower and house. Sometimes the men would play horseshoes, waiting to be called out on a fire.

My brother used to walk the cross braces on the tower. It sure scared me to watch him use it like a tightrope. We dug a hole in the gravel under the tower and played golf. He got into making boomerangs. We had to dodge a lot of them. His next project was snow skis. I will tell you what he made them with and you will know how far he skied. There were nails, a little flashing, and two very green, heavy two by fours. A neighbor boy tried to surf on a small pond with a green sawmill slab. I'm pretty sure he got to see the fish and froggys on the bottom. Dad and mom had my brother plant a very long row of onions one spring. There was only one problem. He planted them upside down!

Dad made us girls a sandbox. We wanted clean, pretty sand, so we gathered sandstones. They were shades of orange, cream, white & pink. We pecked on them with hammers, crumbling every rock into grains. It was fun and took up part of each day.

My brother loved basketball. He had a jump shot that his teammates envied. Both us girls were crazy about volleyball and were cheerleaders as well. All three of us were very competitive.

Playing house on the tower landings was a pastime for my sister and me. We packed stuff up to the first and second landings. Mom would make us carry all our junk down and put it away when we got in a fuss.

One of my siblings would be upset with me most of the time, my brother wanting to play ball and my sister wanting me to play school or house. I was the middle child.

My brother and I liked to fly kites. We didn't have any open areas to fly them. We put our heads together. Where there was a will, we invented a way. We ran & got our rods and Zebco reels. We attached our kites to our reel's fishing line and went to the top tower landing. Talk about fly! They flew!

Dad and Mom played cards with their best friends on weekends. All of them got very good at Rook and Pitch. I know this sounds silly, but when I was little, I would crawl under the kitchen table among their feet and sleep like a puppy. My sleep was more important than playing with the other four kids. Plus, I was the "odd man," or should I say the "odd kid" out.

Every spring Dad would make hickory whistles for us. The bark would slip in the spring, so that was the only time to make them. We always had homemade slingshots. The perfect forked stick, a small piece of leather for the rock pouch, some string unraveled from a feed bag and strips of an old inner tube were all we needed besides our knives.

My Grandma and I shelled corn for her chickens. I saved the sturdiest cobs. I gathered large wing feathers that the chickens lost. We made what we called "whirlymagigs." We put two feathers in the corncob and threw them straight up. They twirled as they came down.

Our parent's love of fishing rubbed off on all of us. I was awarded the middle seat in Dad's johnboat. How lucky I was! It was also the live box. The fish everyone caught went in it, and I had to pass out minnows when needed for bait. My "job" cut down on my fishing time, but somebody had to do it. Dad was among the best at running a johnboat. I was never afraid while riding with him.

Early in the day, we used to cube cheddar cheese up and lay it in the sun to toughen up and dry some. Dad would get in from work, Mom would have supper packed, and we had all our fishing gear ready to roll. All five of us would jump in and head to Turner's Mill to trout fish.

Dad could smell a fish fry just about as fast as Smokey Bear could sniff out a smoke. He was always the last to quit eating. He said he needed a little more of this and a little more of that because nothing would come out even.

We liked camping in the boonies. Our campsites usually had stinging weeds that had to be whacked down so we could set up a tent. Dad always laughed and told us girls to be careful where we squatted because he couldn't put a tourniquet on our butts.

There were two snake events at home. Dad was copperhead bit when moving some lumber. Mom was standing at their yard gate telling my bunch goodbye after dark one summer night. She felt something touch her bare toes. It was a copperhead. Thankfully, it had traveled on before she had a screaming fit.

Dad bought his brother's saw-mill. He always sawed and my Mom and my brother would off bear. My little sister and I were official sawdust doodlers. We were young, so we just played in the sawdust finding turtle eggs and black beetles. The sale of the lumber paid for our family vacation to the West Coast. I'm so happy I was the last person to the sawmill with Dad.

My folks made beautiful furniture from the lumber Dad cut on his sawmill. There are many children who are so proud to own stools that Mom and Dad gave them. Our family reunion always had an auction each year. The stools were donated. The bidding was wild with the stools bringing more than top dollar. They made tables, benches, end tables, chests, trivets, and lazy susans.

One summer Dad wanted to enlarge the porch on our first home. Thanks to his sawmill, he didn't have to purchase lumber. I wanted to help. He handed me a hammer, a small board, and a rusty bucket of rusty and bent nails. My job was to straighten nails to be reused. Nails weren't discarded when bent and rusty. New ones were rarely purchased.

There was a five-gallon bucket hanging on the edge of that same porch. We put all our kitchen scraps in it. Dad slopped the hogs with it.

Our cistern on that porch was close to the kitchen. We had to draw all our water with a rope and bucket. Many times Dad would tell Mom to buy a jug or two of bleach. He told her there was a drowned mouse or rat in our cistern. Sometimes it would have wiggle tails. The bleach got rid of our problems, and we could keep using the water.

None of the three houses my family lived in had bathrooms. Our baths were taken in round or oval galvanized tubs. The youngest went first. Then, water was added, and the next youngest got a bath. Dad was last. If we just got a sponge bath, we would wake up with ice on our wash pan of water from the night before. I kept a brick on the heating stove all day and evening. Each night I wrapped it in a towel and took it to bed to keep my feet warm.

The government house by High Tower only had one bedroom. There was an unfinished basement. All three of us kids slept in the living room which was also where the U.S.F.S. radio was on 24 hours a day. That seemed normal and of course very necessary. Mom even talked on the radio when Dad wasn't there.

Our outhouse at the tower was maybe 30 feet from the porch. So when Mom went down the hill, us girls went to. We played tag around the toilet while Mom was inside. One day I ran one way and then the other and didn't catch my sister. All of a sudden I looked down, and it appeared the ground was swallowing her up. I immediately grabbed her hands and drug her out. The hole that was dug for the outhouse was too big, but we didn't know it because it had been covered with dirt, moss, and leaves. The rotten board broke, and she slid under the toilet. Mom slipped her clothes off, threw them away and gave her a bath. I always told her that her skin was darker than mine from her dip in the toilet.

Dad was a deer hunter most of his life. He put a lot of guys on crossings. There were over twenty deer who met their demise on his favorite crossing. I was happy he asked me to carry his ladder there the last time he hunted that spot.

I remember one season when he killed his deer in his field five minutes before closing time on the last day of deer season. My stand overlooks the same field. So many wonderful memories come to me as I look across the old family farm and High Tower is visible above the tree-tops a mile away. I sure miss climbing High Tower. It was always so peaceful up there.

The U.S.F.S. and tower life was very good for our family. We thoroughly enjoyed it. I can't imagine any other. Our parents gave us security, love, happiness, and their example showed us how to be hardworking and responsible.

We miss Dad and Mom and my brother so much!

Pictured above left at Christmas are Shari, Dana, and Gary.
Above right are Gary and Shari and two of the pets.

My Best Friend and a Life Close to High Tower

By Shari Wolford

Bill Wolford Jr. has been my best friend for fifty years. His parents bought land in the Banner Community in southern Shannon County. They came on weekends to build their home.

The first time Bill set eyes on me I was far from looking pretty. Dad and I were seining fish. I was up past my bellybutton in a muddy, mossy, cow poopy pond. He said he decided right then and there that I was the one for him. It was love at first sight for this old girl. His tanned skin in a snow white tee shirt and that big gaper smile took my breath away.

Our families visited on weekends. Bill was a boy of few words. He never spoke unless he was asked a question. His answers were as short as possible.

He and I were sophomores when he started school here. The farms we lived on were the same farms my parents were raised on. We got to ride the same school bus. Very few kids drove to school back then.

Our first date was a double date with two of our classmates. We went to a movie. Bill's bashfulness didn't keep him from giving me a goodnight kiss.

He came to see me every night. We walked and met in the middle on Sunday afternoon. I always cooked up something, and we walked to his house. No matter what I took he would make instant sweet tea, and we scrambled powdered commodity eggs.

He fessed up to the shenanigans and orneriness he did as a child in Saint Louis. He used to hunt squirrels in the cemetery. The police caught him and his friends. Their BB guns were taken away. Bill's Uncle was a cop, so he was trying to teach them a lesson by hauling them down to the station. They did get their guns back. There was a train track near the cemetery. He and his cronies would throw rocks at people who hitched free rides on the train. I also heard he sewed his wild oats about the same age he gave up his baby bottle of chocolate milk. What a guy!

We dated five years and married on Friday the 13th. We were blessed the first year with the cutest blond-headed baby boy. He was a good kid. We were together twenty-four hours a day. I didn't work. He was born with asthma, so I wanted to take care of him. We sewed and cooked. There are Christmas ornaments we still hang that he made forty years ago.

I guess I made a mistake by teaching him beyond his years. He would come home from Kindergarten so aggravated. It drove him crazy that some of his classmates couldn't color inside the lines and had no idea how to use scissors. He could also subtract and borrow large numbers before he started school. He was so bored at school.

His Dad played with him a lot. He called Bill "Poppy Dad" and got so excited when he knew he was home from work.

They played Yahtzee, War with cards, and practiced trapping in the house with stuffed animals and throw pillows. Bill has always been a great Dad.

Bill knew I would love to live in a log cabin. He liked the idea as well. So in the early eighties, he cut pine trees off our place. He and I loaded them by hand. Dad and Bill milled them on three sides on Dad's sawmill. The fourth side was debarked by Bill with a drawknife. He stacked and stripped them, but they twisted while drying so back to the mill to be resawed. Bill still had to hand plane some to keep the walls level as he connected the logs with eight-inch nails and a sledgehammer.

We didn't borrow a penny to build our log cabin, so progress slowed if we had no cash. Our move happened way before the cabin was completed. We had to sell our mobile home to have more building funds. Five thousand dollars was all we had spent at the time we moved in.

Our eating table was a very rusty, folding camp table in the corner. The floor was cheap particle board. High back, pine board church pews were our couches. They didn't have cushions but did have plenty of splinters and loose nails. We didn't have water in the house, so our baths were in a galvanized tub on the back porch till up in November. My wringer washer came in handy in the backyard. Simple living has never bothered us.

Hunting and fishing were sports Bill enjoyed and still does. Me too! Bill used to quail hunt, and I was the bird dog. We love hunting and eating deer, turkey, squirrels and frogs.

Bill likes trapping as well. Shortly after we married, I was on the trap line with him. He caught two skunks and one civet cat. We were very poor. Bill skinned all three. We needed the money. Each one brought a dollar. We were very thankful, but Bill smelled so bad for so long. So did our house. It was so bad that my eyes watered and I was nauseous.

The skunk story didn't end there. Bill went to his job at the shoe factory. The boss thought a skunk had got in the factory somehow. The search for the skunk went on for a few days. His boss finally figured out the skunk wasn't a striped one. Needless to say, he told Bill to never come to work like that again. I can't remember how we got rid of the stink. But that fiasco didn't stop Bill's trapping career. Since I was his sidekick on the trap line, I made sure he didn't skin any more stinkers.

Bill's parents sold part of their place, so we had to move our mobile home. My folks gave us land. Our move was from a field to a pine forest. Being the oldest native in our community, I have lived six places in over sixty-five years. Those places were all within a mile and a half. Bill and I moved 3 feet once. Talk about a hard move. The only thing we culled was our goldfish. He moved to the pond and lived happily ever after.

We were blessed with a granddaughter who is beautiful inside and out. She has always been wise as well. I gave her and Paw Paw Bill some boiled eggs to snack on when she was very young. He asks for salt. She told him he couldn't eat it because it was bad for his heart.

The summer after she turned eight years old, she spent several weeks with us. We went to farmers markets and bought baby chicks. That called for duding up the chicken house. We put several inches of straw on the mud floor, fixed a waterer and feeder, run a drop cord for a fan, hung a heat lamp, and set up two lawn chairs. She named all the chicks, and we spent several hours every day playing with them. She even fell asleep in the chicken house one day.

Bill has always been a hard worker. The jobs he had early in life didn't pay much. Most fizzled out, and we lived on unemployment, which was less. He cut shoes and mechanized at two factories. Once he worked at a meat plant all day and pumped gas in the evenings. Two jobs he did was turning logs and tailing the sawmill. He always says everyone should tail a mill for a week. Then there wouldn't be so many workers whining when doing much easier jobs for much higher wages.

The Conservation Commission hired Bill twice. They were temporary positions during the fire season. He manned the Thomasville Tower, fought fires, and did timber management. Bill had a chance at a permanent job at Flat Rock Tower near Summersville. He appreciated the offer, but we liked where we lived and didn't want to leave family, friends, and community.

Bill was hired by Howell-Oregon Electric Cooperative. The manager recognized Bill was a great guy and had a good work ethic. There were lots to learn, but Bill was a quick learner. He became a first-class lineman and retired after thirty years of hard and dangerous work.

Bill and I love being together every day whether we work or play. Most would think we are crazy, but we have always enjoyed cutting firewood. We pack snacks for lunch. We also enjoy hunting morel and coral mushrooms. The Mark Twain is only a mile from our home so we can easily enjoy the beauty anytime we please.

I am so thankful and blessed to be Bill Wolford Jr.'s wife and share life with my best friend. I hope you can meet him someday.

Shannondale Tales Information from Max & Trudy Gorman

Several years ago now, I was the recipient of some very good fortune as Terry Cunningham suggested to Max Gorman that he needed to give me a call and "tower talk." It was Steve Orchard who had sent me Terry's way a few years earlier. Not only have all three made me a lot smarter but have all become a part of a long list of "tower friends."

Max and I have worked on several tower mysteries over the last few years. The "east of Shannondale" and "above Brushy Creek Mine" have been discussed in the book already. Another is the "east of Jerktail" question mark. Max remembers being told of a tower that sat where the benchmark symbol is on the topog below. The marker is titled "Asher." We have returned to the site several times and ask around – no answer yet.

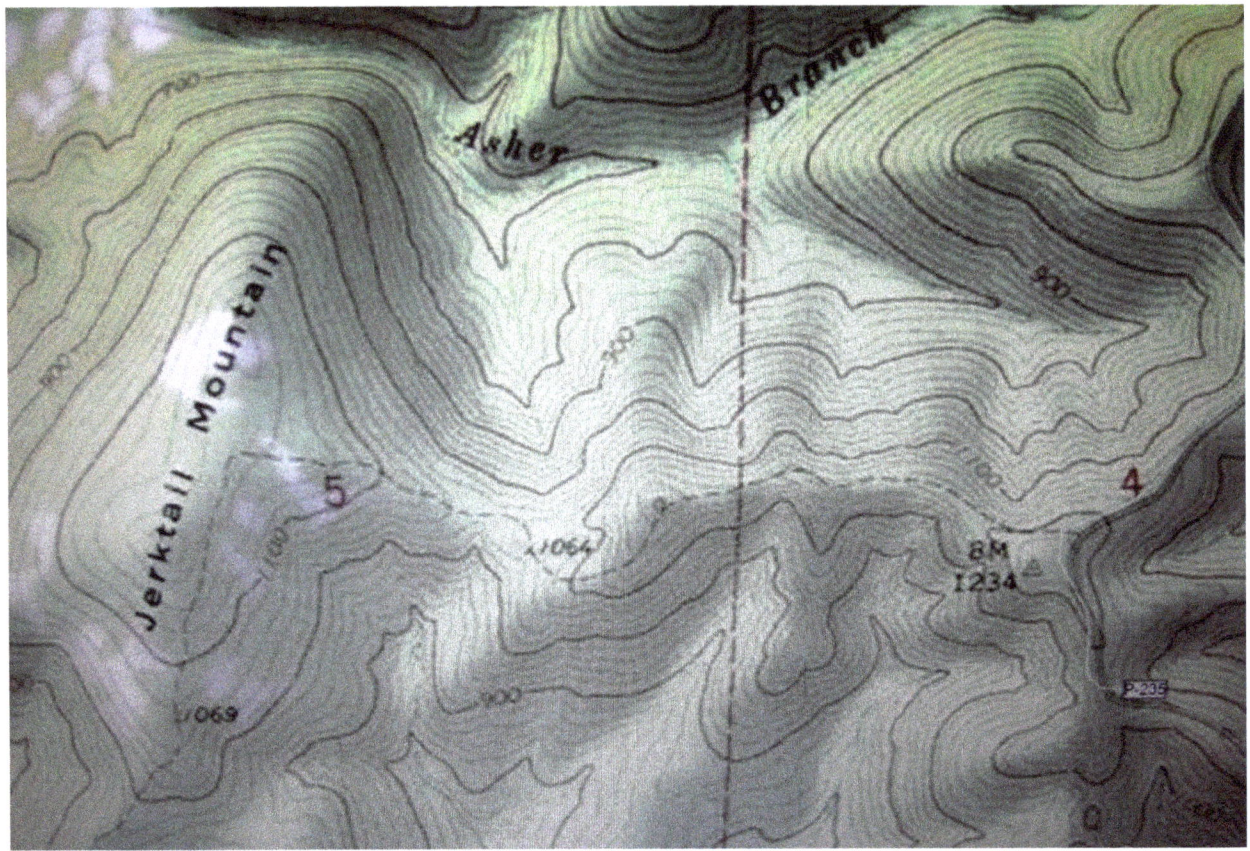

When I approached Max about doing a part for the book, several ideas bounced around over time. What became clear was that Shannondale Tower needed to be at the center of any effort. And so, we began working by phone, email, mail, and visits where to go and what to include.

The story, however, began near Montauk. Max recalls his earliest memory of conservation was when he was about 6 years old – give or take a year. They were building Montauk Wooden Tower at that time. He says you could hear the blasting for the footings (dig if you can – blast if you must). He said when his Dad came home, they all walked about half a mile up to what everyone called the High Knob. There were long black poles and stacks of lumber along with four deep holes and a funny smell – creosote. That smell, he says, stayed with him and he still thinks about towers and conservationists even today.

Max says the conservationists traveled around to the one room schoolhouses and showed movies about wildlife. He says he later started working as a forest firefighter by the hour and worked all through high school. He says he later worked as a temporary towerman in Dent County in the fall of 1967 and spring of 1968 at Montauk Tower

The next stop was the house at Shannondale Fire Tower. Fire detection at Shannondale had been in effect for years.

The original wooden tower at Shannondale was dedicated in January 1945. The Shannon County Democrat noted, "The services at Shannondale next Sunday will give special notice to the dedication of the Community House. Services will start at eleven followed by a basket dinner at noon. After dinner, a demonstration of fire detection apparatus will be given by Tom Chilton and other foresters of the area. There will be a panel discussion on conservation practices and problems by some four or five local men. George White, State Forester from Jefferson City and Charles Kirk , District Forester from Ellington will be there to represent the

State Conservation Commission. The actual dedication will be at the tower itself, just off Highway 19 five miles below Shannondale. It is a sixty-foot wooden structure well located to observe territory on the Current River, Sinkin Creek, Spring Valley and Barren Fork areas. Benton Prugh of Round Spring has charge of the tower and has been employed by the Commission for fire detection and prevention for the past year."

The original wood tower footings are still to be found at the site-

By the time Max arrived, a new Aermotor LS-40 steel tower was in place. Their son Ricky was 2 years old, and their daughter Debbie was born 2 years later. The Shannondale site had a house with a full basement, living room, hall, small kitchen, two bedrooms, and a bathroom. Later a 16' addition was added which included a 5'x11' walk-in closet and 16' kitchen.

With 33' of wood cabinets which Max helped build there was also a two car garage, chicken house, and cow barn as they were allowed to keep a cow and chickens. He said they had him tear down the chicken house. The privy had already been removed. There was a 16' deep cistern, 16' by 8' with a piston pump in the basement. A deep well was drilled later. There was a woven wire two barb fence plus a cattle guard as it was open range and livestock still ran loose at that time. The site also had a flattened spot and picnic table and privy below the parking area. Near that was a barrel for trash that was removed later along with the fence and cattle guard.

Max says he was hired while under District Forester George Graham and worked under District Foresters Charley Santhuff and Loren Leatherman and Regional Foresters Bill Klatt and Tom Draper. There were others not mentioned for fear of leaving somebody out. Max says from the top down, they were all great to work under.

Max then noted the towermen that had lived at Shannondale: a Hefner, Frank Vance, Wayne Stoops, Clyde Lowell (very shortly), Bill Ferguson, Max Gorman, Rodney Rose, James Harlan, and Jason Chilton. Jason was the grandson of Eminence towerman Thomas Chilton. Jason was never a towerman but a district mechanic at Eminence. Roy Light was towerman but lived across Highway 19 about half a mile from the tower. Max said he worked with him until he transferred to the Jerry Presley Education center where he retired. He notes Roy was a true and valuable employee and is still a great friend.

Max then talked about a towerman's life and job as they lived it.

A dedicated employee in the Forestry Division had to mold his and his family's life around his work because of the hours they worked. Many times you never knew when you would be coming home. When there was a fire danger, there was work to do. This sometimes meant missing special family functions and events.

A lookout towerman's wife was asked to climb the tower to look for fires at times when all towers were unmanned because the towerman was firefighting. This was especially true in the early years.

Max says his wife Trudy would bring supper up the tower when the fire danger was high, and the other towermen were down. The wives also took phone calls for fires, accidents, wildlife, and other things that arose. The dispatcher often tried to keep the wives notified when they could as there were no radios in the houses. Max noted the dispatchers in his area were extra good at doing so, and it was much appreciated. The family also often included the dog, which often became skilled at tower climbing.

The tower sitting in high winds involved the wooden towers versus the steel. The wooden towers had four large wooden poles that sat high on top of a concrete footing and was bolted to flat metal embedded in the concrete. In high winds, the complete tower swayed and rocked. The steel towers would sway similar to a metal pipe or radio antenna. Max said he had sat a half cup of coffee beside the fire finder and it would slosh out. Sometimes there would be a big bang like it was trying to tear the cab off the tower. He said he was glad those days were behind him.

Our other duties were many and varied but fire duty always came first unless it was a family emergency, he noted. Max says a towerman was expected to do fire duty, equipment maintenance, mowing the tower site and road signs and conservation areas. There was building maintenance to do and checking forest cropland (private). You needed to get familiar with your area as well as keep records and write reports. There were also district meetings to attend. In later years one of the main duties was making state land improvements and applying prescriptions to accomplish satisfactory results. For that area, Max said they helped with occasional building projects such as erecting radio towers, fire lookout towers in other areas of Missouri. Max noted he helped dismantle the Eminence steel tower but did not help rebuild it at Panther Hill north of Ellington. Eminence Tower was in the center of a circle of towers and in visual sight of Shannondale, Flat Rock, Coot Mountain, and Stegall Towers and was not needed. He said several were ask to help with special projects and events when needed and they went on out of state fires when needed to make a special fire crew. Missouri M.D.C. crews were noted by U.S.F.S. to be specialist backfire crews on out of state fires.

There were always the surprise close calls. Max notes – I had a phone call in the early morning hours that a small fire had been detected in a charcoal warehouse about five miles north of Shannondale Tower. Their water system was not working at the time. There not being a rural fire department at the time they ask if I could come and help them with it being a very small fire about the size of a kitchen table. Upon arrival I surveyed the area as to the location of the fire and escape routes if something went wrong.

Everything was going OK as we were spraying water on the fire when I heard the owners start a forklift and start moving pallets of charcoal in the other corner of the building which stirred up the dust causing a sparking effect that ignited the gas and dust and in turn had a roaring effect with flames totally engulfing the entire building about five feet from the floor. The guy on the forklift abandoned it and ran for the door behind us in the very corner of the building.

The lift was still moving and ran into a post supporting the building and knocked it down. I was running toward where I thought the door was and fell down into a mound of banding or something about a foot high that probably saved my life because when I fell, I could see the bottom of the door. I received burns on both ears, back of my left hand as I was using it to shield my eyes because the fire was roaring toward the end of the building and turning back down lower to the floor. I also had a burn on the very top of my head while wearing a hard hat plus I was wearing a fire shirt.

I have always cautioned others to stay out of burning buildings, away from automobiles and aircraft as they give off toxic smoke.

Another close call happened on 6/2/95 when a soft drink semi-truck crossed the center line as I was watching and trying to avoid it by moving right onto the shoulder of the road. I couldn't move over farther because of a ten-foot embankment. He collided with my front bumper and front axle, sideswiping and tearing out the rear axle. This spun the department truck almost around and off the embankment slinging a push mower and weed eater about 60 feet away. I had James Harlan with me, and it was his second day at work. He said he was glad I was driving instead of him. My left foot was trapped, and it took a while to free it. I had a piece of glass embedded in the top of my head, and my left leg was hurt. My left shoulder was completely dislocated and socked back in place doing irreparable damage to it, and after several surgeries and 23 years, it is still impaired.

The last incident that happened was an Air Force F-15 fighter jet crashed two miles NE of Shannondale Fire Tower on 8/19/99. I was dispatched to smoke that had a degree reading from Shannondale Fire Tower and located after a long search on foot along with two Missouri State Troopers and a Shannon County Sheriff's Deputy. We walked into the crash site and found mostly pieces of the plane varying in size of a marble to a foot and a half except one wing which was mostly intact but in about four sections.

There were two helicopters from the TV station in St. Louis that were flying just above the treetops that stirred up dust and J8 jet fuel causing me to get light burns from the top of my boots to my knees. Also, the Air Force doctor checked me later and sent me to my doctor. I was diagnosed with Pneumonitis and sent for lung tests which were several days later. My condition cleared up later. It took two trips and two days with Timber Volunteer Fire Department to suppress the fires while always being under armed guard by military police.

Commenting on the Eminence Forest District Max noted it was like an extended family. Attempts were always made to get together with our families 2 or 3 times a year to visit and for everyone to get to know each other.

He says he always believed that it was important to share each other's stories and thoughts and to learn from others. Max also saw it as good for morale. He noted you don't realize until you have talked to people for many years and then they meet for the first time and how it affects them. He said he did this at the Conservation Credit Union. He said he eventually went into the credit union and started talking to one of the officers when a bunch of workers came in to look at me to see what I looked like as they knew that name and voice for years but had never seen him.

Max believed that a good moral was good for the quality of work and that a smile promoted good morale. He became famous for "Maxisms." Although partly intended to create a smile, they often contained a ring of truth. One was "The humidity is low, it keeps hangin' fire." This meant that as a result of the low humidity, sparks and embers would blow ahead of the fire and hit branches that might smolder, catch fire, and—hang fire.

Max also recounted another story—"I ate his lunch." Years ago during a busy spring fire season, I was fighting lots of fires and missing lots of sleep and meals. I was sent to a fire a ways off M Highway west of Van Buren, Mo. I went all day without eating since early morning. Butch Frazer (Stegall Towerman at that time) met me on M Highway. I was driving a truck and hauling a tractor plow unit (small dozer with plow). We began on the fire and were still working on the fire until after dark when a man I had never met arrived to help. I completed a containment line around the fire while Butch and Jim Shaddox set the backfire.

I was at the vehicles and very hungry. I started looking through the department vehicles for food. The only food I found was in Jim Shaddox's truck. I then sat down on a very big log and was eating Jim Shaddox's lunch when they walked up. I saw Jim had a strange look on his face but hadn't said anything yet. I said guys I will share this with you if you want. They declined any, so I ate it all. Now looking back on it with Jim meeting me the very first time and Butch only having known me a few days as he had just started working a short while before I must have left them with a good impression. To cut the story short many years later at Jim Shaddox's retirement dinner in Van Buren at the Landing I stopped at Eminence and bought the exact same things as Jim had in his lunch: a double snowball cupcake, two cans of beanie weenies, two bananas, and a package of crackers.

I put these in a paper bag, and after the meal and the presentations, I took the bag up front and explained to everyone and told this story. I then gave him the bag as I told him I wanted to repay him after all these years. He still reminds me when I see him about meeting me the first time, and I was sitting there eating his lunch. Jim & Max always have a good laugh about it!

Max says he was hired under Carl Noren and worked under 4 directors: #3 Carl Noren, #4 Larry Gale, #5 Jerry Presley and #6 Jerry Conley.

Max says he can't begin to name all the people he worked within the Department. He offered a "Thank You" to all and that he has a special place in his heart for each and every one of them. He shared his retirement letter to express his feelings-

---

MISSOURI DEPARTMENT OF CONSERVATION

MEMORANDUM

Date: January 18, 2001

From: Max Gorman, Resource Technician

To: Lorren Leatherman, Forest District Supervisor

Subject:

It is with mixed feelings that I find myself writing this. I don't know if I'm happy or sad, I guess only time will tell. I have decided to retire with April 1, 2001 being that special day. My love of conservation and our natural resources started when I was very young and it still holds a very special place in my heart. I always felt like the Missouri Department of Conservation was a family that I belonged to. It seemed I knew and worked with so many people in all levels and divisions and thoroughly enjoyed doing so.

I feel fortunate to have worked with the people of Eminence, especially the office staff. They are very supportive and helpful when help is needed. I'm also grateful for the respect of the Regional Supervisors in this Ozark Region and would have enjoyed working with them more.

As new leadership at all levels attempts to steer the Department, my concern is for them to not forget how we got to this point and the dedicated people that worked to achieve the accomplishments that we now share. As with all organized groups, good leaders are essential and must be replaced from time to time to keep the vigorous pace with our changing environment. But good leaders should retain the respect of our dedicated co-workers and the support of the public, for we all have our desires and problems too.

As I'm getting ready to leave, my thoughts run about all the things yet undone that I would like to accomplish, but I guess someone else will have to finish them. I always did my best and tried to keep up with the changing times but due to health problems I find myself struggling to keep pace with the heavy work load and day to day problems that arise. However, if possible, I would like to retain a status of official volunteer so I could help on occasion.

c Draper

Max noted his accomplishments and appreciations from 1968-2001. He said that when he was a teenager, his Dad asked him at the breakfast table after Max had been out fighting fires most of the night in what is now the Sunklands Conservation Area, "Where was that place?" His answer was very way down in an awful place in Shannon County, and he could tell him one thing—that is one place I would never want to live. He said he never realized that he would be living near there about 8 or 9 years later and still do after over 50 years—never say never! Max and Trudy live about a mile from Shannondale Tower today and can see it from their porch.

He says he hopes to live there the rest of his life!

Interview with Marvin and Pat Brawley – 3/6/2019

By Teena Ligman/Retired U.S.F.S.

Marvin said though they puzzled about it many times they don't know where the name Sinking Tower came from. I suggested it might have been named for a creek that ran into a sinkhole nearby and Marvin agreed they'd thought that, but there really wasn't any feature like that. They never did figure it out.

Eastwood and Fremont towers had the normal steps that slanted back and forth, only Sinking Tower had a ladder. Pat said she never was totally comfortable climbing up the tower though she did climb it many times. Sinking, Eastwood and Fremont were all 100-foot towers

Marvin said the first tier right below the access door did have steps, so that helped, you didn't actually step out onto the ladder which made it a bit better. Pat said still it always worried her because Marvin had something about if he hit his knee just so, he'd pass out, and she was always worried he'd bump his knee on that access door and pass out and fall down the tower, but he was always careful.

She said they developed a system when Marvin was hungry or thirsty. They had a bucket and a rope on the tower. He could call down what he wanted, and she'd put it in the bucket, and he could raise it up. They got really good at it over the years.

The tower was built in 1935 they think, built by the Civilian Conservation Corps. The CCC also built their house. Pat said when they later did some remodeling and pulled out the kitchen cabinets. The bottom of the cabinet had the names of all the boys who had worked on the house listed. They'd all signed their names.

The Brawleys said they moved into the little house in 1962 right after they were married. They lived there until 1981 when they moved into a new house they built about 5 miles away.

The little house did not have running water but had a good cistern and a pump. He said since there wasn't a bathroom or indoor plumbing and they'd grown up without running water, it's surprising how little water you can get by on. It was rare that the Forest Service had to haul any extra water to them, they just made do with the water in the cistern. They pumped out the water in the bottom of the cistern once in a while and cleaned it, and he admitted it probably wasn't the healthiest water, but they were used to it. They think they paid $5/month rent to live there. The rent was taken out of Marvin's paycheck. The house had an outdoor privy.

Marvin said if the conditions were dry, he put in long days. If he wasn't down by midnight, they'd send someone else out to cover the night shift, but that didn't happen often. If the fire danger wasn't too bad, he could just run up and down and check for smokes every so often and otherwise could work on other things. If the fire danger was high, he'd be up in the tower for the duration. The main towers he talked to and triangulated with to locate fires were Fremont and Eastwood. They didn't really talk to the state towers.

He said the number of fires they had fluctuated a lot over the years. In the early days, a lot of farmers burned their fields, and they stayed busy checking on those. Then there was a period when there were a lot of arson fires, but at other times you might go 2-3 weeks, even in dry times, and not see smoke.

He said there were times it was enjoyable. He handled the boredom pretty well, being up there alone, but it was for long periods of time a boring job that you had to get used to. The hardest thing was if he knew the rest of his crew was out working on other jobs that needed to be done and he could be helping with and instead was stuck up in the tower not seeing anything for days. He said he'd fret about that quite a bit.

I asked how scary it must be to climb down that ladder in the dark, he said you got used to it, but on windy days, it could be tense. Once he said a person climbed up to visit him and look around and then he was afraid to go back down. Marvin said it took quite a while to talk him back down the ladder. Most people just didn't come up. There were easier towers to climb.

I asked about any large fires around the tower that he helped spot or watched from the tower. Pat remembered one that got up into the crowns of the trees- that was exciting to watch. Pat said she didn't really man the tower, but if it was a bigger fire, she'd shimmy up that tower to see what was going on.

I asked Marvin if he still knew his call sign. He did—and still could recite it from memory but said they didn't use them that often.

He remembers how close the crew was that he worked with. There was a group of them from the old Van Buren District which was called the Hallelujah Crew. They were always happy and all religious men. He thinks the people who started calling them that didn't mean it as a compliment, but they liked the name.

Asked what he did in the tower to pass the time he said he read westerns. He liked Zane Grey. And he learned to play the harmonica.

Pat said the site really changed later from the quiet place it was when they moved in. The road crew built a shed next to the house and kept all their heavy equipment out at the site. After that, the road crew came in and out every day. Maxie Williams was in charge of the road crew. Then later they put in a heliport at the site. During fire season they'd station a helicopter there that was on call if a fire was spotted. The helicopter would scoop water out of the pond there near the tower and dump it on fires. If the fire was further out, they'd get water from other sources. Earl Simpson oversaw the helicopter operations.

Geodetic Markers

One of the sideshows to the towers involves the many geodetic markers placed throughout the area. Since my wife is not a climber, she would usually go on the search for markers as I measured and documented the towers or footings. She developed a real knack for finding them.

The National Geodetic Survey Explorer shows the location of many markers. However, because of tree growth or other factors, many can't be found. You can also come across one now and then not on the list.

The markers were set originally at great effort. A new location had to be determined from a known one. Survey techniques had to be used to establish a new latitude, longitude, elevation, etc. Such was the skill then that when I stand at a site today with my GPS the numbers always match those from years ago. Amazing to consider you can push a button today and get numbers it took so much effort to determine back when.

These markers have identification numbers, PIDs. When you check out the information on a PID, it often contains lots of information and even tower notes. Some markers have the same name as a tower. Some do not. Obviously, a marker with the same name as a tower can be very useful. When the setting of a marker came at a time different than the tower construction, other names were used. Here is a piece from the Data Sheet for the "Wolf" geodetic marker on Wolf Mountain. Notice the tower is mentioned in the information.

```
GE0803'THE STATION MARK PROJECTS 4 INCHES, AND THE DISK IS STAMPED
GE0803'WOLF 1956.
GE0803'
GE0803'REFERENCE MARK 1 IS LOCATED AT THE DETERMINED CENTER OF THE
GE0803'BASE OF THE LOOKOUT TOWER.  THE MARK PROJECTS 2 INCHES, AND
GE0803'THE DISK IS STAMPED WOLF NO 1 1956.
GE0803'
GE0803'REFERENCE MARK 2 IS 29 FEET EAST OF THE CENTER OF THE TRACK
GE0803'ROAD.  THE MARK PROJECTS 2 INCHES, AND THE DISK IS STAMPED
GE0803'WOLF NO 2 1956.
GE0803'
GE0803'NO SUITABLE LOCATION COULD BE FOUND FOR AN AZIMUTH MARK.
GE0803'
GE0803'HEIGHT OF LIGHT ABOVE STATION MARK 23 METERS.
```

I looked for some time for the location of a "Horton Tower." Rob Miley sent me to Bob Cunningham who sent me to James Murrell. He told me it was located east of the old town of Horton. When I checked the Survey Explorer, there was a marker there. However, in this case, it was named "West." But, if you read the PID information, it references the tower that was there at one time. Had it been the Horton Marker I would have found the old Horton site sooner. I read PID information now and then, but with thousands of markers, that can be a slow road.

Following is a sampling of markers we have found here and there whose name matches that of the tower.

What's In a Name?

"What's in a name?" Shakespeare once asked. If it is a Missouri Lookout, the answer may be an interesting story. Let me note some of the name tags I have run across and the story behind.

The answer for many lookouts is simple. Many were named for the community nearby. From "A" in the Avon Pole Tower to the "W" in Womack/Whitewater, the nearby locations were very common for name selection. For the tower researcher, this often proved useful. However, it can also be confusing. The Squires Tower is located right at Squires. But, the Thomasville/MDC Tower sits nine miles "as the crow flies" NW of Thomasville. Jim Parker cautioned me that often, but not always, towers are located close to the town that it was named after. When the Blue Slip Tower was built, right between Norwood and Macomb, neither community was used, and Blue Slip was used instead leading to a mini-debate of sorts. It seems the hill there is named Blue Slip after a flower, or a type of Missouri clay? Both sides are loyal to their explanation!

Probably to nobody's surprise, hills and mountains were very popular. Consider the following: Shell Knob, Mountain View, Blue Mountain, Rosehill, Tusher Hill, Timberknob, Lone Hill (twice), Mt. Hulda, Highmont, High (Hill), Stegall Mountain, Sullivan Hill, Twin Knobs, Bell Mountain, Blackjack Ridge, Johnson Mountain, Cottener (also Cottonor at times), Pilot Knob (U.S.F.S. & M.D.C.), Rocky Mount, Stono Mountain, Bunker's Knob, Panther Hill, and Mud Lick (Tip Top at one time – one of several Tip Tops in Missouri).

We find creeks fairly well represented. There is a Sinking Creek Tower located south of Fremont and Missouri that has several "Sinking Creeks" and a Lost Creek Tower. Corn Creek Tower sat just north of Flat and Brushy Creek Tower above Ellsinore. Believe me, as I searched for Brushy Creek Tower, I learned Missouri has many a Brushy Creek. The Caney Towers were named after the cane which grew in the creeks below. There was also a Cedar Creek Tower. Big Springs, Siloam Springs, Climax Springs, and Reed's Spring Towers are names that should be included in the flowing water I suppose as might the Piney Tower that sat above the Big Piney River.

The animals show here and there. West of Poplar Bluff is Beaver Creek and Beaver Mountain which gave rise to Beaver Tower I suppose. Blue Buck Tower was named after a particularly large buck brought in for resettlement. Eagle Tower sat above Van Buren and Deer Run still sits above Ellington. Panther Tower sat just west of the Current River and Bee on Bee Hill. Then there are two of my favorites in Wolf Mountain Tower and Possum Trot (two at that location). Possum Trot is a favorite of mine. Much like "Brushy Creek," "Possum Trot" usage shows on many topography maps here and there.

There are a few oddities. Highway 60 Tower was not on Highway 60, but a few miles down Highway B. Macedonia Tower was named after the community and church, but I have been unable to determine how those rough and tough Greeks gave their name to a community and tower in Missouri. How about Buick Tower? It was named after the community which was named after the first car in town, or Buick was the name of a railroad owner when the line came through? Forestry Camp was named after the University of

Missouri facility there. A "Tram" is a timber train roadbed which Tram Tower south of Winona was built near, Max Gorman told me. Horn Lookout was named after the geographical feature, "Devil's Horn." There is a Kaiser and Czar Tower. Kaiser is German for Caesar and Czar is Russian for Caesar. This means by translation, Missouri has two Caesar Towers. Some of the simplest still elude me – how did Jay Tower get its name? Maybe "Highway J" Darrell Smith speculated.

Tower life can be confusing. There was a Pilot Knob (U.S.), and there still is a Pilot Knob (M.D.C.), and there was a Little Pilot Knob west of Potosi that was changed from Little Pilot Knob to "Floyd" for the community nearby. Don't get your "Dogs" mixed up as in Dogtown and Dogwood (Dogwood, Neosho, Piney, and Doniphan were all taken down by tornadoes).

There is a definite Native American influence on the tower names. Taum Sauk it seems was a Piankeshaw Chief named Sauk Ton Qua. Neosho means "clear cold water," and Tecumseh was chief of the Shawnee nation. It seems Tywappity was a Native American term for the bottomlands below Cape Girardeau (or tribe ?). The term may have been rearranged some by the Spanish. Indian Trail Forest gives its name to Indian Trail Tower. It seems hunting, and movement trails crossed the area in Woodland Indian times. Then, the "Trail of Tears" also passed through. Research continues on trial locations, particularly as they moved west. The name Montauk is used in several ways – the community, park, and tower. It seems "Montauk" was brought by settlers from Long Island, New York who adapted the name from the Montaukett Indians.

Kelleter Tower was named after the Forester, Paul Kelleter – or his mother depending on the source. Coot Mountain was named after Thomas "Coot" Chilton, an early pioneer and ancestor of Steve Orchard of the M.D.C. Hartshorn, as in the community and tower, was the name of a son of an early settler I was told. The Knob Lick Tower is now known as the Glen Skinner Memorial Tower to honor his service. Braswell Tower was named after the Post Office which was named after John Lemuel Braswell who settled the area in the mid-1800s.

The tower name game is a good lesson in Geography/History.

Missouri's two Caesar Towers – Czar left and Kaiser right

What's In a Name?

Below are two of my favorites when it comes to tower names (& blue skies).

Coot Mountain

Blue Slip

View of "Coot Chute" from Coot Tower

A Good Mystery Scrapbook

Sidney Buchman once observed, "If there were no mystery to explore life would get rather dull, wouldn't it?" My tower hobby has often supplied a mystery here and there. Let me discuss some that were solved and some that are "still out there."

Now and then, I look at various topography maps for items of interest. I have always been interested in the topogs, maybe part of the reason I ended up teaching Geography. Several years ago, I was scanning a topog out west of Potosi and noticed a "lookout" dot a few miles east of the Floyd site. My first impression was that it was close to the Floyd location. I checked with my Mark Twain Forest and Missouri Department of Conservation friends, no luck.

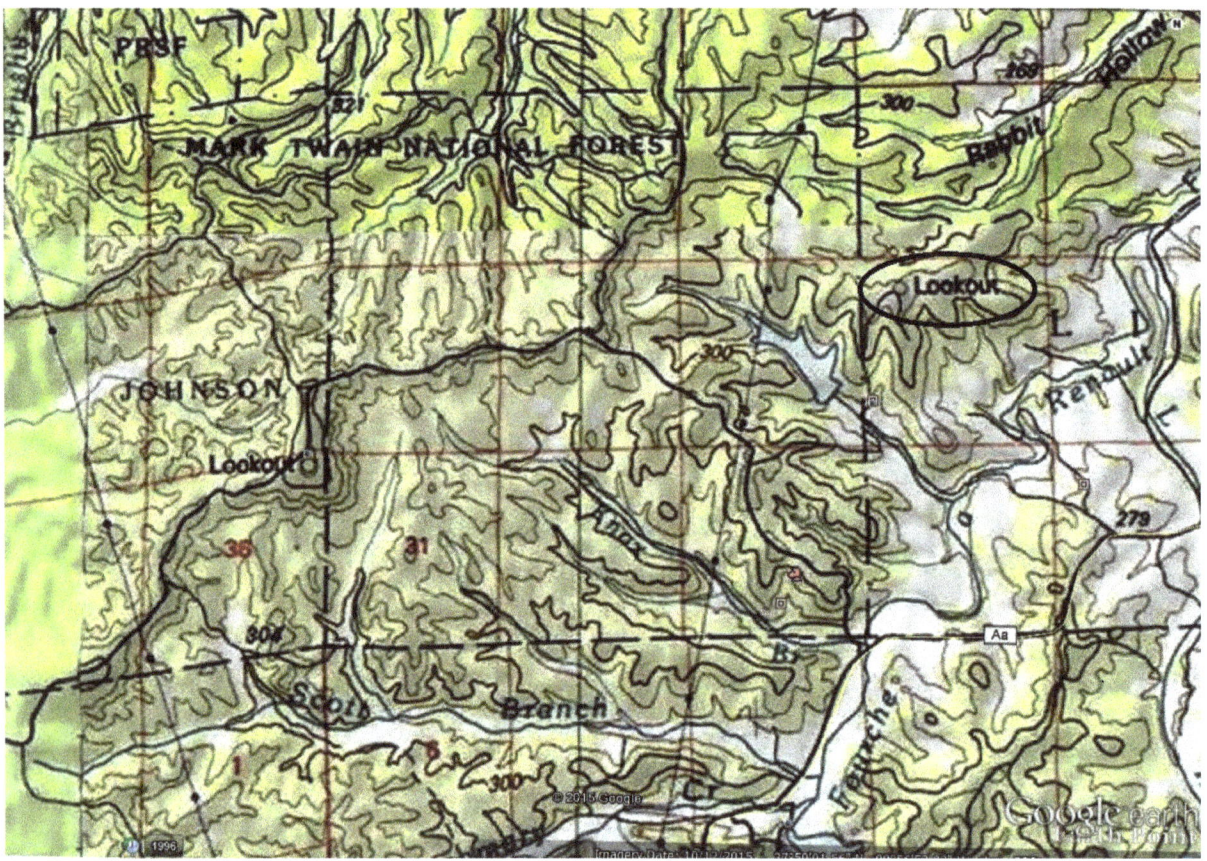

I mentioned it to Chris Polka who created the Google Map on towers, and he simply tried an approach I had not considered since the Floyd Tower was down, he zoomed in on Google Maps. Well, there it was. He was particularly curious since Washington County was the first county he had worked for tower sites and was sure there were none left to explore. He was so curious he headed out the first Saturday to check it out. However, despite which road he went down, he ran into one "Sayersbrook Bison Ranch" gate after another. However, that was a clue.

I then called the Sayersbrook office in Potosi, ordered some Bison meat (very good I might add), and ask a few questions. The girl there was very helpful.

She contacted Skip Sayers, and he provided the answer. It seems H.W. Sayers had constructed the tower in the early '50s to provide fire coverage for the Bison Ranch. The ranch, when running, had been a popular Bison centered park of sorts with its own firefighting unit including the tower. Although never a part of any federal or state system, it did provide "unofficial" fire coverage. I call it the Sayersbrook Lookout. It seems a topog map maker had observed it and put it on the map.

I then did some research on how topog maps are made. Although made from many sources, the observations of the map maker are a big part of that equation. I have found that important to remember now and then.

Another topog mystery appeared out east of Farmington. If you go NW of Weingarten off of "C," you actually turn onto "Tower Road." Several topogs have a "lookout" label at the high point there. It would be a great place for a lookout. See the topog shot here—

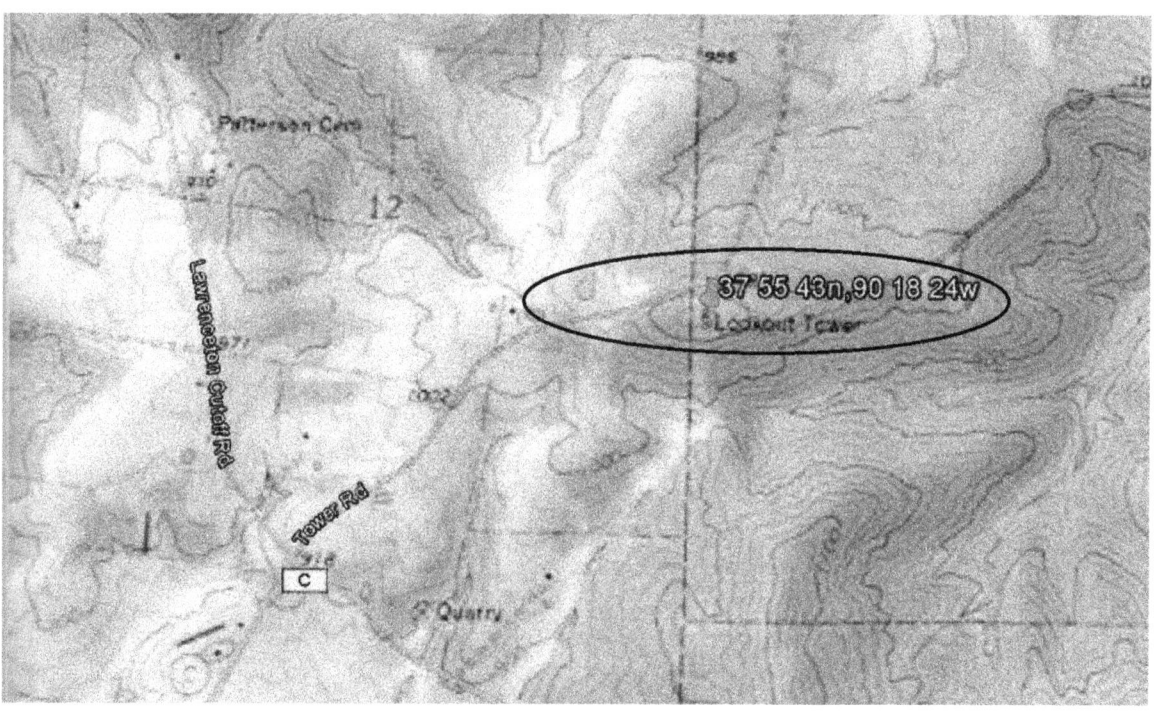

My wife and I stopped by the site the first chance we had and even from a distance noticed that the tower there kind of looked like a lookout and, kind of didn't. At the site it was obvious it was a communication tower of some sort. However, it did have an odd walkway at the top which gave it that lookout look. I jotted down the number from the gate sign and looked it up on the internet. Seems it was originally built for communication and is now used by the Missouri Highway Patrol.

I have an ex-student that I am very proud of that works for the M.D.C. out of Perryville. He connected me with Leon Peterson who has worked the area for some time and was sure no lookout ever stood there. My other area experts Lindell Tucker, Lawrence Buchheit, and Jack Skinner also could remember no lookout. I now believe a map maker looked at the strange tower from a distance and made a visual mistake. However, that would mean the "Tower Road" was so named for the communication tower, and the road name seems to predate the tower, so the mystery still lingers some.

Here is another topog mystery from above Spring Creek.

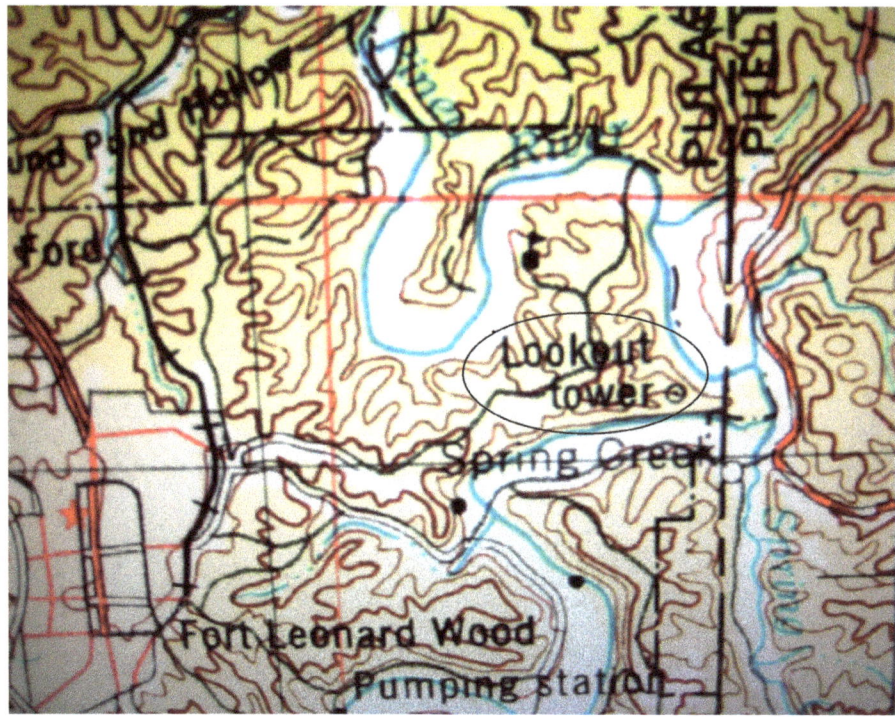

Maps of a different kind also created questions. For many years Missouri Road Maps contained symbols for "Forest Lookout Towers." On a rather curious 28 maps in a row, there is a symbol just south of Competition, Missouri. My wife and I were so curious we stopped at the gas station/café at "O" and "Z" just north of Competition. I walked into a table of those great Missouri people having coffee and a good talk. I spread my maps out, and they jumped in. In fact, it seems one lady had grown up at that site and no tower ever stood there she said. She made a call on her cell phone, same answer. That is pretty good evidence. I also ask them about a "Goose Creek" Tower that shows on one list. They had never heard of it. It must be another name for Phillipsburg at Goose Creek, maybe. My thanks to the "Competition Coffee Club" for allowing me to crash their party and I only hope they enjoyed it half as much as I did.

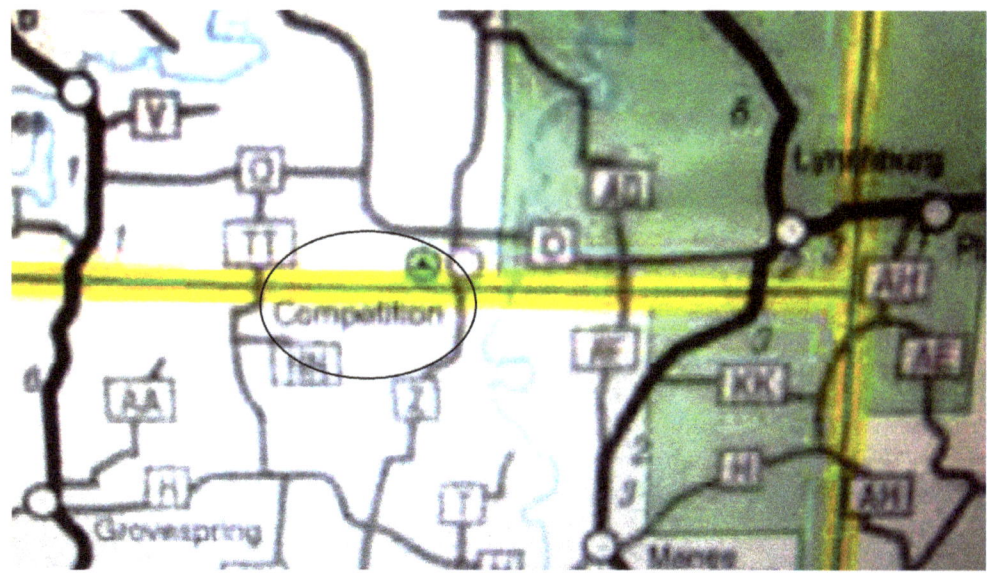

Another Missouri Road Map shows a symbol just south of the Mountain View Airport. I suspect the map maker just misplaced the Mountain View Tower. One thing for sure, a map mistake can get on easier than it gets off at times.

Others still hang there as very odd. One topog shows a "King's Lookout" just north of Mt. Sterling. I and others have checked the area out with no luck. There were some people in the area that helped by putting it out on Facebook. In this case, if a map maker put a visual mistake on paper, nobody can offer an explanation as to what the visual error was?

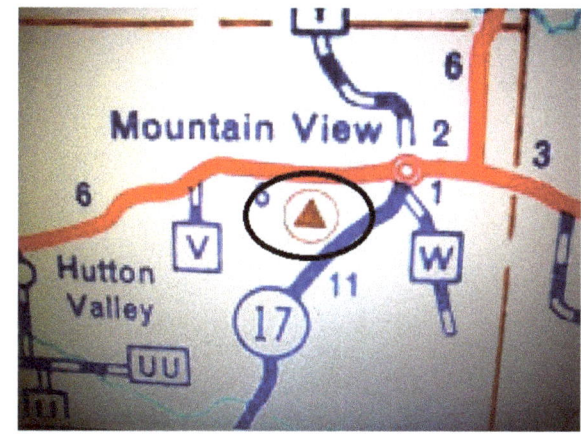

Even "official" maps can create a mystery. This map shows a "Paddy Creek Lookout" north of the Vada Lookout. The Vada Lookout existed. However, only this map shows a "Paddy Creek Lookout," and no trace seems to be there?

However, there are two solid mysteries that persist. They involve footings with no name and a name with no footing! The no-name footings first.

I was scanning a "Boss" topog years ago and noticed, above Brushy Creek/Fletcher Mine, another lookout label. The mine did not show, so the map predated it. The location was @ 1.25 miles east of KK on 2352. So, the next time we were in the area we checked it out. Now, I don't know how many items I would have missed things over the years but for my wife's detail eye. Such was the case here.

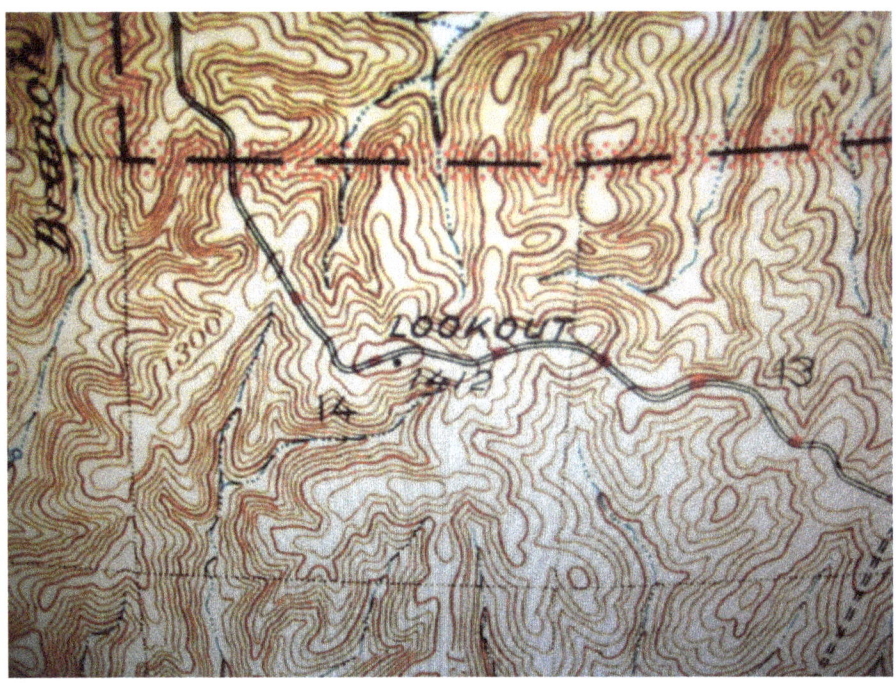

I nosed around at the road's curve for a while and gave up. We then drove back to the west a hundred yards or so, she eagle-eyed another one. There were footings for a small 50-foot tower. I walked between the piers and hit my GPS – 38° 12.162' North and 88° 54.532' West. There was also an odd pipe sticking up in the middle I had not seen before. It seems from the topog the tower predated the mine, but the footings seem to be oddly pristine. I was hoping to find a geodetic marker to give the place a name, but we were unable to locate any. n is below.

I have touched bases with all my "area experts." Kerwin Hafner noted the size of the saplings and Max Gorman the "outgrowths" of several saplings that grew from stumps most likely. The area it seems was cleared at one time and maybe more than once. Max noted the "stress" nature of the anchor bolts – an indication of a steel tower. He also noted the 4-inch pipe was not actually centered, although at first glance it seems to be.

Was it some other kind of tower and the topog maker just made a mistake? The second item on my list involves a name, with no footings.

Update : As I sent this to the publisher I talked to Gregg Mendenhall of Montauk Park who sent me to Jason Stotler at Indian Trail Forest who sent me to Tom Botkin who sent me to Jerry Clements who sent me to Darrell Smith who sent me to Minuard Abney. Darrell, in particular, was able to describe this exact location w/o any input from me. He said it was Seever Tower. The pipe in the middle remains a mystery!

I look through old archival papers now and then although talking to people is my #1 way to gain knowledge. You will notice on the following two old papers a "Plots" Tower. Again, the use of the term tower can be loose at times meaning a single pole lookout or even a tree "tower."

```
                        Willow Springs
Blue Buck Tower:
Dogtown Tower:
Hi Place Tower:
Plots Tower:
Siloam Springs Tower:  [mentioned in WPA guidebook]

Buildings at Siloam Lookout Site are not adequate.  The
dwelling needs a two room addition with bath, or new six-room
dwelling constructed.  This is the district work center, and
from two to three vehicles are stationed here.  There is no
building, at present, to store these vehicles, tools, and
supplies in.  there is need for a three stall garage with
room for small work shop at this location, and for a radio
extension to this building from the tower.  A drilled well
should be provided at this site to replace the cistern.
Regrading and reseeding work is needed at this site.  (Van
Slyke 1961:26-27).
```

Another paper-

MTNF PHOTOGRAPH SUBJECT FILE

SUBJECT		TOPIC	DATE	ENVELOPE
TOWERS		JOHNSON MOUNTAIN TOWER	1937	0299A
TOWERS		JOHNSON MOUNTAIN TOWER	1937	0300A
TOWERS		JOHNSON MOUNTAIN TOWER	1937	0301A
TOWERS		JOHNSON MOUNTAIN TOWER	1941	1354A
TOWERS		JOHNSON MOUNTAIN TOWER	1941	1355A
TOWERS	X	JULIEN TOWER	1930s	0082A
TOWERS		JULIEN TOWER	1930s	0083A
TOWERS		JULIEN TOWER	1937	0351A
TOWERS	X	LOHMER TOWER 351806	1941	0232A
TOWERS	X	MACEDONIA TOWER	1941	1236A
TOWERS	X	NEW LIBERTY TOWER	1935	1056
TOWERS	X	PLOTS TOWER	1935	1456A
TOWERS	X	PLOTS TOWER	1935	1457A
TOWERS		PLOTS TOWER	1935	1458A
TOWERS		POLE TOWER	1937	0286A
TOWERS	X	POSSUM TROT TOWER	1934	1290
TOWERS		POSSUM TROT TOWER	1930s	0075A
TOWERS		POSSUM TROT TOWER	1930s	0076A

Another paper sets the size at 40 feet. This is the only name I don't recognize from either list. They seem to be correct in the use of "tower." James Murrell, who helped me find the Horton location seems to recall something at the entrance to Knoblett Lake. The Willow C.C.C. camp was also in that neck of the woods. It had a water tower with footings it seems. Maybe that was used as a "lookout." There were also some small wooden "patrol" towers back when and 1935 is a pretty early date. It seems Plots was a very early notation that disappears from later inventories. All of this is speculation. I was also told that "Plot" or "Plots" is a type of Coon Hound. The pictures are long gone or at least that part of the mystery could be figured.

You will note, the postcard above is labeled "U.S. Forest Lookout Tower in the beautiful Arcadia Valley." However, the tower is not named. My best efforts have not produced the name. By the process of elimination, several of us guessed the Crane Tower. District Ranger Becky Ewing posted the picture at a "Crane Lake Community Forum." Lots of those in attendance looked, but there was no sure answer. Look familiar to anyone?

"Seeing Double at Possum Trot" has been on my mystery radar screen for some time. Here is an article I wrote for the Spring 2018 FFLA Lookout Magazine.

career. He simply said, "Kid if you want to make a career in this outfit you're not going to get it just being a lookout, you need a variety of experience". He did say if I was set on going back to the lookout he would honor my request and I could man the lookout again. It was a very difficult decision for me, but Johnny was correct, I did need varied experience. So I turned down the lookout job and it was the last year I applied for such a position. I eventually turned down the fire crew position and went to work that summer at the Regional Office, in Juneau, Alaska. I graduated from college the spring of 1972 and my dog and I headed to Alaska.

In the early 70's jobs were filled from a Civil Service Roster. If your name was on there in good standing you just never knew what type job, when or where it would be offered. I held a variety of positions over my 40 year career with the government that took me to one B.L.M. District and 9 National Forests in four Regions of this country. I accepted what was offered me and none were in fire. My varied jobs consisted of entomology, land surveyor, check cruiser, log scaler, para archeologist, felling timber for a net volume study, timber sale layout and logging systems. I was not officially in fire but kept active by assisting in District slash burning, fire assignments, blaster, Class C faller and 14 years with a Northern Rockies Type 2 fire team. During all the years I worked, my fondest memories go back to when I was young and free, "looking out my back door" as a fire lookout.

(L.E. Smith (Smitty) retired in 2011 from the Kootenai National Forest in Montana and resides at a log cabin outside of Libby, Montana)

Possum Trot Double Footings

For decades my wife Brenda and I have enjoyed a tower hobby in Indiana, Illinois, and especially Missouri. Over the years we have come to expect the unexpected. We were still taken back however when in September of 2016 we sought out the historical Possum Trot site for documentation. Located south of Winona, Missouri just the name "Possum Trot" had always caught my eye. Working with my GPS, the site was located exactly where you would expect.

The location was expected, the site layout was not. Instead of four footings, or piers, there were eight. Finding smaller and larger footings at a site was not uncommon. However, in this case, the smaller set was located concentrically inside the larger. The assumption was a smaller tower was replaced by a larger and the new larger footings were just set outside the smaller. That in itself was not a usual pattern.

Just the other day, I crossed paths with another tower hobbyist, John Timmerman, and the subject of Possum Trot came up. He told me the pattern of the eight footings was simple, the two towers stood at the same time in the same place. He also suggested I take a look at some pictures he would send or take a closer look at the one I had. Upon close examination there they were hidden in plain sight.

What the images show is a 50 foot Aermotor "windmill" set right inside what appears to be an IDM 100 footer. This is what the pictures show. What they don't tell is why this was done and nobody seems to have any idea. I was loaned a book, "50 years of the Winona District" by Bill and Shari Wolford.  Her Dad, Everett Chaney had worked for the U.S.F.S. in the area on Forestry and Hydrology. That book lists "Possum Trot 1938" as a 50-foot steel tower with Charlie Knight as the tower man.

As a rule, when a larger tower replaced a smaller, the smaller was moved for usage elsewhere. It was suggested maybe the smaller tower was used to erect the larger and the larger then used to dismantle the smaller. The picture might have been taken at just the right time. However, in 50 years of towering, I have never heard that before.

Sidney Buchman once observed, "If there were no mystery left to explore life would get rather dull, wouldn't it?" Trust me, there seems to never be a dull moment in the forest lookout world.

Bob Frakes, *frakes2@mvn.net*

Firetowers

I have a canoe book I picked up years ago. It has several unexplained tower symbols. Here is one east of Shannondale.

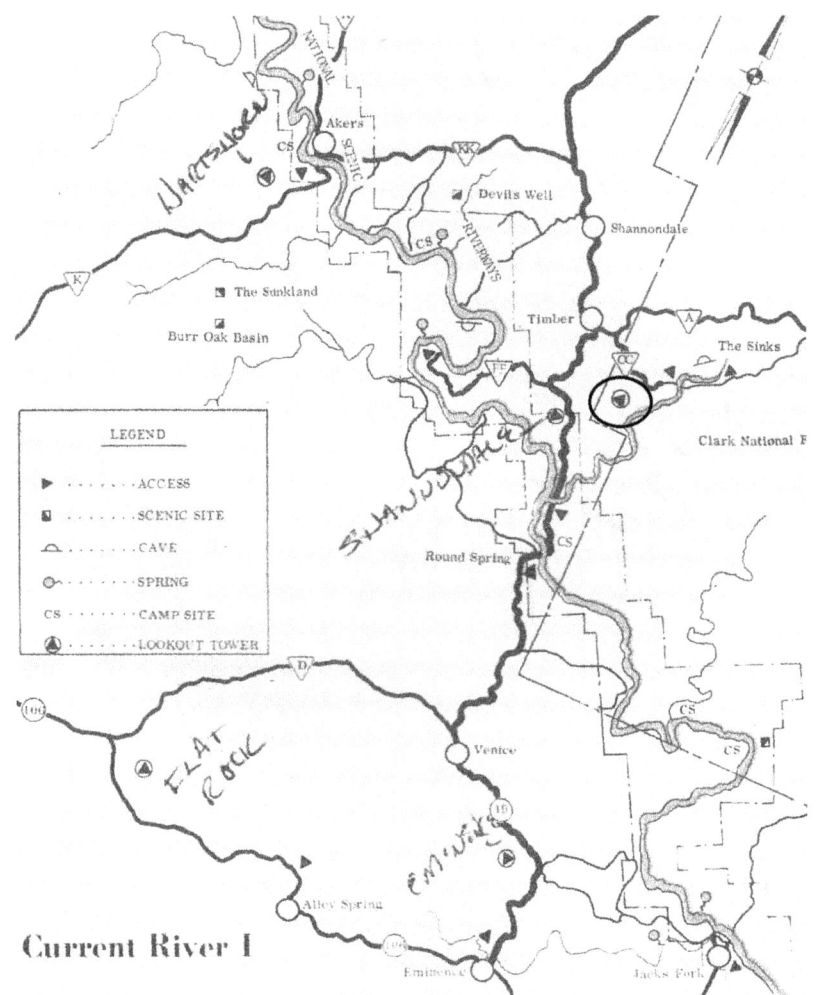

East of Smallet

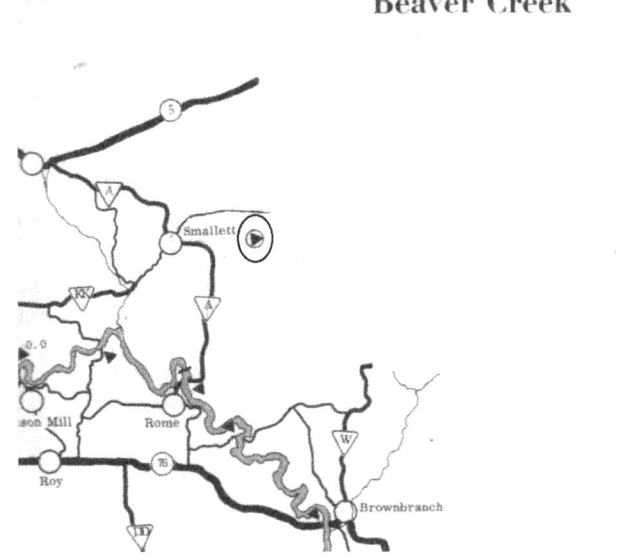

South of Twin Knobs

I received the above picture from Tim Lutes. It serves as a good example of how many questions can be answered by reaching out to the experienced. I first sent the picture to Jim Ruble (whose Dad, Avery worked the Vulcan Tower) and then Lawrence Buchheit. The "Old Foresters" Reunion gave it a look as did David Hurlbut and Gene Brunk. The names that emerged were Front Row – Ted Eudy (Forest Assistant), Harry Stroup (Taum Sauk Tower), Walter Holland (Dispatcher), Milton Trammel (Assistant District Forester).

Back Row – Melvin Harper (Mudlick Tower), Beauford Overton's Son (Gipsy Tower), Don James (Grassy Tower), unidentified (only worked a short time?), George Graham (District Forester), Earl Lutes (Forest Assistant, Lutesville), and Harold Shell (Cascade Tower).

Two of the names stuck out as I had met them, in the case of George Graham, or received information on them , as with Earl Lutes.

Here I have two more mysteries to look at. The first is a picture from I know not where of a wooden tower in Missouri – not labeled. I have shown it to several tower veterans with no answer. The second is the top of what appears to be an MC-39 steel tower. The picture is from the Missouri Historical Society but is only labeled as part of a Lynn Morrow collection. The citation is on the picture citation page. It is also referenced as a "deer stand" in Osage County. You would be surprised by the number of deer stand uses for former towers. Many I have tracked down what tower it came from and where it is now. Maybe you can help with this one?

George Graham

I met George at several "Old Foresters" Reunions I was allowed to attend, hang around, and ask questions. Two things about George became obvious: 1) he was a very witty and funny guy and 2) he was held in very high regard by the other foresters.

George graduated from Michigan State University. He worked in North Carolina and enlisted in the Air Force serving 4 years. George served in West Virginia where he met his wife, Ruth. He worked for Kirby Lumber in Texas for 7 years before going to work for the Missouri Department of Conservation. From 1963 to 1965 he was the Assistant District Forester and then District Forester. From 1965 to 1971 he served as the District Forester at Eminence and the District Forester at Perryville until his retirement in 1991.

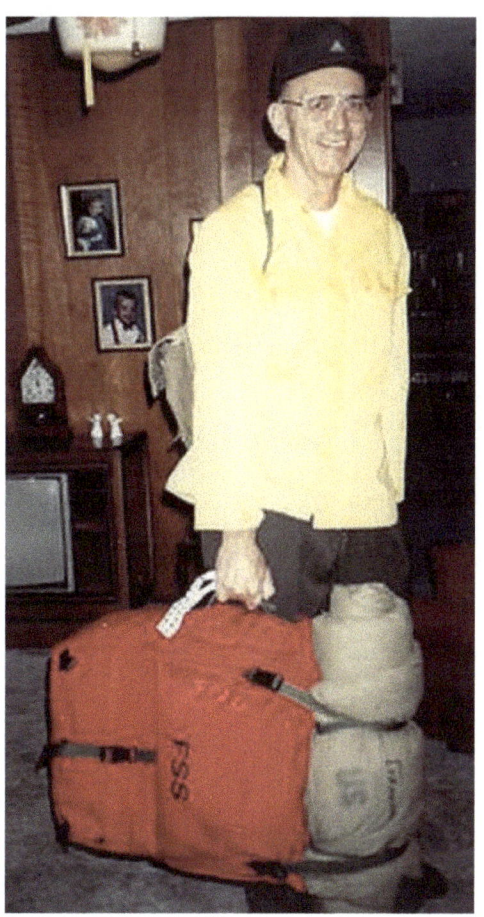

George fought fires out west (California, Idaho, Montana, Oregon) nine times for the federal government.

He is also a person of hidden talents. Duane Parker recalls George as a master paper doll cutter outer. He says his daughters still recall the works of art he created. He was also a jokester. Ron Woodland recalls that even in the middle of summer, a tower call for a look-see always came back, "north slope, covered with snow." I feel very fortunate to have had the chance to spend a little time with George and all the "Old Foresters."

George at a 2012 sign dedication recognizing his building of a nature trail and outdoor classroom at a public school.

George is shown accepting recognition at his retirement dinner. Smokey shown at a parade - he was the same height as George, hum?

Ed Ponder, who worked with George noted his dry sense of humor. He also mentioned that although George watched the money very closely, all you had to do was convince him of a need and it would get done.

Earl (Minnie) Lutes

To many, he was always called "Minnie." According to his son Tim, the name was commonly used even back in grade school days. I had talked to some who thought the name was connected to Minnie Pearl, but Tim thought it harkened back to his Aunt Minnie somehow. I found out though that is you say, "Earl Lutes," most of the locals and MDC will quickly say – "Minnie."

His son Jerry reflected

I guess my earliest recollection of Grassy Fire Tower was sitting on the steps of the old wooden tower as the new one was being built. This was around 1959, so I was probably was only around 4-5 at the time. I remember my Dad always leaving for work in the morning and coming home around 5pm in his conservation pickup – the earliest one I can remember was probably around a 58/59 Chevrolet pickup. Later, he got a 63 Ford pickup, then a 68 Chevrolet (that's the kind I am currently building into a conservation truck.)

He would always have to go to Salem, MO. to the maintenance shop for major service and repairs. Every year he would also have to have his truck inspected at headquarters, and several of my brothers and I would help clean up the truck beforehand (only wash/wax job for the year). The interior was always a chore because I think every piece of paper and other small items he acquired ended up on the dash or the bench seat. It was a work truck!

These trucks were always plain, stripped down version – vinyl floor mats, manual transmissions, no A/C, no radio- just a plain work truck. The only truck that I ever heard him complain about was a 1971 International Pickup. These were just a plain ugly looking truck (and the first ones with the new Conservation triangle decals). It didn't have power steering, but it did have power brakes, and as my dad said, "Not enough power to pull the hat off your head." After a couple of years, it popped out of gear on a hill one day and rolled off into a ravine. It was damaged enough that the Conservation Department decided not to fix it, and he eventually got a replacement truck – a Dodge.

One thing about these trucks, as well as all of the other equipment, they were all painted the same dark "Conservation Green" color- not like today's Conservation Department vehicles. To me, it may be a money-saving feature, but you lose some of the cohesiveness and team building spirit that I think the department is lacking today. Same with the uniforms (plus I like the old Hawthorne patch better).

It was always a treat as a young boy to be able to ride in the Conservation truck, made you feel special. Didn't really go hardly anywhere, but most of the time it was a short ride uptown for my Dad to go make contact. Back then, radios and coverage were pretty sparse. In order for him to be able to talk to Headquarters (Piedmont) at the time, he would have to drive up on the hill at the highest point in Lutesville. The trucks were equipped with the old Motorola radios and had a 10' whip antenna mounted on the truck bed rails. Usually, contact was around lunch time and then in the evening around 5 pm. It was always neat to drive down our home street (Magnolia) which had some trees with lower hanging branches, and listen to the sound of the antenna banging on the branches.

Occasionally, when the fire danger was high, he would bring the big truck hauling the dozer home with him. Getting to ride in that was an extra special treat, and as a young kid, you felt like you were the most important person in the world. You hoped that all your friends would see you, (and as you got older- the cute girls as well!)

I do recall the time that the tower man/forestry assistant at Gipsy – Buford Overton, had a heart attack on his way home from Piedmont, and ran off the road, wrecking his International Scout. I don't remember if he died from the heart attack or the wreck, but in any event, it was sad news. My dad took the big truck and loaded the wrecked scout on the back, to haul over to Salem. I remember him bringing it by the house and me crawling up to look inside. The scout was a tangled mess, with blood and broken glass everywhere inside.

My dad worked with several different guys at Grassy over the course of the years. The earliest one I remember was Jim Boyer. After he left, the Conservation Department hired Don James who was there for several years. Later, when I started working at the tower site, I can remember riding with Don on numerous occasions to go check out potential fires. He usually drove an International Scout as well, and it had a brush guard on the front, which got a good workout going through the woods at times. After Don decided to go into construction with his brothers, Russell "Pete" Kirkpatrick took his spot. Later, Joe Garvey took that position, but by that time, I was in the Air Force and didn't really get to work with him.

During fire season my dad would recruit my brothers and me at the various times, as well as other of our school classmates as necessary. I'm amazed at the age levels that we were at (starting around the age of 13/14, - about the time we were starting high school). I guess child labor laws were a little more relaxed back then. Usually, we would have at least four or five people at the tower on the crew at any one time. Most of the time was spent playing card games down in the shop building, waiting for the next call, as well as having at least one or two people up in the tower looking for smoke. Most of the time in the tower was pretty boring, but it was nice to sit with the windows open on a nice spring or fall day, and have a soft breeze blowing through the cab. On cooler fall days, the tower cab had a little electric space heater built into the wall for heat. Although we did have an overhead light bulb in the cab, I didn't like to turn it on much in the evening as it really cut down on being able to see out of the cab after sunset. I remember sitting in the cab by myself in the dark, while the rest of the crew was out on a fire call. With the light off, you could see all of the lights from various homes and villages for a great distance.

For most of the time, Grassy was a popular spot with visitors, especially on the weekends. The tower site had a nice stone path from the parking area and a wooden sign welcoming visitors to the tower. There was even a barbeque grill and picnic table, and more than one family enjoyed a picnic at the tower site. From time to time, we would have many visitors who would climb the tower to see the view from the cab. A lot of the time, many would only make it only part of the way up before they chickened out and went back down to the ground, but quite a few did make it, and we were always glad to welcome them and allow them to view the surrounding area from the cab. We would show them how the Osborne fire finder worked and let them use the binoculars while pointing out local points of interest.

There wasn't much equipment in the tower, usually just a set of binoculars, the Osborne, a Motorola radio to make contact with (report fire conditions during hourly contact or when necessary), and a telephone connected to the shop building. Scanning for fires was about 90% boredom, but occasionally you would see smoke on the horizon. After watching for a while to see if it got bigger or smaller, you had to make a decision whether to call it in or not. I was pretty good with the Osborne, at least with the azimuth, but getting the distance was a little harder to do. Usually, I would call down to the shop, and tell my Dad about the smoke. His usual response was to continue to watch and let him know if it got bigger. If it did look like a fire (instead of someone burning a trash pile), a quick call to the shop and Dad would be up in the tower cab in a matter of minutes. He knew every inch of the territory and could just look out the window and pinpoint the fire ("That's old man so-and-so on county road 403, burning his woods off again"). Usually, Don or Pete would go to check it out and call back if they needed the dozer.

We looked forward to having to go on a fire and getting to ride in the "big" truck with the dozer, especially if you got to go through town (so your friends could see you!) Once you arrived at a fire, the first step was to unload the dozer. At that time the truck had a tilt bed which had to be tilted up to about a 45-degree angle to get the dozer off the bed. My Dad would hop on the dozer and fire it up. We would go back to the control panel that had two levers – one to raise/lower the bed and the other to run the winch. We usually weren't much older 15/16 doing this, and I couldn't imagine trusting a 15/16-year-old today to do that. After Dad had got the dozer pretty much off the truck, we would have to climb under the raised dozer blade to unhook the winch cable. Again, couldn't imagine anyone that young doing that today.

My Dad had an instinct on how to best plow around a fire, and usually, off he would go as soon as we unhooked the cable. If the landowner was around, he might listen to him on where to go through a fence. IF this was the 3rd or 4th time to the same place, my Dad would just go through their fence whether new or not! The remainder of us would grab broom rakes and start following behind the dozer, raking leaves out of the line so the fire couldn't jump over, while one of the other crew would start setting a backfire, either with a fire backpack or in most cases, a broom rake full of leaves.

Usually, most fires were fairly small, and the terrain not too rugged so you could get a fire under control in an hour or two. After that, we would reverse the process to load up the dozer. Dad would usually talk to the landowner and/or fill out the paperwork, while he would have us walk the fire line and pace the fire (count steps). By pacing the fire, you could get a rough size of acreage burned.

Several memories from fighting fires- I remember one time following fairly closely behind the dozer and the smoke and fire were pretty intense. We were busy raking leaves and setting backfires, and at one point, my legs felt like they were on fire. They weren't really on fire (at least from the fire), but while plowing the fire line, my dad had plowed up a nest of yellow jackets and they were swarming all around and stinging my legs. Fortunately, the smoke was keeping them fairly low, but I got several nasty stings and welts from that.

One other time, we were on a fire, and I was with my brothers Ron and Gary on the fire line. The wind was pretty brisk that day, and at one point, the fire jumped up into the trees and was pretty intense. Usually, most fires just burned the brush and undergrowth on the ground, but getting up into the trees was pretty serious. Needless to say, the fire jumped the fire line, and my Dad was already well ahead of us. Knowing that the fire could really get out of hand quickly, my brother Ron told me to run ahead and let Dad know that it had jumped. I started out, and in just a short time, I was surrounded by smoke and flames. The heat was intense, and I couldn't see because of all the smoke and my eyes were burning. Panic was setting in, and I thought I had had it, but I dropped low to the ground and saw a small opening. Once I got through, I made my way back in the direction of where my brothers were. By the time I got back, there was my Dad with the Dozer. After a few minutes of a good ass-chewing, he replowed a new fire line, and we were back on track. Fortunately, the wind died down, and the rest of the fire was finally controlled. I fully expected that I was in for round two of the ass-chewing, but my Dad never said another word. I guess he figured that learning the hard way was sufficient enough, and was a good life lesson. It sure stayed with me through the rest of my (short) firefighting career.

Going to the Fair- One of the more exciting times of the year was getting to go to the SEMO District Fair in Cape Girardeau. This usually took place in early September, and it was always fun going with my Dad to the Missouri Conservation Exhibit. Usually, the big truck and dozer were on display, with some of the other equipment. In addition to the wildlife displays, the forestry division had a small portable sawmill set up by the exhibit pavilion. My Dad and some of the other guys would work the sawmill, cutting up logs into tiny plaque boards. My job (and some of the other brothers' as well) when we were there was to stamp the various logs with ink pads. The stamp pads were available for the various types of wood (Oak, Elm, Cedar, etc.). Also, there were a "Compliments of the Missouri Conservation Commission" and a stamp of Smokey Bear. It was a great time, and the little wood plaques would be gone as soon as we finished stamping them.

Dad's other Conservation Department Job—One of my Dad's best friends in the Conservation Department was L.T. "Corky" Wilder. Corky was the assigned game warden for Bollinger County, and he and dad were pretty much inseparable for the length of their careers. Although my Dad was in the Forestry Division, I think he spent about half of his time, working in the game protection division with Corky. I'm sure Tim can fill you in about this a little better than I can, but I believe that my Dad was the only Forestry Division person in the state that also carried a Game Warden badge. I'm not sure who got his badge and service revolver after he passed away, but I think my brother Jeff got those. I don't think that there was a person in Bollinger County that didn't know Dad or Corky, and vice-versa.

One of the main problems that they always faced was dealing with 'spotlighters' – people who would go out in the evening and shine deer with spotlights and shoot them. Daddy or Corky would get a call and no matter what time of night it was, he was out the door in a matter of minutes and rendezvousing with Corky to go where the spotlighting was going on. I do remember them talking about being shot at a few times, and also on one occasion chasing a car with spotlighters in it down one of the narrow gravel roads that crisscross Bollinger County. In order to get away, the spotlighters turned their spotlights on Corky who was driving, and he lost control and struck a tree head-on. Both came out of the wreck okay, with only minor injuries, but it was a scary moment.

Since my Dad knew most of the people in the area, he had a good idea who was usually doing most of the spotlighting. Being in a relatively rural, poor county, my Dad looked the other way when it was someone who was just trying to put food on the table versus someone who was breaking the law just for the thrill of it. Times were lean and desperate.

During my last few years of College, the Conservation Department got sophisticated with their patrols and brought a conservation owned plane – an Aero Commander, down to Cape for looking for spotlighters. Area Game Wardens would be stationed at various points on the ground, and my Dad would go up (with a couple of the brothers and me too!) with the Conservation Pilot to fly around and look for the tell-tale sign of spotlighters on the ground. Once a spotlighter was spotted, agents would be vectored in to apprehend the violators. Most of the time it was routine, but every once in a while, it was a real chase to catch someone. We had a great viewing position from around 5,000 feet above. Again, my Dad seemed to know where we were most of the time, even though I was lost as last year's Easter Egg.

When my Dad finally retired in 1991, he was the longest-tenured employee of the Missouri Department of Conservation, with a career lasting 43 years. Both he and Corky Wilder have granite markers outside of the Conservation Building in Cape. See below from the Missouri Conservationist–

I'm sure that I have just touched the tip of the iceberg here with stories, and when Tim and I talk it starts bringing out other memories as well. It would be nice to get some of the brothers together, and I'm sure that you would get a lot more information, but as the saying goes, it would probably be like "herding cats" to do that. Anyway, I'm copying Tim on this as well, and he can correct me if I am in error on anything, or add more to what I have written. Hope this helps!

Tim Lutes has completed a beautiful restoration of an MDC "Dozer." The perfect lead into a chapter on "Dozers!"

"Dozers"

(Information supplied by Jim Parker, Max Gorman, Lawrence Buchheit, David Lane, and the Lutes Brothers.)

My basic aim in getting a book going was to document the pictures, stories, information and facts collected in my 50-year tower hobby. I was contacted by several to add what I had collected in a few other related areas. One of these involved the "dozers."

The dozer could cut a fire line fast. Jim Parker noted that 20 % of the time this line was meant to stop a small fire. Eighty % of the time this line provided a good base for backfiring.

John Deere models seem to be the preference of most. They were gas operated with some models only having two cylinders. These at times tended to be underpowered and worked much better going downhill than up. Later models used diesel. Some features are noted –

A – A cage provided some protection from the brush etc. The back was open, however, and some saplings tended to roll under the pads, bend over and come back up and whack the driver on the back of the head. Guards were improved over the years. A fully enclosed cage, however, would make escape difficult in a rollover.

B – A tank contained 5 gallons of water. This could be used for fire suppression or keeping a fire off the machine. It could also be used for drinking water if you didn't mind it warm. Jim Parker's wife Judy says he still drinks his water warm!

C – Each unit had its license plates. Conservation Commission is noted on this unit, albeit inverted.

D – Most units had blades that could also be used to fight a fire. In fact, Jim Parker notes the blade was often every bit as useful as the plow. The blade could cut a fire break and after was very useful in clean-up. Items still smoldering could be pushed back onto the burned side to prevent a flare-up.

E – The plow was controlled by a hydraulic unit to raise or lower the cut.

F – The plow actually cut the fire break. This model is an Anderson. SECO was another model. Each seemed to have advantages and disadvantages. Some models were more prone to jam up. The idea was to cut a trench and throw soil over to quickly create a fire line for stoppage or backfiring. The unit could be transported quickly by truck or trailer and unloaded for usage.

Earl "Minnie" Lutes (on dozer) and Don James unloading at a fire.

Different color schemes were used, but in later years brighter colors or white on top became more common to allow aerial units to locate the dozer in the woods and fires.

In the picture below you see a dozer being used to create a fire break and several workers using that break to start a backfire to rob the fire of fuel.

The first picture below is a "dozer" with a broken axle. The second is the same dozer restored by Tim Lutes. Thanks, Tim for the use of the pictures! They have become collector items of sorts and bring back memories to some I am sure.

"Dozers"

On this model, the plow is a SECO. Some models had no blade but pulled an attached plow that a worker rode on and operated manually.

Vintage Conservation Commission "Hawthorne Bloom" photo of a dozer ready to go fight.

On The Move

Once the Jay/Botkin tower move surfaced, I became more interested in finding out how big that story might be. I was aware of many "institutional" moves. To meet changing conditions, towers had been shuffled now and then to maximize their use.

Here are some examples: Gipsy to Cascade, Swedeborg to Proctor, Eminence to Panther Hill, Rocky Mount to Runge, Benton to Cimarron National Grasslands (if they come get it), Caney I to Caney II, August Busch to Guthrie, original Cottoner (or Cottener) to Womack/Whitewater, or Black to Oates.

Several towers were purchased from Michigan for $1 a piece if you came to get them. Jim Parker, who went to Michigan to take down and transport recounted the lodging and food were good, but the trailer and bridge back were too small!

The lower part of the Hollister Tower serves as a viewing platform at the Ruth and Paul Henning Conservation Area. The old water tower at Steelville was moved and used as the base for the Rosati Tower.

There has also been an interesting collection of private purchases and moves. The Mulvinia Tower was purchased and moved to a farm in Indiana. In fact, a New York Company made the move and specializes in the purchase, take down, move, and put up all for a package price. The Hurricane Deck Tower was bought by a local businessman. A campground at Arlington, Missouri bought a tower and moved it in for an attraction, but nobody seems to remember where it came from.

The Bunker Tower was moved but to where evokes a spirited debate. James Ruble, who is always right, says you can "take it to the bank" that it was moved to the south of Sullivan. Some paperwork I have has it sky-craned to Fort Leonard Wood. Another version has it going off to a junkyard in Marion, Illinois or to the camp at Arlington. A newspaper article I have has the Warrenton Tower sky craned to Fort Leonard Wood, also for range observation.

Now, I received a newspaper clipping from a tower friend – Rolla Daily News, Monday , May 9, 1983, page 3. The headline reads, "Man Gets Better View With His own Observation Tower."

The article relates that a John Satterlee, of Rolla, had purchased a Forest Service Forest Lookout Tower. It seems John was an employee of the USGS and had often climbed the towers to get a good look at the land. When the CCC built Shell Knob Tower came up for sale, he bid $101 and was the winner.

The story recounts that John and a friend, Abert Guill spent September in 1980 taking the tower down and moving it down the hill to a truck. The pieces were hauled back to Rolla, and the concrete footing poured. When they dried, the tower started going back up. The article says Ray Collier assisted with the re-assemble. Lights were strung at Christmas to make a Christmas Tree.

Now for the mystery. The article contained many names. There was the author of the article and photographer. Those who took the tower down and put it up are mentioned. The tower seems to be gone but I can make out footings from a Google view, maybe. But as I have talked to tower friends in the Rolla area and searched for contact info in regard to the names involved, I have not been able to gather any information on this tower story in recent years.

The second tower at Cottoner has an odd history. I was looking at a collection of tower pictures and noticed one labeled "Stockton Lake." Since I was not aware of any tower ever standing there, I called the Corps of Engineers there. They confirmed it was not a government tower but did point me toward Hawker Point where it stood. You could see the shadow on Google. I called the nearest business, and they said a Delaney Dunn had erected the tower, but he now lived near Branson. I was able to talk to him, and he had quite a story.

He had become interested in locating a surplus tower to move to his property. The Forest Service offered the Floyd or Cottoner Towers. Since Cottoner was in better shape, he put in for it.

The Cottoner Tower actually had a radar unit atop it at one time and was sturdier than most. DeLane and his brother Forrest would work 5 months taking the tower down and moving it to the farm at Stockton Lake. On a typical weekend, DeLane would drive to his brothers in St. Louis, and they would head out on Saturday morning for the hour and fifteen-minute drive to Marquand. Saturdays were spent taking things apart and staging the parts on the ground. After working Sunday morning, they would load the trailer up and go their separate ways. Making their way down the road at Cottoner with a trailer loaded with steel was one of the most interesting parts of the process. The hardware alone would fill 27 five gallon buckets.

Back in Stockton, they dug 4 eight foot by eight foot holes four feet deep and then poured 6.5 yards of concrete in each hole along with 2-foot piers on the top of each. Over the next three years, they put the tower back up. The tower framework was 8 feet shorter which made the cab larger. They made most of their tools including the booms and winches used to move the steel.

The cab had windows on each side with a steel door. Inside it had laminate flooring, tongue and grove wood walls, a skylight, furniture, electricity, and a small heater. The cab was custom made on the ground, disassembled and raised, and reassembled.

Needless to say, DeLane and Forrest showed much determination and craftiness! Next, you see the result located at Stockton Lake.

The Grassy Tower is an interesting tale. A few years ago while my wife and I were driving into Montauk for "catch & release" my wife noted a tower just west of Ellsinore. Since I was aware no tower had ever stood there, we wheeled around to the local café to get the story. I was told the tower had been moved by one fellow and sold to another. It was to be used as a "deer stand" I was told.

Digging a little deeper, it turns out that tower is the old Grassy Tower and is now owned by Raymond McGarrity. He has plans to move it again to another site near Ellsinore. The moved Grassy/McGarrity Tower is pictured on the next page.

Now, several years ago I was looking through some papers given to me by Conservationist Jim Lyon. One paper noted the purchase and move of the Goodman tower by Larry Newton. It also noted the move was not far away. I went to Google Earth and, there it was! A tower I thought was gone hidden in plain view.

I stirred up a mailing address and contacted Larry by mail. He sent me several papers and a phone number. I was doing a tower series for the River Hills Traveler Magazine and traveled to Larry's place near Goodman to get the story and take some pictures. It was also a chance to use my drone that I had started working into my documentation.

Parts of this are reprinted with permission from the article I did. It seemed when the Goodman Tower was put up for sale, Larry Newton and others could not stand to see it go. Larry would submit and submit again as he became concerned his bid was not high enough. He said he had a limit in mind and was more than willing to offer. He said, "he just could not stand to see it go."

Now came the hard part. The purchase stipulated the tower had to be moved. Larry soon found he was not alone in his wish to see the tower remain standing and was able to call in several who shared his view. Ken and Don Ruby would help with the "take apart" and "back together." Marshall Long would work on the footings or piers. These have to not only be level but spaced at an exact distance. Carson Bunch would work on the electric hookup and Colt Wise would apply a fresh coat of paint. S&S Erectors would set the cab.

The tower is a 120-foot Aermotor MC-39 or IDM clone. It may well be the most popular design of all time. It has 160 steps, standard for this model. Following the setting of the footings and base, the rest of the tower was re-created in the 10 sections it was removed in. It was just a matter, Larry notes, of lining up the holes and bolting them together. He noted the great condition of the original bolts and the tower in general. Galvanized steel is indeed tough stuff. The tower is stamped with "Bethlehem" for the steelworks in Pennsylvania where the pieces originally came from.

Larry noted he would "do it again in a second." He has never hesitated in his belief that he seized a very rare opportunity.

There were once hundreds of "forest lookout towers" across Missouri. About sixty some remain. They go on sale now and then. Every now and then the site and tower are sold, but often the tower has to be removed. Keep your eye open, and you might be able to make an interesting purchase and keep a part of history alive.

I enjoyed my tower visit with Larry. After 50 years of my tower hobby, the climb has gotten a little harder, but I made it. As I always say, "towering" is lots of fun but the real joy is meeting the "tower people" of Missouri.

Below is a drone shot of Larry in his tower, and if you look closely at the arrow in the second picture (right center), you can see the green area that was the original location for the tower.

Now, some "moves" fell into a category all their own. These involved moves of nature. Towers, by nature, were erected in high and exposed areas. They demonstrated a remarkable ability to resist the elements. However, nature could win. In my documentation, I have come across four examples : Dogwood (3/15/1973 as per Stan Lovan), Piney (4/1947), Doniphan (2/1985), and Neosho (5/2008). Even galvanized steel and construction skill could be no match for a twister.

Doniphan

Neosho

Charles Tatum putting the Doniphan Tower back up.

Drone Shots

Over the last few years, drones have offered the chance to view the lookouts from a perspective never seen. The following shots were taken by Damian Goodman. **These flyover shots were fully within guidelines at the time taken many years ago. The U.S.F.S. and M.D.C. have and are working up rules and regulations for their use. Make sure and check on the latest guidelines before using a drone on state or federal land.**

Below is a shot from a Coot Mountain flyover. You can see a section of the Current River known as Coot Chute in the background.

Coot Mountain

Shannondale Sunset

Shannondale Tower

Drone Shots

Flat Rock Tower

Summersville Tower

Hartshorn Tower

Hello Down There/Hello Up There

Since my wife is not a "climber," she would go to locating the geodetic markers while I checked out the tower. One of our traditions was taking a "hello" picture from any tower I climbed. Here is a sampling –

Blue Slip Lookout

Thomasville Lookout

Sunridge Lookout

Squires Lookout

Rosati Lookout

Perry Lookout

Camdenton Lookout

Keysville Lookout

Managing Fire Tower Sites on Federal land: The Mark Twain National Forest

James A. Halpern

Zone Archaeologist/Mark Twain National Forest, Missouri
Management of Historic Properties

Administration of historic properties located on Missouri's federal lands is guided primarily through the National Historic Preservation Act of 1966, as amended, and its accompanying regulations. In creating the Act (often referred to as the "NHPA"), Congress declared that such properties should be managed "in a spirit of stewardship for the inspiration and benefit of present and future generations" (54 USC § 300101). Under the NHPA, historic properties are defined as "any prehistoric or historic district, site, building, structure, or object included on, or eligible for inclusion on, the National Register [of Historic Places], including artifacts, records, and material remains relating to the district, site, building, structure, or object" (§ 300308).

In accordance with the NHPA, Heritage Program staff working on the Mark Twain National Forest are responsible for the identification of historic properties located in areas where federal undertakings are proposed, for assessing potential adverse effects of project activities to both new properties and those already documented, and for long-term management of all such properties across the Forest. The Mark Twain must also consult with the Missouri State Historic Preservation Office, Native American tribes, and other interested parties, as appropriate, on the adequacy of its efforts to meet the requirements of the NHPA as well as the anticipated effectiveness of any measures recommended to mitigate potential adverse effects.

Thousands of cultural resources, including archaeological sites, historical structures, isolated artifacts, and historical features have been identified on Missouri's National Forest System lands, to date. While many of these resources have been found to be ineligible for listing on the National Register of Historic Places for a variety of reasons and are therefore released from ongoing management, a fair number have been found to be significant. However, a majority of known sites have not been investigated sufficiently to allow for a credible evaluation of their historical significance; they are therefore managed as National Register "unevaluated" properties and, out of an abundance of caution, are afforded the same protections from adverse effects as properties found to be eligible for the National Register.

Mark Twain National Forest

On June 8, 1929, the Missouri General Assembly passed an Enabling Act that authorized the US Forest Service to begin purchasing qualifying lands for what would eventually become the Mark Twain National Forest. Following several amendments to the Enabling Act, broad-scale land acquisition began in earnest during 1935. Within five years, these lands were officially designated as two separate National Forests: the Mark Twain and the Clark, with administrative headquarters in Springfield and St. Louis, Missouri, respectively (McConnell 1963:9-13). By November 1939, Forest Service employees and their designated representatives had been able to purchase from willing landholders approximately seventy-seven percent of the Forest's current total land base of more than 1.5 million acres, at an average cost of $2.02 per acre (US Forest Service 1940:20). On February 17, 1976, all of the National Forest System lands in Missouri were combined into a single administrative unit headquartered in Rolla, Missouri: the Mark Twain National Forest (US Forest Service 1985:2).

Today, the Mark Twain extends across 29 counties in central and southern Missouri, and it is the largest administrator of public lands in the state. Forest management objectives include restoration and enhancement of diverse natural landscapes and watershed protection in collaboration with a variety of interested partners and neighboring communities, and in so doing to provide a range of forest products and recreational opportunities to the public.

At the time of their acquisition, many of the lands comprising what would become the Mark Twain National Forest were in poor condition due to unrestrained timber cutting, over-grazing, indiscriminate burning, and the resultant erosion of soils (US Forest Service 1961a:9). However, they had not always been so: for many thousands of years, Missouri's aboriginal peoples inhabited the area and successfully exploited its plentiful natural resources in groups of varying size, including relatively small, nomadic bands occupying seasonal camps to somewhat larger populations dwelling in villages and towns. Following federal designation of tribal lands as public domain, widespread Euro-American settlement of the region began during the late eighteenth and early nineteenth centuries, leading to the rapid displacement of native peoples—sometimes forcibly so. Pioneer families dependent on wild game and the yield of relatively small gardens were followed in turn by subsistence farmers who occasionally reaped a modest surplus which could be sold at local markets or traded in exchange for goods not procurable on the family farm. Each of these groups left their mark upon the landscape: stacked rock or concrete foundation remnants and abandoned field clearings of the family farm overlie flakes of stone and tools created through their artful removal, persistent indicators of the campsites and more permanent dwelling places of Missouri's indigenous peoples, most traces of which remain hidden beneath the ground surface.

Benefitting the Land and the People

Almost from its inception in the 1930s, the establishment of the National Forest System had a profound impact on both the land and people of Missouri. A significant proportion of the Mark Twain's early land management objectives were realized in large part through public emergency works programs implemented under President Roosevelt's "New Deal," initiated during 1933 in response to the Great Depression. One of the most effective and popular of these programs was the Civilian Conservation Corps (CCC); its benefits to local economies were substantial (Conrad 1997:67,97; Halpern 2012:13).

Throughout the entire state, more than 100,000 Missourians would serve in the CCC between 1933 and 1942; they planted more than 43 million trees, constructed 240 bridges and 1,600 miles of roads, and carried out hundreds of erosion control, recreational, and wildlife rehabilitation projects. During the latter part of October 1933, the first of twenty-three CCC camps in operation at various locations began to be established on recently acquired National Forest lands, each housing 150 to 200 enrollees supervised by co-operative teams of Forest Service and US Army personnel. In the woodlands that would eventually be designated as the Mark Twain, CCC enrollees and other workers hired locally under the Emergency Relief Administration performed intensive reforestation activities, built and improved roads, constructed and maintained telephone lines, quarried and dressed stone for buildings, established game refuges, developed water impoundments, controlled erosion, and—in conjunction with their US Forest Service counterparts—fought fire. To that end, they raised a strategically distributed network of wood and steel observation towers with interconnected viewsheds to assist in their suppression efforts (Crowell 1953:1-2; Malouf 1989:1; Williams 1983:4). These towers comprise perhaps the most conspicuous site components present on the Mark Twain National Forest and form the basis of the discussion to follow.

Forest Lookout Towers

Although the records are sometimes contradictory and incomplete, according to Michael Elliot's draft *National Register of Historic Places Multiple Property Documentation Form for Fire Lookouts, Towers, and Associated Structures on the Mark Twain National Forest, Southern Missouri* (2010:17,42-43,56-65), which is the most comprehensive synthesis of fire tower data produced on the Forest to date, the Mark Twain has identified 108 fire tower sites that are thought to have been constructed on the Mark Twain or in its vicinity by CCC enrollees and/or members of other New Deal programs during the period 1934-1941. The location of 90 of these sites can be placed with reasonable confidence inside current Forest boundaries; they appear to have included either ca. 100 foot-tall primary steel towers surmounted with open platforms or enclosed cabs or secondary towers of pole or lumber construction, standing 40 to 80 feet tall. Primary tower components were fabricated by various manufacturers, including Aermotor and Bethlehem Steel. Only 21 of the 90 fire tower sites known to have been located on the Mark Twain National Forest actually retain standing towers. All are fabricated of steel and rise to approximately 100 feet in height; each also possesses an enclosed cab of galvanized sheet and steel frame construction measuring ca. 7 feet square (Elliot 2010:51).

A variety of additional structures, usually built according to standard Forest Service plans, were often associated with the primary towers. In addition to the tower itself, these site complexes might have included a small domestic residence for the towerman and his family, a latrine, a garage or warehouse, a tool cache, an oil house, a well or cistern, ornamental vegetation, as well as parking and picnic facilities for the public. Information derived from archaeological investigations of these properties suggests that some towermen also kept chickens and/or pigs and likely maintained small garden plots.

For decades, these complexes continued to be used as an integral component in Forest wildland fire operations; however, by the 1950s the Forest Service's determination to educate the public about the dangers of uncontrolled burning as well as the agency's unrelenting fire suppression efforts led to significant reductions in both the frequency and intensity of forest fires. As time progressed, the fire towers and associated complexes were less frequently manned, particularly as aircraft (due to their ready availability and the comparative affordability of their operation) began to assume a major role in fire detection. During the late 1960s and early 1970s, tower-based fire spotting was superseded by the exclusive use of aerial detection flights (Elliot 2010:16). Ultimately, many of the remaining towers and associated facilities fell into disrepair or were dismantled and removed from federal lands.

Considering Historical Significance

For federal land managers, a number of factors must be considered in determining whether or not archaeological properties—including the Mark Twain's lookout tower sites, either individually or collectively—comprise properties that may be eligible for listing on the National Register of Historic Places. Foremost among these are the National Register "Significance Criteria" set forth in the Code of Federal Regulations (CFR) and further clarified in a variety of National Park Service technical bulletins in accordance with its authority under the National Historic Preservation Act.

As delineated under 36 CFR 60.4, historical significance is present in districts, sites, buildings, structures, and objects [typically at least 50 years of age] that possess integrity of location, design, setting, materials, workmanship, feeling, association (or various combinations thereof), and at least one of the following Criteria as properties that…

A. Are associated with events that have made a significant contribution to the broad patterns of our history; or
B. Are associated with the lives of persons significant in our past; or
C. Embody the distinctive characteristics of a type, period, or method of construction, or that represent the work of a master, or that possess high artistic value, or that represent a significant and distinguishable entity whose components may lack individual distinction; or
D. Have yielded, or may be likely to yield, information important in prehistory or history.

In order for a property to attain National Register significance, at least one of these Criteria must be met. Additionally, sites must retain a degree of physical integrity sufficient to convey their significant characteristics.

Tower Property Types

Each of the 90 fire tower sites reasonably certain to have been erected on Mark Twain National Forest System lands can be categorized as one of four basic "fire tower property types" according to their current morphology. Elliot (2010:56-65) describes these property types as follows: *Fire Tower Archaeological Sites* with no standing tower or other associated structures represented solely by artifact scatters, tower footings, and/or concrete structure foundations (n = 69); *Standing Fire Tower Sites* with associated structural remnants, such as foundations, artifacts, and/or other potentially significant archaeological remains or landscape features (n = 8); *Partial Fire Tower Complex Sites* characterized by the presence of standing fire towers as well as additional intact structures, such as a garage or forge, artifact scatters, and additional features, however, the towerman's residence is no longer standing (n = 11); and *Complete Fire Tower Complex Sites* with a standing tower, the towerman's residence, artifact scatters, and a majority of the significant structures and other features originally present on the site (n = 2).

As can be seen above, some of these property types are far more common than others (e.g., *Fire Tower Archaeological Sites*); this can also factor into evaluations of site significance because highly redundant property types are less likely than more unique examples to yield significant data beyond that which can be obtained through basic site recordation—even if they retain a measure of integrity. By no means should it be inferred that such sites deserve to be discarded wholesale; to the contrary, even redundant sites or those appearing to lack significance for other reasons merit a reasonable degree of historical documentation, particularly if they're likely to be declared ineligible for the National Register and released from future management.

Determinations of Eligibility

Of the 90 fire tower sites known to a reasonable degree of certainty to have been constructed within the current boundaries of the Mark Twain, nine have previously been determined to be ineligible for listing on the National Register because they fail to meet any of the above Significance Criteria, lack sufficient integrity in their physical attributes to adequately convey significance, or both. All of these former tower locales are purely archaeological in nature (i.e., they retain no fire towers or other standing structures). This does not in and of itself disqualify them from listing on the National Register; however, a number also display signs of post-occupation ground disturbance (e.g., bulldozing or other forms of site preparation). As a consequence, it is highly likely that the archaeological components of these sites occupy disturbed contexts and thus their physical attributes (artifacts, structural remnants, and the associations between them) lack integrity. Accordingly, they were determined to be incapable of conveying meaningful information or significance beyond that obtainable through basic documentation.

The remaining 81 purported or confirmed tower sites vary considerably from each other with respect to form and condition; however, a number of them could be historically significant under as many as three of the four National Register Criteria, including Criteria A, for their association with the various New Deal programs, such as the CCC; with Criterion C, as being stylistically representative of the distinctive characteristics of the type, period, and/or method of construction used on the Forest during that period; or Criterion D, as being capable of yielding archaeological and/or historical information important in history (Elliot 2010:56-65).

Sixty-two of the 81 fire tower sites known to lie within the boundaries of the Mark Twain have not been investigated to a degree sufficient to allow for credible eligibility determinations, and are therefore being managed as National Register unevaluated properties. Sixty of these no longer have any existing towers or other structures, and correspond with the *Fire Tower Archaeological Site* type; they are comprised entirely of archaeological remnants of the towers and associated structures, such as tower footings, artifact scatters, and/or structure foundations. Two additional sites do have standing towers: one is consistent with the *Partial Fire Tower Complex Site* type; the other with the *Standing Fire Tower Site* type with no associated structures; neither of these properties has been formally evaluated with respect to their suitability for inclusion on the National Register.

Nineteen tower sites identified on the Mark Twain have previously been determined to be eligible for listing on the National Register of Historic Places, each of which still has standing lookouts. Eight of these sites can be characterized as *Standing Fire Tower Sites* that have only the tower standing; other associated structures (if originally present) have either been dismantled, been destroyed or have decayed with the passage of time, however archaeological evidence of such structures or other features of the landscape may be present. Nine additional sites are considered to be *Partial Fire Tower Complex Sites* with standing towers and at least some remaining contemporaneous structures and/or features, though they lack the towerman's dwelling. Lastly, two National Register eligible sites correspond with the *Complete Fire Tower Complex* site type and include standing fire towers with towerman's dwellings, garages and/or woodsheds, latrines, and possibly other period structures and features.

It should be noted that where lookout towers and/or associated infrastructure may have previously been removed, those actions were most likely taken well before the sites had attained 50 years of age. As a consequence, considerations relating to their historical significance would not have been required under existing preservation statutes prior to removal.

Multiple-Use Assets

In addition to a wide variety of natural and cultural resources, Mark Twain National Forest personnel are charged with responsibly managing roads, dams, and the Forest's inventory of standing structures, including fire lookout towers. Not only are the latter considered historic resources, fire towers being actively utilized in furtherance of any Forest management objective—fire-related or not—are also be considered to be "administrative facilities" (Amy Wilson, personal communication January 2019). The Mark Twain has mounted radio repeater antennae near the apices of several National Register eligible fire towers to help provide communications across the Forest; still other standing towers are being used by federal, private, state, and local government organizations under permit as similar platforms to facilitate "911" emergency services dispatch, rural bus route communications, and amateur radio operations. Thus, even in ways not directly related to their original purpose, these towers continue to benefit the public.

Although a handful of National Register eligible standing towers are not being put to current use, as existing Forest infrastructure, they nevertheless require inspection by qualified civil engineering specialists every five years to ensure they do not constitute a hazard to the public or to Forest employees. As a result, at a minimum Heritage Program staff are kept apprised of their condition. For the most part, all remain fundamentally sound, even if their cabs may have suffered by long exposure to the elements or their wooden stair treads have been affected by extended disuse and a corresponding lack of routine maintenance.

During the past decade, at least 11 eligible towers have been restored (or are in the process of being restored) to a safe operating condition in order to be used for fire detection once again. Not only have tower stairs been repaired and cab enclosures been made whole again, but where available the original Osborne Firefinders (alidades used by fire lookouts to plot fire locations) have been refurbished and are being employed in the use for which they were made more than three-quarters of a century ago. This revival is due in large part to the growing cost of aerial operations, but also to the seasonally irregular assignment of aircraft to the Forest and to an increase in the number of fire specialists available to staff the towers on an as-needed basis (Reggie Bray, personal communication January 2019).

Moving Forward

Lands comprising the Mark Twain National Forest have borne witness to a tremendous amount of history, the vast majority of which occurred prior to the Forest's organization in the 1930s. Countless generations of indigenous peoples lived among Missouri's wooded hills long before the state's boundaries were drawn. They were eventually displaced through federal designation of their former territories as public domain lands and a subsequent influx of Euro-American settlers seeking the promise of better lives for their own families and heirs.

Settlement of what would become National Forest System lands was definitively ended by National Forest development; however, the occurrence of historically significant events in the region did not end with formation of the Mark Twain. Roosevelt's New Deal programs helped restore a measure of vigor to areas withered by the Great Depression; enrollees of the Civilian Conservation Corps, the Emergency Relief

Administration, and their US Forest Service counterparts began the long process of stabilizing and restoring lands altered from their historical natural condition by indiscriminate deforestation, overgrazing, and uncontrolled burning—a restorative process that continues to this day.

The Mark Twain's fire tower sites are emblematic of these early- to mid-twentieth century federal conservation efforts in Missouri, and as such their preservation is deserving of thoughtful consideration even as competition for budgetary allocations becomes ever more intensive. Moving forward, the agency will need to focus its efforts where they can do the most good. This means making a reasonable and good faith effort to strike a balance between preserving those resources most capable of conveying their historical significance while wringing what data can be drawn from less promising sites before releasing them from future management.

While opportunities for public/private partnerships in tower preservation may exist, durable, legally-binding commitments can be challenging to secure and administer. However, a very good case for long-term federal preservation can be made on behalf of those towers that can be economically rehabilitated, maintained, and employed where they stand for their original purpose, and possibly in other ways not directly related to fire suppression—or as "multiple-use assets." With respect to the Mark Twain National Forest's fire towers and associated structures, ongoing use that benefits the Forest, as well as the people of the United States, is perhaps the best chance such properties have to survive into the future.

Travelogue

Over the course of decades, my wife and I have covered many of the highways and byways of Missouri as we documented standing towers, historic sites, mysteries, etc.. There were often interesting and curious side stories that emerged. On the following pages, I hope to share some of those. At times it will just be a good tower picture and at times the unexpected.

Asher Lookout – Asher Lookout was located about halfway between St. James and Salem just off Rt. 68. It started out as a wooden tower that was replaced by a "windmill" tower which was possible moved from Buck Mountain. The location today is on private ground. Below are two pictures of the tower. It was taken down on 10/11/1984. Pictured are Gene "Geno" Farrow, Jim Parker, Max Dunn, and Justin E. "Mac" McMillen who removed the tower.

Avon Lookout – Avon was a single pole lookout located @ 3 miles SW of Avon on Bidwell Creek Road. Vivert Moran had placed the lookout on a map he sent to Conservationist Jim Lyon. Bruce Barron had contacted me to get a hold of his father-in-law, Lindell Tucker who is retired from the M.D.C. Lindell confirmed the Avon story. In April of 2017, my wife and I stopped by the site. There was an elderly couple in their yard a few miles from the site, and I stopped to touch bases. I might add I have never stopped to ask a question about a search we were on that somebody was not willing to help. The Missouri hills are full of friendly people! We were told just where to turn but were cautioned a logging road had been cut through and although some cable and guy wire footings had been there at one time, they might be gone. We took this shot of a suspicious mound of this and that but could find no remaining evidence. The view down the road cut was wonderful, however.

Baldridge – The Baldridge site is located NW of Roby. Local Historian Terry Primas says Bald Ridge refers to Baldridge Creek named after John Baldridge , a 19th-century rafter and lumberman. There is a Baldridge Creek and was a Baldridge School at one time. Here are the 50-foot tower footings we took pictures of several years ago.

Beaufort – Although we never traveled to Beaufort, Google Tower Map creator Chris Polka did which started a search for the owner of the footings. Zach Gillihan turned out to be the owner of the site now and sent some pictures of the footings. The Washington Missourian paper announced the opening of the tower in an 11/24/1955 issue. It named Virgil Fritz of Spring Bluff as the tower man and located the tower 3 miles SW of Beaufort on EE.

Beaver Lookout – The Beaver Lookout was located out west of Poplar Bluff. We were not able to locate the footings. At times you can see them 100 yards away and at times you trip over them in the brush. I suspect we were a little off in regard to the area we were searching. We did find a very nice Geodetic Marker and what appears to be an open area used for "deer camp." I recall what a nice fall day it was and the large number of "whispering pines" that surrounded the area. We had to come in the back way. Seems a road straight up was used at one time. The Beaver cab sits in a pasture south of Poplar Bluff.

Big Springs Lookout – Located SW of Van Buren, it is @ a 1.5-mile walk in, and 1.5 miles out if the gate is closed. We were there on a beautiful fall day and enjoyed the walk. The tower was closed.

Black Lookout – The Black Lookout was located NW of Centerville. It seems the Black Tower was moved to what is now the Oates site a few miles west. My GPS shows the Black and Oates sites at the same location. We were never able to locate the original Black footings, but Chris Polka located several concrete items at the latitude and longitude where Black was listed.

Update – Darrell Smith confirmed the Black Tower was moved to make the Oates site literally as I sent this to press.

Blue Buck Lookout – Blue Buck is located out west of Willow Springs. The tower is closed, but the view out through the power line cut was very scenic. I have a long history of the animals at the towers taking a dim view of my documenting and as you can see the buzzards at Blue Buck did not roll out the welcome mat!

Blue Slip Lookout – Located to the west of Norwood, Blue Slip is a very enjoyable tower stop. As you can see, a freight train rolled through as I was enjoying the view providing a seldom seen perspective.

Branch Lookout/Virgil Swanigan

The original Branch Tower (wooden) was put up in the mid '40s when the site was acquired. In the mid '50s, that tower was replaced by a steel lookout.

I received the following email note from Janet Shannon –

My father, Virgil Swanigan manned the Branch Fire Tower from 1963 to 1975. We rented the house there which was a nice little house for a young married couple with small children. He spent a lot of time up in the tower during fire season. Occasionally, he would let us go along on a call to investigate a fire as long as we stayed in the truck. The tower was the center of our lives, and it attracted tourists during the summer. Our Dad used every opportunity to talk about fire safety and even had a cool trailer with a giant automated Smokey Bear for a few summers. It was lots of fun for the kids. He handed out many posters, Smokey comic books and coloring books. The community looked up to him as their helper and protector against fires. He was their first responder. Dad passed away in 1994.

Brandsville Lookout - The Vultures from Blue Buck must have phoned ahead as the flock at Brandsville was waiting for me!

Braswell Lookout - NE of Alton was found to be very overgrown. You could actually see it easier from a distance than you could from the road up close.

Breeze Lookout – The Breeze Lookout is located out west of Poplar Bluff. A Mr. Taylor, who worked the tower, told me the foundations were never used due to the war.

Briar Lookout – Briar is located near the community of Briar. The tower is fenced and the road gated but it is just a short walk.

Brushy Lookout – Brushy was a 50-foot secondary tower. It was listed in Wayne County. A fellow NW of Ellsinore told me it was out east of Twin Ponds and we looked several times with no luck. I even wrote about it in the Wayne County paper. On one trip through Ellsinore, I asked outside the post office and was sent to a house and then to the quilting circle at the community center. Viola Crites, in particular, remembered the Brushy Lookout, and again it was east of Twin Ponds. The road going east from Twin Ponds plays out just into Wayne County, and since the list has it in Wayne County, we looked there – again no luck. It was then that I received a call from Owen Brown, who had read my article, to call Richard Brown who could answer my question. It seems Richard had hunted the area and had even stood on the old footings while there. He told me right where to look, offered to even ride with me up there, and has answered many questions since. We again made the drive up to Twin Ponds and surprise – the tower area was mowed and even had ribbons tied to the trees! Our Brushy Creek Lookout search had come to an end. It had been so much fun we were almost sad. It turns out Viola's son-in-law, Michael Pomeroy knew exactly where the lookout had been located and made it very easy for me to find. Viola called later and told me this. It turns out the Brushy Creek Lookout was not in Wayne County, but the site is a few hundred yards into Carter County. We were looking in the wrong place and had passed the footings several times, hidden in the brush. I could mark Brushy off and thanks to all my "helpers!"

Buick Lookout – You will notice when we were there on 11/11/2010, the fire danger was high, the tower was being used, and the windows open.

Bunker Lookout – The Bunker Lookout was located south of Bunker. A single pole lookout preceded it. How the tower was removed and where it went to was discussed in the "On the Move" Chapter. A geodetic marker is set in one of the footings.

Cabool Lookout – This tower is located north of Cabool. A tower friend of mine had climbed the tower and was checking out the view when several motorcycles roared up and began checking out the parking lot. He made his way down to converse with a group of leather and tattoo riders. One asked, "what is that?" He explained the lookout principle and urged them to climb for a view. One of them remarked, "No way man that looks dangerous ---------." Here is a view from Cabool.

Camdenton Lookout – The lookout at Camdenton has been modified to make it very safe for climbing. If you don't like heights, it would be a good place to get the tower experience. My wife and grand-daughter are shown resting at the tower.

Caney II Lookout – Was moved from Caney I for whatever reason – built originally in the wrong place or a better location? Located on the beautiful Glade Top Trail .

Cascade Lookout - This tower was moved from the Gipsy Site to replace an "oil derrick type."

Center Lookout – This site is located east of the Little Shoal Creek. Also called Shoal Creek Tower?.

Coot Mountain Lookout – On our first trip we thought we were lucky, the gate was open. This was until we encountered the large hornet ball under the first landing!

Corn Creek Lookout – This site is located NE of Flat near – Corn Creek.

Cottoner (or Cottener) Lookout – As discussed earlier in the book, a site of several towers and stories. Here is a drone shot from last year.

Czar Lookout - Located near the community of Czar. On my top ten list of impressive tower pictures.

Deer Run Lookout – Deer Run was one of the first towers I ever visited. It also was the first steel tower built in Missouri. However, on our first visit, we barely got out of the car. The top of the tower was engulfed in what looked like smoke but was actually the largest swarm of hornets I have ever seen. The picture below was taken just last fall.

Doniphan Lookout – Doniphan site is another place to get a great shot of an LS-40 Aermotor Tower. As noted in the "towers moved" chapter, the tower was knocked down by a tornado and put back up.

Flatwood(s) Lookout – I always wondered about the (s). When we stopped by the site, I began to understand. We found not one but two sets of footings. One set was small and the other large. Maybe a smaller tower replaced by a larger? There is no certain answer I could find.

Freeburg Lookout – Chris Polka's/Google Map journey began here.

The Gipsy Tower was located just south of Gipsy. Even though the tower is not there anymore, it is still standing. The tower was moved to Cascade. The tower at Cascade was one of the "oil derrick" styles that required a climb up a steel ladder and as a result were never very popular. The Gipsy site was very interesting as the walk up was surrounded by whispering pines, and the site itself was on an open area atop the rise. There were a number of concrete foundations nearby as the site was a primary tower at one time with living quarters and other buildings. There is also a very nice geodetic marker that was very easy to locate.

High (Hill) Lookout – It seems the official name is High Hill but most call it High it seems. Following an article I wrote on the tower in the Eminence Current Wave I received a call from Marguerite (Scoville) Barkley who had grown up at the site when her Dad, John Scoville was the tower man. That conversation led me to Shari Wolford whose Dad, Everett Chaney had also worked the tower, and she was raised there. You will enjoy the "Bucksnort Foodstand" connection as well as the submissions from Bill and Shari.

Himont Lookout – Located in the Roger Pryor Backcountry south of Bunker, the site now serves as the trailhead for several trails in the area. As you can see, the footings have been turned into seats around a fire pit. It was a beautiful fall day the day we stopped by.

Horton Lookout – No picture here but a story on the trail that has to be traveled "by phone" on occasion to nail down a location. Rob Miley first gave me an area for Horton out west of Willow Springs. With that, I called Bob Cunningham, an expert in the area. He told me to call James Murrell as he would know. He did. Horton was a timber town located a few miles north of Siloam Springs. It seems no town still exists, but there is a Horton Cemetery. I had not noticed that in any of my topography map scans. He said to go back east from the old town site to Rt. AP and the footings were on the NW of the crossroads. He had even come across them while working a fire once. I checked my geodetic marker map, and there is a marker there. It is however labeled "West" and not Horton although once you read the description, it does mention a tower there.

Hunter Lookout – The Hunter site is located north of Hunter. The gate is usually closed some distance below. The story goes that on one occasion the tower man at Hunter heard a noise outside. He lifted the trap door to find a goat standing there looking at him. Well, goats do like to climb!

Indian Trail – Indian Trail is located north of Salem and has an "animal on the climb" story of its own. We have been to Indian trail many times, but this was the first trip years ago. Much like the tower man at Hunter Tower, I heard a sound. This was as I was climbing the tower. I turned around to take a picture of a dog who lived at the house there I assumed and had learned how to climb. I assumed he would stop at some point, but he was up for the full experience. When we made our way down, I stopped and rubbed his ears for a few minutes leaving this as one of my fondest memories. I assume he is gone now but not forgotten!

Knob Lick Lookout (Glen Skinner Memorial) – It was the day after Thanksgiving in 2009, and we decided to enjoy the nice day and head out on a tower tour. One of our stops was the Knob Lick Tower north of Fredericktown. We had been there before and noticed the Glen (Glenn also at times) Skinner sign on the tower. As we walked back to the parking lot, we began talking to a fellow who turned out to be Glen's son Jack. It seems the 28th is the anniversary of his Dad's birthday. We talked for a while, exchanged email addresses, and have communicated now and then since. We were able to make a new tower friend, and Jack is contributing a piece on his Dad in the submission section.

Lone Hill – You will actually find two Lone Hill sites in Missouri. One is located SW of Poplar Bluff and is on private land. We have tried to get access, no luck. The other is a historic site at Meramec Park south of Sullivan. If you park at the foot of Lone Hill (also called Love Hill), it is a nice walk up to the site. Jim Ruble has a piece on his Dad, Avery in the submissions and there is a bridal trail there also named in his honor.

Lost Creek – Lost Creek is located SE of Greenville above – Lost Creek. In addition to the footings, there are foundations for several other buildings that once stood there.

Montauk Lookout – The Montauk Lookout is located north of the beautiful Montauk State Park.

Mud Lick Lookout – This is the first tower I climbed, at least part of the way, over half a century ago. My Grandparents (Roy & Ella Kinnison) lived south of Patterson on Rings Creek and trips to Sam A. Baker were a part of the summer season. Mudlick Tower stands on Mudlick Mountain, once known as Tip Top according to some topography maps. The tower is no longer open for climbing.

New Liberty Lookout – The New Liberty Lookout was located right by Rt. 19 to the west end of the New Liberty C.C.C. Camp. I had actually misplaced the site on the Google Map Project. I give my thanks to Steve Orchard for this picture of the site which we visited recently. We also took in Falling Springs nearby. Remains of the C.C.C. Camp can be found scattered in the woods.

Oates Lookout – This site is a bit confusing. It seems there was a Black Tower (named after the community) and an Oates Tower (named after the community). It also seems the Black was moved to Oates, at least that is what the paperwork says. My GPS unit has some tower sites noted, presumably because they are on the topography map the unit is based on. In this case, the Black and Oates are indicated by symbols right by each other. This has to be the Oates site because a state GPS marker labeled "Oates" is to be found there. Although Black and Oates show on some topography maps, they would have been only a mile and a half apart. My wife and I have traveled to the sites as has tower expert Chris Polka. Tower documenter Ron Kemnow has studied the question. It remains a question mark. Sites are NW of Centerville on the "Karkagne Drive." (See Black Tower)

Update – Darrell Smith confirmed Black was moved to Oates. He climbed the same tower, in two places!

Panther Hill Lookout – This site was originally a wooden tower (wooden tower chapter) and is now a steel tower. The tower was moved from Eminence when a tower at that site was no longer needed. We have visited the site several times. It is a stately tower to photograph and offers a view of Missouri lost in a sea of trees. Hardly any man-made structure is visible. You can see, with field glasses, the Proffit Mountain Reservoir at Taum Sauk located @ 18 miles away. This is also the area where the Tri-State Tornado of 1925 either began or certainly turned deadly. As tornados are also a hobby of mine, it is hard to imagine as you stand atop Panther Hill a tornado starting there and traveling over 200 miles before ending in Indiana. Panther Hill is also the location for several "Jessie James & Gang camped here" local legends.

Perry Lookout – The Perry Lookout is located SW of Perryville. Lawrence Buchheit, who worked the tower for decades and is the subject of an article in the "submissions" chapter, gave me a tour of the tower. Here you see Lawrence scanning the horizon.

Possum Trot Lookout – Possum Trot Tower was located south of Winona on Rt. 19. I suspected from the paperwork that a small 50-foot tower had preceded a larger 100 footer. However, when my wife and I visited the site, I was surprised by what we found. As you can see in the picture, there are four small 50 foot footings located concentrically inside four larger 100-foot footings. I have never seen this before or since. I remained puzzled until John Timmermann shared the second photo below with me. If you look close, you can see a small 50-foot tower standing inside a 100 footer. There are only speculations as to why this might have been done.

Proctor Lookout - The Proctor Tower is the Swedeborg Tower moved. It is a very interesting site with the footings for the wood tower that preceded the steel tower still there. The picture I took is one of my favorites. It almost looks like a painting.

Roby Lookout – The Roby site is located just north of Roby. We had driven by the site many times, and the gate was always closed, so all I had was a distance shot. Last fall when we drove by the gate was open, so we pulled in. It seems with the very dry weather and deer season open they were on standby just in case. I was fortunate to be able to talk with the group about the site and other questions. One fellow, Greg Painter, had a real tower interest and he has been able by email to answer some of my questions and provide some information. I was aware the tower there originally had a steel ladder up to the cab but was converted to a diagonal design. That was not uncommon as the steel ladder was very unpopular. My thanks to all there for the question and answer session.

Rolla Lookout – I stopped by the Rolla Office a few years ago to ask some questions. I found the staff there to be very friendly. They had a picture on the wall of the tower that stood there at one time and one fellow, Doug Gall made a copy for me. It turns out he had lots of tower experience, and he was able to answer many of my questions then and by email. It was Doug who connected me with Jim Parker who is always ready to "tower talk." Jim would provide me with several Rolla pictures, but I will use the one from the wall at Rolla as a remembrance as unfortunately, Doug passed away suddenly. My thanks to him for all the help he provided. I miss the "tower talk."

Rosati Lookout – The Rosati Tower is an unusual design as the bottom is the old water tower from Steelville. The tower is located on "Knobview," and in fact, the town of Rosati was known as Knobview at one time. Some papers list a Knobview Tower, but many believe this is just another name for the Rosati Tower. I exchanged several emails with Steve Zulpo who grew I up in the area. He mentioned the Chestnut trees that grew there at one time. It seems the Conservation Commission shipped seedlings out from there. There were also efforts there to address the blight that devastated Chestnut trees in this country.

Seymour Lookout – The road to Seymour turned out to be as interesting as any. It all started when I was told the Bunker Tower had been moved to Seymour. I called the Webster County Courthouse, and they connected me with the Historical Society and Helen Lamb. Now, Helen had always been interested in the Seymour Tower and had memories of it when up. Her granddaughter had married a nephew of Vonnie Johnson who had worked the tower along with other duties. Helen was able to stir me up some pictures of Vonnie and the tower. She also got me a phone number for Richard Stirts. Richard, having worked for the M.D.C., was very helpful with answers and had some pictures to share also.

I was "tower talking" with Jim Sorenson some time ago. Jim was head of the Lebanon District at one time. He shared a picture with me, and there Vonnie popped again. Jim described Vonnie as a good employee that you could give a job to, and it would be done right. Vonnie also operated a "Dozer" that was used to fight fires, and his picture could be found there also.

Now, Seymour comes up now and then when a discussion of the highest cab in Missouri is in the table. Taum Sauk is the highest point in the state. If you put a lookout there it must be the highest cab that ever existed in Missouri, right? Well, not so fast. The tower at Taum Sauk is only 72 feet high, so if you take the height at the base of 1,759 feet and add a 72-foot tower, you get 1,831 feet. But the base at Seymour was 1,740 feet, and if you add a 100-foot tower, you get 1,840.

Travelogue

We visited the Seymour site a few years ago and documented the footings and geodetic markers. Left you can see a picture of the Seymour Tower when up.

Shannondale Lookout – Shannondale will always be on my top ten list. It was a view of the tower from the Current that first caught my "tower attention." It was the first tower I climbed all the way. I have stopped by the site more than any other. Although fenced now we still always stop by hoping to get lucky. I crossed tower paths with Max Gorman several years ago. Max and his wife Trudy lived at the tower for years. Max was able to show me various things, like the footings for the wooden tower that preceded the steel. Max shared a drawing of the tower that in the front of this book. Next Page I have a picture of Shannondale taken many years ago. In fact, it goes all the way back to the film days taken with an "old school" camera and zoom lens. You may notice the canoes on the river. They were slapping their oars on the water and provided a good science lesson that light travels faster than sound. You could see the slap and then hear the sound a few seconds later (below).

Squires Lookout – This tower is located right at Squires. Jim Parker noted Squires was one of the towers where the footings were a little off. That meant some loosening and adjustments as the tower went up to make it work.

Stegall Mountain – We have stopped by this tower several times. Every stop has been eventful. In May of 2009 we stopped by, but the effects of the recent derecho made the road up impassable. We were by again and on August 8, 2011, we received the thrill of a lifetime when a mountain lion ran right in front of our car at Peck Ranch. Think you can outrun one? Think again, it was a blur. If you want to get a picture, better have your camera up and ready to go! We had stopped to watch some wild turkeys and may have spoiled the lion's lunch? Then on October 11, 2012, we finally made it up for some pictures. There was a wooden tower there at one time. The area is very rocky and an attraction of its own.

Sun Ridge Lookout – This tower is located south of St. Louis at the Jefferson County/Sun Ridge Park.

Taum Sauk Lookout – The cab height was discussed in the Seymour section. The style is more like that out west, shorter and with living quarters. I mentioned with Panther Hill you can see the water storage for a power plant on Proffit Mountain to the north. From Taum Sauk you can see the same to the south.

Thomasville (MDC) Lookout – The tower is actually located a good nine miles as the crow flies NW of Thomasville. There was also a Thomasville (US) lookout NE of Thomasville located high in a Maple Tree. Pictured is the MDC tower.

Twin Knobs Lookout – This tower is located SE of Vanzant. We enjoyed the tower visit and a chat with a kid from the area who was out walking her beagle. I have always felt the Twin Knobs Tower was one of the more impressive shots of a tower from a distance. It is leased from the U.S.F.S. by the M.D.C.

Runge Conservation Center – The lower part of the Rocky Mount Tower was moved here and made very safe for public education. An Osborne Fire Finder is also on display. As you can see in the picture, my Grand-Daughter quickly went to work scanning the horizon for smoke. If you don't like heights, and many don't, this is the place to taste what the tower workers experienced under very safe conditions.

Firetowers

Now, the preceding lookouts have been those that stuck in my mind for some reason or happenstance. The following pages of our Travelogue will contain pictures of the other impressive lookouts we have visited. It has been quite a journey filled with towering sights, history, and interesting people!

Can you identify the tower types? (I noted this earlier)

Eastwood Lookout

Fairview Lookout

Flat Rock Lookout

Fort Leonard Wood Lookout

Fremont Lookout

French Village Footings

Firetowers

Garwood Lookout

Grandin Lookout

Grassy Footings

Hartshorn Lookout

Hercules Lookout

Higdon Footings

Highway 60 Footings

Houston Lookout

Julian Footings

Keysville Lookout

Knotwell Footings

Leasburg Lookout

Travelogue

Lenox Lookout

Lynchburg Footings

Marcoot Lookout at Sunset

Mountain View Lookout

Oak Lookout

Pilot Knob View

Piney Footings

Plad Lookout

Rockwoods Footings

Rosehill Lookout

Siloam Springs Footings

Sinking Creek Lookout

Sterling Footings

Summersville Lookout

Tecumseh Lookout

Texas Footings

Tram Footings

Vada Footings

Vichy Lookout

Vulcan Lookout

Washington Park Footings

West Plains Lookout

Westover Footings

Whitewater/Womack Footings

Gone, But Not (here) Forgotten

I used several pictures in the book already of towers no longer standing: Rolla, Baldy, Asher, etc. I also have several pictures of historical towers to offer. Most of these have a credit source at the end of the book, a couple are just out there. A few of these still stand such as Eminence to Panther Hill, Gipsy to Cascade, French Village and Grassy to private, and Washington Park to Keysville I have been told.

The Warrenton Tower shown being "sky craned" to the gunnery range at Fort Leonard Wood and the Ulman Tower being taken down by regular crane.

Beaufort Lookout Tower *Gulf Lookout Tower*

The Washington State Park Tower (moved to Keysville?) and Washington II which was removed just a few years ago (2012).

Powell Lookout Tower *Eminence Lookout Tower*

Stono Mountain Lookout Tower

French Village Lookout Tower

Rockwoods Lookout Tower

Meta Lookout Tower

Firetowers

Grassy Lookout Tower

Gipsy Lookout Tower

Jenkins Lookout Tower

Wharton Lookout Tower

Ellsinore Forest Lookout Tower

Information by Barbara Kingen Alcorn

After writing a piece on the towers of Carter County in the Current Local paper, I received a call from Barbara Alcorn. She said it was her Uncle, Waldo Kingen, who worked the tower in the late '30s and early '40s. He left the tower when drafted into the Army at the beginning of W.W. II.

The C.C.C. camp there, #1738, was built in 1934 and tore down in 1946 she noted. The lookout tower was erected in 1937 and closed around 1975.

She said the tower left lots of memories for lots of them. The park-like setting around the tower provided a place where school groups, church groups and family groups gathered for years for meetings, get-togethers and reunions. Other important occasions such as marriage proposals also occurred. Eugene Oakley noted to Barbara he proposed to his wife of many years, Judy at the tower.

Barbara also spoke with her cousin about a tower that stood on the Butler-Carter County line – the Breeze Tower. I talked about the Breeze Lookout Tower earlier in the book. Her cousin spoke with Bob Taylor's wife about the Breeze Lookout Tower. Bob had worked on the Breeze Lookout Tower.

A view of CC Company #1738 at Ellsinore. They built the farm-to-market roads, the telephone line to Williamsville, and the forestry tower. They also surveyed land and timber, and did fish counts. The camp was torn down in 1946.

Ellsinore Forest Lookout Tower and tower worker Waldo Kingen with Lou Ellen (his 12-year-old sister) and Barbara (the contributor here/his 6-year-old niece). Below is Barbara's 12-year-old sister, Donna Kingen Knodell (Waldo's niece) and Waldo who joined the Army and went to England in 1942. In between is a drone shot of the grown-up area today.

The Evolution of the Fire Tower in the Missouri Ozarks
A Look at Then and Now

By Steve Orchard

Forest resources have changed tremendously since Missouri's first permanent fire tower was erected at Deer Run Park in 1926. Typical of towers of the day, Deer Run was set to protect the State's 6,625-acre Deer Run Park from the uncontrolled wildfire that ravaged the Ozarks at such frequency that tree growth and quality was limited to hardwood sprouts and a few scattered fires-scarred trees of no commercial value. Deer Run Park was the state's first refuge where forest protection was needed to restock the state's depleted whitetail deer herd, as well as to serve as a model of forest protection.

The Ozark's Forest had been under the same intense fire regime since eastern Native Americans began moving westward across the state and continued as European Settlers began filtering in after Missouri became a state in 1821. Fire-tolerant shortleaf pine was notoriously present in the Ozarks most likely due to large pine tree survivability in fire, and attrition by fire in other species. The human population was relatively low, so forest and related resources were not being used much beyond subsistence farming on a small scale during this era. The land's carrying capacity was not exceeded, and use was occurring intermittently and in small patchwork homesteads. A milk cow, hogs, and goats were common and permitted to roam across the forest foraging off the land where burning created openings and increased plants.

Around 1880 the forest underwent one of many large-scale changes as outside interests from Pennsylvania, and other locations discovered Missouri Pine, and as markets opened for pine lumber to build new towns in the treeless plains such as Kansas. Between 1880 and 1930 most of the commercial size pine was removed from the core of the Missouri Ozarks. Forest resources were heavily exploited during this era as pine lumber, and oak railroad ties were sawmilled and shipped elsewhere. With the sawmills came many new people who were accustomed to a steady income from the manufacturing industry. After the mills left many of these people stayed and attempted an agrarian living. With so many people living across the landscape, forest and wildlife were depleted and the land's carrying capacity was far outstripped by human use.

The 1920s and 1930s ushered in forest protection as the U.S. Forest Service, and the State of Missouri purchased tracts of undesirable cut and burned over forests with a vision for protection and restoration of plants and animals living there. During this era, the main threats were uncontrolled wildfire, and overuse of resources from open range livestock grazing. The first line of defense was the fire tower where workers could be stationed to watch over the surrounding area and catch and suppress fires while they were relatively small. Prior to World War 2 and during the Great Depression, the Civilian Conservation Corps played a huge part in the restoration of our forest.

Fire towers and suppression efforts appeared futile for a time, as forest managers literally watched their protection and restoration work go up in smoke during dry periods each spring and fall. However noticeable headway was being made. Deer and turkey were making a comeback in refuges, and 323 whitetails were shipped out of Deer Run Park alone. Float fishing became popular, and a testament to good water quality and erosion stabilization, and trees began growing into commercial sizes again and free of fire scars. Fire towers no doubt provided the early fire detection and suppression needed to keep refuges viable, and to make inroads of positive public sentiment for the benefits of forest protection.

Fire towers and their small coverage area soon made a transition as fire districts, the telephone, and two-way radio became available to protect larger areas known as protection areas. Many towers including the Deer Run Tower were moved to watch over more centrally located and larger areas than just a refuge. The Smokey Bear Campaign began in the 1940s and continues today as an aid in spreading the fire prevention message. As fire towers remained an important part of the firefighting arsenal, changes to the forest continued. One of the most radical of changes was the closing of open range in the late 1960s. Now local farmers were required to contain their own livestock, and keep fences up to prevent livestock damage and associated burning on the property of others. With the new law for maintaining a closed range, woods value increased tremendously since the law was conducive to management without destructive fire and grazing practices of the past.

Fire tower use slowed by the 1990s, and aircraft detection had been part of the reason as it allowed forest workers more time to getting management work done and less time lost while manning towers during dry periods. The efforts of fire prevention, the advent of the cell phone, and highly trained and equipped rural fire departments were making a huge impact on the fire situation. Today even the most remote areas often have rapid fire department response to catch and suppress most fires while relatively small. Forest managers continue to retain wildfire suppression skills and credentials as they focus on management work in the restored forest resource that those now lonely towers made possible by keeping fires out and protected.

Today fire towers are far fewer in number than they once were. Victims of technology, efficiency, leaner budgets, vandalism, and a changing society where the forest is used much differently. Forest managers now focus on tending woods that often have three times the board foot volume than the forest had during the period around 1900. The forest was restored, and it thrives today, ironically controlled fire is used in some areas as part of forest ecosystem management. Fire calls are generally reported via cell phone, and fire department response is usually rapid. Towers are used when convenient to provide a quick reference for fire locations by area staff who know the area, but only the worst fire days see the required tower staffing and dispatch support in numbers to get that important 3-way cross from fire finders and a dispatch map.

In the foreseeable future, it is anticipated that fire towers will continue to dwindle in numbers and in use. Some will undoubtedly remain as artifacts of forest history from the era after the big cut through the forest regrowth. Fire tower history is a great way to document these steel and wood giants that have stood sentinel over the Ozarks for nearly 100 years.

Footnote:

Steve Orchard is a Forester with the Missouri Department of Conservation and is currently the Area Manager of the 29,000-acre Current River Conservation Area and home of Deer Run Tower, Missouri's first permanent fire tower. The original tower cabin still stands on the site, and the Deer Run Tower was moved to its present location in 1935. Steve's career with the MDC began in 1991 as the Hartshorn Towerman near Summersville, Mo., and was later assigned to the Hunter and Stegall Towers in Carter County. Steve recalls having the task of roof painting, and window repairs to most towers on the Eminence District including Coot Mountain, Stegall, Hunter, Thomasville, Flatrock, Hartshorn, and Shannondale Towers.

Steve grew up near Eminence Missouri, in view of the Eminence Fire Tower, and very close to the Missouri Lumber and Mining Company's mill site where pine logs and lumber were processed during the Big Cut after 1909.

Picture Credits

Note: Pictures are my Personal Private Collection or Public Domain except as noted below

Angel, Gerald – Deer Run wooden tower

Beasley, Verlin and Faye – two pictures of the Earnest E. Beasley White Oak Lookout Tower

Botkin, Dewayne – The "Botkin/Jay" Tower

Courtesy Glen Kennedy - Electronic File # P1080 Digital Collection/Mark Twain National Forest Supervisors Office- Rolla, Missouri / The Ancient and Honorable Order of Squirrels Certificate

Ellsinore Lookout Tower- Barbara (Kingen) Alcorn

Gall, Doug – The Rolla Tower

Gillihan, Zach – Beaufort footings

Goodman, Damian – The drone shot section

Joplin Globe – Goodman Wood/Goodman Steel Tower

Lamb, Helen – Seymour Tower

Long, Frances (Christopher) – Kelleter Tower section

Lutes, Andrew-French Village, Stono, Gipsy, and Grassy Lookout Towers

Lyon, Jim – Backfiring (glossary & dozers), backpack pump, blower, dispatch map and five items, Meta Lookout Tower

Missouri Department of Conservation – the clear cut hillside, "free range" picture #1, Hawthorne Bloom, MDC Triangle, Black Locust ravine, wooden tower going up, three canoeing book/tower symbol diagrams

Mountain View double towers – Charley & Carol Santhuff

Orchard, Steve – New Liberty Tower footings

Parker, Jim – Asher Tower, Asher Tower coming down, climbing Rolla Tower

Pioneer Forest Section – The Pioneer Forest

Polka, Chris – Black Tower footings, Mudlick Tower, Washington II Lookout Tower

Ruble, Jim – Vulcan Tower section

Sorenson, Jim – Blue Slip and Marshfield Tower builds, fire finder and dispatch map section

The State Historical Society of Missouri, Photograph Collection – Baldy Lookout 16/09 947A & Baldy Lookout Joe Donley 16/10 948A Macedonia Tower 19/03 1236A Neosho Wooden Tower R1000 Lynn Morrow collection, box 17 & file 855 Tower top/Deer stand R1000 Lynn Morrow collection, Box17, folder 858

Stirts, Richard – Seymour Tower removal

Tatum, Charles – Doniphan Tower tornado damage, Les Carson safety test, Panther Hill wooden tower

Timmermann, John – Several Aermotor and IDM tags, double Possum Trot towers

Topog and Map shots – Taken from old maps I have.

USDA Forest Service Mark Twain National Forest (on file at the Supervisor's Office, 401 Fairgrounds Road, Rolla, Missouri 65401) – Beamer Handle Company, CCC toolbox and workers, Chess and Waymond Stave Company, "free range" picture #2, increment borer, tie capital of the world, tree lookout.

Bibliography/References Cited

Clark National Forest Map (1936)

Crowell, Ralph E. (1953) . History of the Mark Twain National Forest/Unpublished Manuscript

Hoffman, Mike . Fire Towers and Wildlife in Missouri – A Brief History

Jefferson City Post-Tribune (1972)

Keefe, James F. (1987) . Missouri Department of Conservation / The First 50 Years

Kelleter Paul D. (1936) . Clark National Forest Purchase Unit, Missouri.

Koenig, Frank (1984) . Pages From the Past/History of the Winona Ranger District

KWTO (1936-37) . Radio Interviews with Gardner National Forest.

Lawter, William Clifford Jr. (1994) Smokey Bear 20252 A Biography

Malouf, Richard (1991) . Thematic Evaluation of Administration and Fire Tower Sites of the Mark Twain National Forest, Missouri

Price, Jay (1940) . R-9 Facts & Figures. Milwaukee: USDA Forest Service, North Central Region.

Rose, Margaret (1990) . Fire Towers: A Vanishing Monument. The Ozarks Mountaineer 20-21.

Steyermark, Julian (1959) . Vegetational History of the Ozark Forest, The University of Missouri Studies, No. 31.

Turner, Chapman (1938) . Rebirth in the Missouri Forest. The Kansas City Star 8/14/1938.

The First Eden, The Mediterranean World and Man (1987) . B.B.C. Documentary

James Halpern Tower Piece References

Conrad, David E.

1997 The Land We Cared For: A History of the Forest Service's Eastern Region. Jay H. Cravens, Editor. United States Department of Agriculture, US Forest Service, Region 9. Milwaukee, Wisconsin.

Crowell, R. E.

1953   Mark Twain History: 1940-1952 Statistics. United States Department of Agriculture, US Forest Service, Springfield, Missouri. October 1953.

Elliot, Michael L.

2010   Draft National Register of Historic Places Multiple Property Documentation Form for Fire Lookouts, Towers, and Associated Structures on the Mark Twain National Forest, Southern Missouri. USDA-Forest Service, Mountain Heritage Associates. March 2010.

Halpern, James A.

2012   A General History of the Mark Twain National Forest. Unpublished paper on file with the Mark Twain National Forest, Rolla. Missouri.

Malouf, Richard T.

1989   The Civilian Conservation Corps and the Mark Twain National Forest: A Preliminary Compilation. Unpublished manuscript on file at the Ava Ranger Station, Ava, Missouri.

McConnell, H. P.

1963   Historical Summary of Land Adjustment and Classification, Mark Twain National Forest, 1933-1962. Mark Twain National Forest, Rolla, Missouri.

US Forest Service

1940   Report of Forest Conditions in Missouri. United States Department of Agriculture, US Forest Service. Prepared for the Joint Congressional Committee on Forestry. Mark Twain National Forest, Rolla, Missouri.

1961   The National Forest Reservation Commission: A Report on Progress In Establishing National Forests. United States Department of Agriculture, US Forest Service. September 1961.

1985   1985 Forest Fact Sheet. United States Department of Agriculture, US Forest Service. Mark Twain National Forest, Rolla, Missouri.

Williams, Ed

1983   The Mark Twain National Forest Salutes the Civilian Conservation Corps. *In* Sho-Me Smoke Signal, Mark Twain National Forest. United States Department of Agriculture, US Forest Service, Rolla, Missouri. August 1983. Pp. 1-7.

Index

A

Abney, Minuard-145
Aermotor-xii, 84, 89, 90, 177, 200
A-Frame-xii, 33
Aley, Tom-113
Alidades-105
Alphabet Agencies-10
Amendment 4-7
Ancient & Honorable Order of the Squirrels-13
Arcadia Valley-146
Ad Council-15
Ash, Jack-27
Asher Lookout-29, 64, 124, 182
Attenborough, Sir David-Title Page
August A. Busch Lookout-64, 162
Avon Lookout-29, 137, 183
Azimuth Line-106

B

Back Fire-xii, 60, 158
Back Pack Pump-xiii, 60
Bald Knob Cross-67
Baldridge Lookout-29, 184
Banner Community-116
Barkley, Marguerite Scoville-112, 203
Barren Fork-127
Barrett, Joyce-113
Battle of Lapanto-4
Beamer Handle Company-11
Beasley, Earnest-26
Beasley, Verlin and Faye-25
Beaufort-184, 233

Beaver Creek-137
Beaver-184
Bedell, Don-74
Bee Hill Lookout-29, 137
Bell Mountain 1&2 Lookout-29, 137
Belts & Braces-33
Benton Lookout-162
Bethlehem Steel-99, 103, 177
Big Piney River-137
Big Springs Lookout-137, 186
Birch Lookout-29
Black Lookout-162, 187, 209
Blackjack Lookout-28, 136
Bloomfield Lookout-64
Blooming Rose-10, 27
Blowers-xiii
Blue Buck Lookout-187
Blue Mountain Lookout-137
Blue Slip Lookout-85, 139, 173, 188
Boss-143
Botkin, Pete & Dewayne-89
Botkin, Tom-145
Boulay-Eaton, Kathleen-79
Boyer, Jim-154
Branch Lookout-189
Brandsville Lookout-190
Braswell Lookout-191
Brawley, Marvin & Pat-133
Breakline-68
Breeze Lookout-192
Briar Lookout-192
Broom Rake-xiv
Brown, Owen-192

Brown, Richard-192
Brunk, Gene-149
Brushy Creek Lookout-137,192
Brushy Creek Mill-22
Brushy Creek Mine-124
Buchheit, Lawrence-67,78,149,158,211
Buchman, Sidney-140
Bucksnort-110,112,203
Buick Tower-137,193
Bunch, Carson-166
Bunker Lookout-194
Bunker Pole Lookout-28
Bunkers Knob Lookout-136
Burn Index-25,68

C

Cabool-194
Camdenton-174,195
Caney 1&2-98,137,162,195
Cantilever Sign-xiv
Carkin, Jim-xvi
Carnage-xv,98
Carnegie-99
Carson, Les-87
Cascade Lookout-162,196,202
Catwalk-59
Cedar Creek Lookout-137
Center Lookout-196
Centerville Lookout-29
Chaney, Betty & Everett-112,115,203
Chess & Waymond Stave Finishing Company-12
Chilton, Jason-128
Chilton, Thomas-128
Chilton, Thomas Coot-138
Chilton, Tom-126
Christopher, Ed-50
Christopher, Eddie-50
Cimarron National Grasslands-162
Citizens Committee for Conservation-9
Civilian Conservation Corps-10,27,51,59,133,176,208,240
Clark National Forest-175
Clark Purchase Unit-9

Clear Cut-5
Clements, Jerry-145
Climax Springs Lookout-137
Coffman Lookout-67
Competition-142
Conley, Jerry-131
Consent Acts-7,9
Conservation Commission-8,26
Conservation Federation of Missouri-7
Cooperative Forest Fire Prevention Program-15
Coot Chute-139,169
Coot Mountain-59,129,139,169,197,241,
Corn Creek Lookout-87,137,197
Cottoner (Cottener) Lookout-67,137,163,197
Creosote-xv,34
Crites, Viola-192
Cross Out-106
Crow's Nest-xvii,25
Cruising Timber-xv
CT-4-37
Cunningham, Bob-135,204
Cunningham, Terry-22,124
Current Local-xi,74
Current River Conservation Area-35
Current River Lumber Company-22
Current River-127
Current Wave-xi,112,203
Czar Lookout-138,198

D

Dare, Tom-x
Deer Run Park-239
Deer Run Tower-35,199,241
Deer Run-59,83
Design for Conservation-9
Devil's Horn-138
Dirkson, Senator Everett-6
Dispatch Boards-106
Dispatch Map-xv
Dixon Lookout-64
Dogtown Lookout-138
Dogwood Lookout-138,166
Doniphan Lookout-166,200
Donley, Joe-97

247

Dozer-69,155,157
Drift Pin-xv,78,84
Drey,Leo-22
Dry Valley-59
Dunn, Forrest-163
Dunn,Delane-163
Dunn,Max-182

E

Eastwood Lookout-133,222
Elkhorn Lookout-38,64
Elliot Lookout-25
Eminence Lookout-129,162,234
Enabling Act-176
Eudy,Ted-149
Ewing ,Becky-146

F

F-16-130
Fairveiw Lookout-222
Falling Springs-208
Ferguson,Bill-128
Fire Factors-xv
Fire Finders-104
Fire Parts-xviii
Fire Types-xix
Flat Rock Lookout-129,171,222
Flatwoods Lookout-201
Fletcher Mine-143
Floyd Lookout-138
Footings-xvi,84,86
Fort Leonard Wood Lookout-223
Fordland Honor Camp-87
Frakes, Marge (Kinnison)-x
Frazer, Butch-130
Free Range-4
Freeburg Lookout- 64,202
Fremont Lookout-13,223
French Village Lookout-223,235
Fristoe Purchase Unit-9
Fu Go Ballons-15

G

Gale,Larry-131
Gall,Doug-63,215
Galvanized Steel-xvi
Garvey, Joe-154
Garwood Lookout-224
Gasconade Purchase Unit-9
Geno Farrow-182
Geodetic Marker Survey-135
Gillihan,Zack-184
Gin Pole-xvi,84
Gipsy Lookout-162,196,202,236
Glade Top Trail-195
Goldie Bear-16
Goodman Lookout-38,64,164
Goodman,Damian-169
Google Map Project-xi,55,202
Goose Creek-142
Gorman,Max
 -x,25,34,83,93,123,128,138,144,158,217
Gorman,Trudy-123,217
Graham,George-128,149,151
Graham,Ruth-151
Grandin Lookout-34,224
Grassy Lookout-38,154,163,224,236
Great Depression-7,240
Green,Junior-43
Greenley Lookout-38
Gulf Lookout-233
Gutherie Lookout-31,162

H

Hafner, Kerwin-77,144
Hallelujah Crew-134
Halpern,James-175
Harlan,James-128
Harper,Melvin-149
Hartshorn Lookout-172,224,241
Hawthorne Bloom Logo-8,161
Hefner-128
Hercules Lookout-38,225
Heiskell,Wilmer-60

Higdon Footings-225
High Hill Lookout-52,112,121,137,203
High Knob/E Highway Lookout-25,29
Highway 60 Footings-225
Hilda Lookout-29
Hilltop Lookout-38
Himont Lookout-136,204
Holland,Marvin-59
Holland,Walter-149
Hollister Tower-162
Horn Lookout-30,138
Hornaday, William-2
Horton Cemetary-5
Horton Tower-135,146
Horton-5,204
Hotfoot Teddy-16
Houston Lookout-225
Hunter Lookout-38,204,241
Hurlbut,David-149
Hurricane Deck-162
Huzzah State Forest-53,82

I

Increment Borer-xvii
Indian Trail Tower-62,205
Inland-99
International Derrick & Equipment-xvii,90,98

J

James,Don-149,154,159
Jay Tower-138
Jay/ Botkin Lookout-89
Jenkins Lookout-38,236
John Derre-158
John Lemuel Braswell-138
Johnson Mountain-137
Johnson,Vonnie-87,216
Joplin Lookout-38,64
Julian Footings-226
Junior Forest Program-16

K

Kaiser Lookout-138
Kampschroeder, Laura-79
Kelleter Lookout-49,138
Kelleter,Paul-4
Kelleter,Pauline-51
Kemnow,Ron-xi,209
Keysville Lookout-174,226
King's Lookout-143
Kinnison, Roy & Ella-x,207
Kirk, Charlie-59,126
Kirkpatrick,Russell-154
Klatt,Bill-128
Knob Lick Lookout-71,205
Knobview-216
Knotwell Footings-226
Knuckles,Gene-59

L

LAD Foundation-22
Lamb,Helen-216
Lanagan Lookout-64
Lane,David-158
Leasburg Lookout-226
Leatherman, Loren-128
Lenox Lookout-227
Leptis Magna Principle-1
Leptis Magna-1
Leptis Magna-Title Page
Light,Roy-128
Ligman,Teena-133
Little Shoal Creek-196
Lone Elk Park-53
Lone Hill Lookout-137,206
Lone Hill/Meramec-38
Lone Pine Lookout-30
Long, Francis Christopher-50
Long Marshall-166
Lookout-xvii
Lost Creek Lookout-137,207
Lovan,Stan-166
Love Hill-206

Low Wassie-25,30,74
Lowell,Clyde-128
LS-40-93,127,200
Lutes, Earl "Minnie"-149,153,159
Lutes, Jerry-153
Lutes, Ron & Gary-155
Lutes,Tim-149,157,158
LX-24-93
LX-25-93
Lynchburg Footings-227
Lyon,Jim-xi,56

M

Macendonia Lookout-32,34,137
Marcoot Lookout-227
Mark Twain National Forest-9,140,175
Marshfield Lookout-64,85
Maxism-130
MC-39-95
McGarrity, Raymond-163
McCormack,Eugene-31
McMillen, Mac-182
Mendenhall, Gregg-145
Meramec State Park-51
Merino Sheep-3
Meta Lookout-235
Miley, Rob-135,204
Millman Lumber Company-59
Missouri Conservation Commission-40,51,122
Missouri Department of
 Conservation-7,71,74,79,141,221,240
Missouri Forestry Commission—71
Missouri Historical Society-150
Missouri Lumber and Mining Company-241
Missouri Outstanding Forester-26
Model 33&37-96
Mondy, Howard-43
Montauk Lookout-x,125
Montauk State Park-207
Montaukett-138
Moran,Vivert-183
Morey,Bill-59

Mountain View Lookout-35,38,143,137,227
Mt. Hulda Lookout-137
Mud Lick Lookout-137
Mud Pond Ridge-25,30
Mudlick Mountain-x,42,207
Multiple Use Assets-180
Mulvinia Lookout-162
Murrell,James-135,146,204

N

National Association of State Foresters-16
National Distillers Products-22
National Forest System-176
National Historical Preservation Act-175
National Registry of Historical Places-178
Neosho Lookout-35,38,64,167
New Deal-10
New Liberty-208
Newton,Larry-164
Noren,Carl-131
Norwood-64
Nottinghill Lookout-30

O

Oak Lookout-228
Oates Lookout-162,187,209
Old Baldy-97
Old Foresters-viii
Olin Ashleck-29
Open Range-239
Orchard, Steve-124,208,239
Osborn Fire Finder-xviii,41,106,155

P

Paddy Creek-143
Painter, Greg-214
Panama Pump-xviii
Panther Hill Lookout-36,58,129,162,209,219
Parker,Jim-34,62,83,88,158,182,215,217
Patrol Tower-33
Patterson, Mo.-x
Patterson,Elsie & Curt-113

Peplow, Wayne-66
Perry Lookout-174,211
Peterson, Leon-141
Phillipsburg Lookout-64
Piankeshaw-138
PID-135
Piers-xvi
Pike Lookout-30
Pilot Knob Lookout-137,138,228
Piney Footings-228
Piney-166
Pioneer Cooperage-22
Pioneer Forest-22
Plad Lookout-228
Plots Tower-146
Pole Tower-27
Polka, Chris-xi,55,187,202,209
Pomeroy, Micheal-192
Pond Fork Purchase Unit-9
Ponder, Ed-152
Possum Trot Lookout-137,147,211
Potosi Lookout-64
Powell Lookout-38,64,234
Prairie State-2
Presley, Jerry-74,131
Primary Tower-xviii
Proctor Lookout-32,162,213
Prugh, Benton-127

R

Reavis, Mike-82
Reeds Spring Lookout-137
Reeves, Bill-59
Reform Lookout-31
Reynolds County Courier-xi
Rings Creek-x,207
Risers-xviii,84
River Hills Traveler-xi,56,112,164
Roby-90,94,214
Rockwoods Footings-229
Rockwoods Lookout-235
Rocky Mount Lookout-136,162

Roger Pryor Back Country-204
Rolla-215
Rombaurer Lookout-30
Rosati Lookout-162,174,216
Rose, Rodney-128
Rosehill Lookout-137,229
Ruble, James Alan-43
Ruble, James-39,149,206
Ruble, Myrtle-47
Ruby, Ken & Don-166
Runge Conservation Center-162,221
Ruth & Paul Henning Conservation Area-162

S

Sam A. Baker Park-x,42,207
Santhuff, Charley-58,128
Satterlee, John-162
Sauk Tonqua-138
Sayers, H.W.-141
Sayers, Skip-141
Sayersbrook Bison Ranch-141
Schnurbusch-68
Scoville, John-112,203
Seco Plow-160
Secondary Tower-xix
Section, Range, Township-109
Seever Tower-145
Seton Porter Forest-22
Seymour Lookout-86,217
Shaddux, Jim-130
Shannon County Democrat-126
Shannon, Janet-190
Shannondale Lookout
 -x,38,59,93,125,148,170,217,241
Shawnee National Forest-9
Shell Knob Lookout-136,162
Shell, Harold-149
Siloam Springs Lookout-137,229
Simpson Lookout-30
Simpson, Earl-134
Simpson's Crow Nest-27
Sinking Creek Lookout-133,137,229

Skinner, Glenn-70,205
Skinner, Jack-70,141,205
Sligo-25
Smallet-148
Smith, Darrell-145,187,209
Smokey Bear 20252-15
Smokey Bear Historical Park-17
Smokey Bear-15,156,240
Sorenson, Jim-15,65,78,83,104,216
Spring Valley-127
Spud Bar-xv
Squires Lookout-64,84,136,173,218
Stamps-99
State Forester-7
Stegall Mountain Lookout-25,36,129,136,218,241
Sterling Footings-230
Stirts, Richard-217
Stono Mountain Lookout-235
Stoops, Wayne-128
Stotler, Jason-145
Strange, John-113
Straps-32
Stroup, Harry-149
Styron, Emery-xi
Sullivan Hill Lookout-30,137
Sulser, Chester-59
Summersville Beacon-xi
Summersville Lookout-171,230
Sunridge Lookout-38,64,173,219
Swanigan, Virgil-189
Swatter-xix
Swedeborg Lookout-162,213

T

Tags-99
Tasmanian Tiger-2
Tatum, Charles-168
Taum Sauk-41,97,217,219
Tecumseh Lookout-230
Tee Lookout-25,30
Texas Footings-230

Texas Soil and Water Commission-25
The First Eden-Title Page
Thomasville Lookout-137,173,220,241
Timber Knob Lookout-136
Timber Stand Improvement—xix,68
Timber Volunteer Fire Department-130
Timmermann, John-147,211
Tip Top Mountain-x,137,207
Topog Map-140
Trail of Tears-138
Tram Lookout-90,110,138
Trammel, Milton-149
Triangle Logo-8
Tucker, Lindell-141,183
Turner Mill Cave-113
Tusher Hill Lookout-137
Twin Knobs Lookout-137,148,221
Tywappity Lookout-64,138

U

Ulman Lookout-233
United States Forest Service-15,115,133,221,239

V

Vada Footings-30,231
Vada Pole lookout-29
Vance, Frank-128
Vichy Lookout-65,231
Visibility Assessment-xix
Voyles, Jim-112
Vulcan Lookout-39,231

W

Wappapello-9
Warrenton Lookout-162,233
Wartime Ad Council-15
Washburn Lookout-38
Washington II Lookout-234
Washington Park Lookout-232,234
Wayne County Journal Banner-xi
Wendelin, Rudy-16

West Plains-232
Westover Footings-232
White, George O.-3,78,126
Whitewater-Womack Lookout-136,162,232
Wilder,Corky-156
Williams,Maxie-134
Willow C.C.C.-146
Windmill Towers-xix,87
Wise,Colt-166
Wolf Mountain Lookout-135
Wolf Mountain-135
Wolford, Bill Jr.-112,120
Wolford,Shari-110,115,121,203

Woodland, Ron-50,79
Woodlands Award-26
Woodsey Owl-16

Y

Youngblood,Doug-60
Younger, Charlie-65

Z

Zulpo,Steve-216

Epilogue

In 2015 wood product industries contributed almost $10 billion dollars to Missouri's economy. Some 47,000 jobs were created with a payroll of $2.3 billion dollars. $91.5 million in sales tax was generated with Missouri sawmills processing about 760 million board feet of lumber. Clearly, no bad "Leptis Magna Principle" at work here. In fisheries and wildlife, the story is similar. Rivers no longer choked with gravel and run off promote a healthy fishing experience. Deer seasons now exist because there are many deer to hunt.

It is easy to see why many "in the know" consider Missouri to be the nation's #1 Conservation success story. Clearly, an effort has been made to "support nature." Through resources and the work of many, the Missouri one sees today stands in stark contrast to a century ago.

In any undertaking of this magnitude, there will always be a need for evaluation and direction. Not every idea will fly, and some ideas will be in need of discovery. But, an occasional bump in the road will not deter from the big picture.

No book could ever, regardless of how big, credit all who might deserve it. I have attempted to cover by experience, job performed, and location in the state to provide a good sampling. If you are one who feels they deserved to be in this book, you are probably right.

My aim was to get things down before they were lost, to give credit where it was due, provide some technical information, but also do a "fun book" and to tell my story. Today, cell phones, local fire districts and the public do much in regard to detection and fire suppression.

I hope you enjoy checking the book out as much as I have enjoyed working on it.

The Author

The author was born in St. Louis mid last century. He still has relatives scattered here and there in Missouri. His Dad was transferred to Southern Illinois where he would grow up and live. However, he and later with his wife would "keep the road hot" between there and Missouri.

Always a big believer in hobbies, he had several that followed him for much of his life. "Towering" was one of them. More than just a hobby, it would provide a source of many smiles shared with many "tower friends."

A public school teacher for over 30 years (American History, World History, Geography, Government, Civics, Yearbook, and Golf Coach) he holds undergrad and graduate degrees from SIU and EIU.

Following his retirement, he began to write tower articles here and there reflecting an interest held by many in Missouri. He would do tower series for the Reynolds County Courier, Wayne County Journal-Banner, Summersville Beacon, Current Wave, and Van Buren Current Local.

As a contributing writer, he would do a multi-part tower series for the River Hills Traveler and also do pieces on canoeing and the towers of Southern Illinois. He recently had a piece on the Possum Trot Towers published in the National Forest Fire Lookout Association magazine.

In addition to visiting most of the standing towers in Missouri (he has left a few unvisited so as to not be sad at finishing such a fun journey) he has documented many historical sites as well as towers planned but not built and a few tower mysteries. He has also done research in Illinois and Indiana. He is often called by others seeking information and shares his experiences and pictures for free. As much as he has enjoyed working on the book, he is looking forward to doing more research and finding a few fire trails he has not navigated and friends he has not met.